Flu

A Social History of Influenza

Flu

A Social History of Influenza

Tom Quinn

NEW
HOLLAND

First published in 2008 by New Holland Publishers (UK) Ltd
London · Cape Town · Sydney · Auckland
www.newhollandpublishers.com

10 9 8 7 6 5 4 3 2 1

Garfield House, 86–88 Edgware Road, London W2 2EA, UK
80 McKenzie Street, Cape Town 8001, South Africa
Unit 1, 66 Gibbes Street, Chatswood, NSW 2067, Australia
218 Lake Road, Northcote, Auckland, New Zealand

ISBN: 978 184537 941 4

Editorial Direction: Rosemary Wilkinson
Senior Editor: Kate Parker
Copyeditor: Naomi Waters
Design and cover design: Peter Crump
Production: Melanie Dowland

Reproduction by Pica Digital Pte Ltd, Singapore
Printed and bound by Replika Press PVT Ltd, India

Note: The author and publishers have made every effort to ensure
that the information given in this book is safe and accurate, but they
cannot accept liability for any resulting injury or loss or damage to
either property or person, whether direct or consequential and
howsoever arising.

Front cover: A British couple attempt to ward of the flu with nose
caps to protect from the virus, 1929.

To Wado

Contents

Acknowledgments

'The greatest part of a writer's time is spent in reading, in order to write;
a man will turn over half a library to make one book.'

When Samuel Johnson wrote that, 250 years ago, he was certainly thinking of libraries containing at most a few tens of thousands of volumes. Today, the author is faced with the prospect of turning over far more books – not to mention magazines and journals – than ever before, particularly if he is treading a well worn path.

Writing this book presented a curious mix of problems – specialist journals are a rich source of material about flu and viruses in general but they do not touch on the social aspects of disease or if they do it is only, as it were, incidentally. Similarly, books – with a few notable exceptions – tend to concentrate on the scientific aspects of influenza. The history of influenza as it affected individual lives is much harder to come by, especially when it comes to primary material – the nitty gritty of real lives reported in real time. Given that difficulty it has to be said that this book would hardly have got off the ground without the generous assistance of a large number of individuals and organizations, but particularly specialist libraries.

We tend to forget that libraries – specialist libraries – would not and could not function without the skills of the staff who run them. Books and journals may be available for all in these institutions but it is the librarians who provide the route map that makes any major collection of material genuinely accessible. Their efforts on behalf of specialist researchers usually go unnoted and unsung. My own experience in a number of libraries across the UK and elsewhere reminds me that few books – apart perhaps from works of fiction – would reach the booksellers' shelves without the efforts of these individuals who work in obscure corners yet provide enormously helpful advice to anyone who needs their help. Authors draw hugely on the experience and knowledge of librarians to short circuit what might otherwise be a long and tedious journey towards the right journal, the appropriate reference work. At the same time librarians tend to be a rather self-effacing lot, which may be why those who gave me the most help tended to be least keen on being publicly thanked. So without mentioning them by name I'd like to thank all those librarians who pointed me in the right direction or saved me from obvious blunders and fruitless searches.

One of the most extraordinary things about writing a book such as this is that the process of research brings one not into the dry history of kings and queens, of impersonal and imperial development, but rather gives one a rare glimpse into the personal everyday lives of long vanished individuals. These individuals left no great monuments but took part in, or were victims of, some of the most exceptional events of the past century and more.

Without the personal testimony of survivors of, for example, the great flu pandemic of 1918-19, a book such as this would not be possible. It must have been immensely painful for the survivors of families almost wiped out by Spanish flu to recall again for contemporaneous researchers the horror of those days, but their memories have helped scientists, medical researchers and historians immeasurably. I would like to thank those descendants of survivors who were unfailingly patient and polite in the face of what must have sometimes seemed an endless stream of enquiries from me. They were also diligent in answering my often lengthy letters.

In earlier centuries many doctors, struggling with the weight of history and their own inadequate equipment, were also prepared to spend a great deal of time writing in journals and in letters to colleagues. These accounts frequently contain remarkable detail on patients' symptoms, the progress of the disease and their own attempts, however futile, to cure the sick.

Doctors were particularly good correspondents and much of what they wrote survives in record centres and libraries up and down the country – finding one's way through these documents is a nightmare for the uninitiated and I would like to thank a number of individuals including Tom Pike, Tim Kehoe, Andrew Hall and Pietro Lampedusa for helping me through a mountain of documents.

I would also like to thank a number of living doctors who didn't hesitate to share their expertise and knowledge of influenza – particularly avian influenza – with a layman.

Virologist Patricia Davis deserves a huge thank you for carefully reading the book and rescuing me from numerous foolish errors of both emphasis and fact. Errors and misjudgments that remain are, of course, all my own.

For help with practical, emotional, logistical and general historical matters I'd also like to thank Wado Wadham, Barbara O'Flaherty, Richard Jarman, Karen Warren, Faith Glasgow, Sarah Storey, Juliet Quick, Mr Scrivens, Deborah Fisher, Mary Corbett, Eric Gray, Mr Busby, Rachel Lennox, Richard Smith, The Latimer Road

Fishing Club, Tom Marmoset, Lol Plummer, Louise Davies, Lord Sharpe of Bromley, The Hon Mel Capper, Nicola Bird, Emma Westall, Katy Quinn Guest, Alexander Quinn Guest, James Quinn Guest, the late Deborah Anne Quinn, Jessie Cooke, Nina Porter, Sara Doak, Corinna Marshall, Jane Smith, Robert Pike, Frances Jackman, Julian Bell, Jane Simms, Minky, Mona and Captain Swing.

If I have missed anyone in my relatively restrained list above, I'm sure they will understand but to what might best be termed the inner circle – that is, my children and partner Charlotte not to mention London's most intelligent dog, Nutmeg – I'd like to say an extra thank you.

And last but by no means least I would like to thank the person with the most difficult job of all – Kate Parker at New Holland who has been unfailingly patient despite having to put up with shortfalls of text, late changes of heart, mis-spellings, obscure phrasing and occasional bouts of authorial lunacy!

Introduction –
The Barbarian at the Gate

Biblical references to plagues and famines reveal one of our deepest and most entrenched fears. In the era before science it must have seemed that the gods had turned against human society when the crops failed or when, for no reason that could be discerned, people began to sicken and die. Across the Old World, abandoned villages and towns – many now buried beneath desert sands or on windswept promontories – bear witness to an ancient visitation by epidemic disease.

In England abandoned medieval villages are common – bubonic plague, the Black Death, was often responsible for mortality on such a scale in some communities that the survivors moved away for good, partly because the community was no longer capable of sustaining itself and partly, no doubt, because the villagers feared that the place itself had somehow been cursed by the gods or by evil spirits.

Punishment of the gods

For millennia the arrival of plague was among the most feared of all events and offerings to placate the gods were made when the first members of the community began to die – perhaps as in the case of smallpox – horribly disfigured and in great pain. When the sacrifices did not work the people would perhaps have believed that they had offended the gods so greatly that no amount of sacrifice could placate them. The curse of the gods that came in the form of disease would have reached a level of particular intensity some time between 10 and 20 thousand years ago when, according to the best archaeological evidence we have, settled communal life for human beings began in earnest.

Settled community living had at least one massive drawback that could not have been recognized at the time – it ushered in the dawn of epidemic if not pandemic disease as virulent bacterial and viral infections began to exploit the large numbers of potential victims concentrated in particular areas. Before the era of settled villages and then towns of increasing size, human groups would have typically been small and either nomadic or semi-nomadic and probably based around extended families, much as chimps and bonobos – our nearest relatives – still live today. Isolated communities containing small numbers of related individuals were far less likely to suffer devastating epidemics.

The ability to domesticate animals and to grow crops was a key factor in the earliest development of settled communities and the life and prospects offered first by the farmstead and village and then by the walled town must have been compelling. We have never looked back and the number of people who live in cities and towns still grows year by year across both the developed and the developing worlds.

As the scale of early settled communities increased so too did the scale of viral and bacterial attack whose impact would previously have been minimal. The risk of attack by disease was analogous, if you like, to the risk of attack by those still unsettled tribes drawn to the concentrated and immovable mass of a settled town with its wealth of potential plunder. A walled town would have seemed an easy target for a marauding tribe tempted by the lure of money, slaves, women and food. Greek and later Roman society's greatest strength and paradoxically its greatest weakness was the city. Living in a city brought the perennial, almost mythological fear of attack from outside whether by disease or by barbarian hordes. Germanic tribes – who typically moved about rather than choosing to live in cities as the Romans did – always posed a threat to those who lived a more settled existence.

The diseases that periodically struck at cities were at least as deadly as these human attackers, and it was impossible to stop them. The plagues came out of nowhere to lay waste to whole populations and, having done their evil work, they disappeared as mysteriously as they had come, leaving baffled and weakened survivors or a ghost town inhabited only by the dead.

We know from archaeological evidence that infections, including some that are still with us today, destroyed some of the ancient world's most famous cities. Viral and bacterial disease took a firmer grip on people's lives at this time because they were perfectly fitted to thrive where humans gathered and lived in large numbers. Man had no knowledge of the relationship between hygiene and infection; no awareness of bacteria, let alone viruses; ancient peoples could only wait and hope to placate their gods.

If placating the gods failed, they might try a host of different approaches: isolating the afflicted (not a bad idea even by modern standards, but difficult to do effectively) or wearing red, or sniffing vinegar-scented nosegays. Even if these things did no good in reality they must have been comforting – better than doing nothing at all.

Superstitious remedies

Other ideas had disastrous consequences. During the terrible outbreak of bubonic plague that afflicted England, particularly London, in 1663–4 it was assumed that dogs and cats were spreading the contagion so as many as could be found were killed. The result was actually to make the situation far worse since plague was spread by fleas carried by rats. With the cats and dogs almost eliminated there were no predators left to control the rat population and the plague spread more easily as rats (and their fleas) multiplied.

Practical but mistaken measures like this were matched by what we now see as equally mistaken ideas for looking after those who had already succumbed to a particular disease. Bizarre practices with no basis in science developed, and not just for viral and bacterial disease. As recently as 1700 it was still medically accepted practice following surgery for gallstones for the wound to be sewn up and then old milk poured over it. This must have increased the risk of infection at a time when the operation was highly dangerous anyway – one in two died. The fact that 50 per cent of those cut for the stone survived presumably made 17th-century surgeons believe that they had been saved by the application of milk. In fact far fewer would probably have died had the milk not been applied in the first place – the bacteria it contained would certainly have been more harmful than beneficial.

With epidemic disease, attempts at curative measures seem, from a modern perspective, to have been almost random – bleeding the patient was popular, mercury was sometimes given and there was a near obsession with the need to empty the bowels, the latter idea derived from the ancient Greek physician, Hippocrates.

Such ignorance lasted well into the 20th century, as we will see. By then of course we did not rely on guesswork for all our medical procedures but on science. Science was applied in many areas but it has only recently – much more recently – begun to catch up with what is arguably our greatest medical adversary, the virus. This is why, as recently as 1918, in addition to sensible scientific measures all sorts of crackpot cures were tried for flu that had no effect at all and may even have made things worse. Desperate situations call for desperate remedies and in this respect modern man – faced with a disease he cannot control – is not that different from his ancient ancestors.

But if city and town populations were woefully ignorant of the risk of infection through open wounds, lack of hygiene and overcrowding they were even more in the dark when it came to understanding how or why a third or even half their numbers might suddenly be struck down by something that severely incapacitated then killed quietly, quickly and inexplicably.

A combination of a superstitious suspicion that malign influences must be at work combined with a vague sense of being enveloped by a mysterious and invisible miasma gave us the name of what is probably the most infectious of all illnesses – influenza. Various dates are given in various sources for the origins of the word but late medieval Italy is probably the most likely. According to the Oxford English Dictionary the word influenza (Italian for 'influence') was first recorded around 1504. The Italians thought of flu as a malign influence somehow linked to the position of the planets – whenever influenza struck, astrologers explained that the planets were misaligned, which resulted in this strange malady that could not be seen or heard or smelled, yet had the power to kill.

The scientific method

By the standards of the time the attribution made sense. Western society was only beginning to understand some aspects of the study of science, or natural philosophy as it was then known. The Renaissance involved a return to the questioning that had typified the ancient Greek and Roman search for knowledge. The medieval church was beginning to lose its grip on a world it had insisted humankind should not question or try to understand. To do so was blasphemous. Still the old ideas lingered, however, and it was to take several centuries – until the invention of the electron microscope in the 1930s in fact – until the last barrier to understanding some of our most lethal diseases was removed.

For those at the dawn of the modern scientific age some headway could be made in treating some diseases, but flu and other virus-borne diseases were attributed to a malign influence because there was no alternative explanation. Diseases that weakened and often killed yet seemed to come from nowhere were made to fit into a world view that saw the influence and intervention of gods and demons as a daily reality.

It is highly unlikely that influenza made its first appearance at the time it was first recorded. It has, like so many viral and bacterial diseases, flourished since those first settled communities, and has probably been around in some form since *homo sapiens* first evolved. Without concentrations of people it would have been far less noticeable and perhaps even milder in its effects.

Bacteria and viruses reproduce incredibly quickly relative to human reproduction and the greater the number of generations of an organism the greater the chance of genetic mutation – genetic mutations are errors in the process of DNA (deoxyribonucleic acid), or in the case of flu, RNA (ribonucleic acid) copying. Most mutations do not give the organism a reproductive advantage. But every now and then a mutation does give an organism a reproductive advantage over individuals who do not share that mutation. Individuals with the mutation are more likely to reproduce so they come to dominate the population. Mutations often confer an advantage on viruses because they enable the virus to avoid the immune response of the human body, which would otherwise destroy it. As we will see viruses – and particularly the flu virus – mutate at an astonishing rate.

This book is about the flu virus and its effects on humanity over the past four centuries and more. I've looked briefly at reports of disease from much earlier – from ancient Greece for example – but it is very difficult to be sure we are talking about influenza in the sense that we now understand it when we read ancient accounts of disease and epidemics.

Epidemics and pandemics

A pandemic is defined as a disease that crosses between countries and whole continents. The word pandemic is derived from the Greek *pan* meaning all, and *demos* meaning people. An epidemic spreads across particular countries. Much has been written about the most infamous flu outbreak of all – the great pandemic of 1918 – but historians have tended to concentrate on the medical rather than social side of what happened, and they have largely ignored earlier epidemics and pandemics.

There were a number of significant flu epidemics and pandemics before 1918 and there have been several since. Most worryingly, however, is the fact that despite the best efforts of modern science we are permanently in danger of a new flu epidemic if not a pandemic.

The early part of this book looks at the evidence for flu infections since the time of Hippocrates, who is popularly supposed to have first mentioned what may have been flu or a flu-like disease. Without the benefit of science it was difficult during earlier epochs to define and clearly demarcate various illnesses – even today many of us find it difficult to distinguish between a cold and a mild bout of flu. In earlier times the difficulty was much greater as communities, though often substantial in size, were relatively isolated by the difficulties of travel and communication, and what afflicted one community might not seem quite the same as an illness that seemed to spread rapidly through another community.

In England the 'sweating sickness' mentioned in various documents during the 15th and 16th centuries may have been a virulent form of flu or it may have been a form of what we now call hanta virus. Again, at this distance it is difficult to know. In Edinburgh at the end of the 16th century an ailment called 'the new acquaintance' was almost certainly flu, but again it is difficult to be certain.

I hope that to a lesser or greater extent we can untangle the knot that surrounds early reports of flu and see how much those reports had in common across wide geographic areas. We can then see how society coped and developed in the face of repeated infection, sometimes mild, sometimes far more severe. And we will see how influenza and the possibility of prevention and cure was perceived by some early commentators and how it was seen in relation to other types of infection.

By the early 19th century or possibly earlier most people had a pretty shrewd idea that flu was a distinct illness, though of course they still had no idea what pathogen (disease-causing agent) caused it, nor how it was transmitted. The pandemics and epidemics of that century are reasonably well documented. Less well known and until now unexplored is the fascinating story of how society coped with the effects of flu, who died and who lived.

Chapter 5 covers the 1918–19 pandemic not just from a national perspective – that has already been done, particularly in regard to America – but from a global one. This section also examines the attempt not just to save lives but to stem the seemingly inexorable spread of the disease. The range of tactics adopted both socially and in the strictly medical sense was astonishing, and at times when we see what our great-grandparents did during this period we realize that in many ways their actions were not unlike those of 17th-century Londoners who killed cats and dogs to try to stop the spread of the plague.

Like those 17th-century Londoners our great-grandparents were working blind against a strain of flu which had never been encountered before. The 1918 pandemic shows that what people lacked in precise medical skills and knowledge they made up for in ingenuity. All kinds of treatments were tried in the hope that almost by chance something might be found that really would work.

The future threat

The final section of the book takes a look at the very real threat from flu that faces us in the future and the means we now have to guard against that threat.

Avian and pig flu viruses are seen as the main danger, but it is their complex relationship with human flu viruses that will almost certainly lie at the heart of future pandemics. Vast concentrations of potential human victims live in our great cities and they must be protected from new and emerging viruses to which, in the worst cases, they will not have immunity.

It is among immense concentrations of livestock, particularly birds and pigs living in close proximity to large numbers of humans that the real risk of a pandemic lies. The situation in this respect is particularly difficult in certain parts of the world, most notably Southern China where humans share living space with large numbers of birds, increasing the chance of avian flu viruses jumping species. Most, if not all, new and particularly deadly strains of flu virus probably originate there.

The history of influenza is to some extent the history of medicine and how it has developed over the past few centuries from a largely unscientific endeavour in which appeals to authority always mattered more than hands-on experience into the modern fact- and evidence-based science we know today. The story of medicine reflects also the growing sophistication of the communities that doctors have served.

In a sense the history of flu splits into two major phases. The first phase was complete ignorance, during which time doctors simply tried out a range of traditional remedies, some of which – particularly opium – may have alleviated symptoms but none of which could possibly have tackled the central cause of the disease, which was not to be discovered until the 1930s.

The second phase of the history of flu begins with the biggest and most appalling loss of life in human history – that devastating outbreak of influenza that came just a decade or so before the discovery of the virus that caused the disease. So the second phase of our history starts with devastation and moves quickly into the post-1930s period of enlightenment when doctors at least knew what they were dealing with. The second phase brings us to the present when there is at least a reasonable chance that a truly effective antiviral drug or vaccine may be created.

A third and final phase is beginning now and involves the future terrors of avian flu – a disease to which we have no historic immunity and one which, if it mutated into a form that could be passed from human to human (rather than only from bird to human) might make the 1918–19 pandemic seem relatively benign.

Before we look at how society was affected by influenza in the distant and not so distant past and may be affected in the future we need to start with some basic science, for only science will enable us to define and understand the enemy we face. The most important initial question is: what exactly is a virus?

CHAPTER 1

Viruses – What Are They and How Do They Work?

The human body is a rich breeding ground for microscopic and submicroscopic life. The mouth for example is a mass of alien life forms – mostly fungal and bacterial – in fact there are far more microbes here even than in the rectal area! We are quite literally covered with bacteria, fungi and other forms of life – like some bipedal planet, each individual human provides a home for more microscopic and submicroscopic forms of life than there are people in the world! Imagine – you are a source of life and nourishment, permanently and for the whole of your life, for more than six billion creatures. Some of these creatures are beneficial, even essential to our continued health, others highly dangerous.

Bacteria

Against the latter our bodies wage constant and unremitting war. The discovery of the immune system and the way it works by Paul Ehrlich (work for which he won the Nobel Prize in 1908) revealed that the healthy human is not in a state of perfect balance and quiet equilibrium. Rather, the healthy body is like a magnificently defended castle, under constant siege. Some battles against would-be invaders have been partially won – the discovery of antibiotics, for example, gave humans a massive advantage over bacteria. What was once thought to be an outright victory for humanity, however, has turned out to be a temporary respite from the battle as various strains of bacteria become resistant even to our most powerful antibiotics.

But if bacterial infections were once among humankind's great killers, that is no longer the case. The discovery of penicillin in the mid-20th century and its antibiotic derivatives has saved tens of millions of lives that would undoubtedly otherwise have been lost to tuberculosis and a host of other now commonly treated infections. Although the war against bacteria may never be completely won – numerous drug-resistant bacteria always threaten – we have, as it were, got the measure of our adversary. The situation with viruses is far more complex.

The problem with viruses is that we have as yet no cure for any viral infection and vaccination is usually, at best, only partially successful. Smallpox eradication is a happy exception to this and no cases have been reported since 1980 following a worldwide campaign of inoculation. Polio is well on the way to eradication, too, but with other viruses the situation is far less promising. Vaccination is still our main line of defence against an adversary whose existence has been firmly established for fewer than 100 years. Before the 1930s no microscope could even see a virus and their existence was a subject for doubt and speculation.

Three great world killers – Human Immunodeficiency Virus (HIV), malaria and flu – are still with us. HIV infection can now be controlled by a complex and expensive drug regime but in poorer countries, particularly in Africa, it is still a major killer because the drugs are too expensive for local populations. Malaria, caused by a protozoan parasite and so not a virus, is nevertheless a huge problem and kills more than a million people, mostly children, every year. But in world history the biggest killer among a host of unpleasant viral enemies is flu.

This may come as a surprise, but the history of flu is the history of a virus so successful that it can and has killed on a scale that dwarfs deaths from war, smallpox and HIV. The reason flu is such a powerful adversary is that even among viruses it is singularly difficult to deal with.

One of the most fascinating things about the flu virus and indeed all other viruses is that scientists are not even agreed about whether they count as living things. Bacteria are certainly living – they are the smallest of all life forms in the sense that they can survive independently of other creatures. They are single celled and contain DNA like every other living thing. DNA (deoxyribonucleic acid), is the double-stranded, helical molecular chain found within the nucleus of every living cell. It carries the genetic information that encodes proteins and enables cells to reproduce and perform their functions.

A bacterium is roughly 500 times bigger than a virus. A bacterium can read DNA messages, convert them into ribonucleic acid (RNA) and then make proteins from that RNA. RNA is a chemical found in the nucleus and cytoplasm of cells that plays an important role in protein synthesis and other chemical activities of the cell.

What viruses do inside our bodies

Bacteria can take in and use oxygen to fuel the work of making proteins and release, as a by-product, carbon dioxide. Scientists believe that bacteria are the blueprint cells for all life and, as we have seen, modern bacteria are, in a sense, direct descendants of the earliest life that appeared on earth.

A virus, on the other hand, is just a scrap of genetic material surrounded by a protein. It cannot reproduce on its own, yet the sole reason for its existence is reproduction. Although it does contain genetic information – viruses have up to 400 genes (although exceptions with over 900 genes have been found) compared to a human with 30,000 – it cannot make proteins itself and must enter a living cell to coerce that cell into doing its reproduction for it.

Once a virus gets inside another living creature's cells it stops those cells performing the function for which they were designed. Instead the cells are forced to start churning out copies of the viruses that have infected them. Viruses don't take over our cells deliberately in order to make us ill, but the flood of chemicals we release to combat them combined with the damage they do as they infect cells – an infected cell almost always dies – leads to the various and sometimes fatal diseases we experience. For example, if all or most of the cells that make up your liver are taken over by a virus and your immune system cannot destroy them quickly enough you will die for the simple reason that you cannot function without a liver.

Viruses may also weaken the immune system as it battles to get the upper hand to such an extent that the body becomes prey to secondary bacterial infection – in the case of influenza, pneumonia is the most serious secondary infection. And when pneumonia takes over the lungs the patient can quite literally suffocate, in the worst cases turning blue from lack of oxygen in the process – a condition known as cyanosis.

Different viruses cause different diseases because their proteins are designed to lock on to and infect different cells. In simple terms the virus tricks the cell into allowing it in. The viral protein of a particular virus will match the protein the human cell expects to recognize on the chemicals that it must admit in order for it to function. Once the cell allows the virus to enter it is doomed.

When we are infected with a cold or flu we cough because the cells in the respiratory tract are damaged by the viral attack and the antibodies we produce to fight them produce the cough reflex – coughing may help remove the disease from our bodies, but it also helps spread many kinds of virus to others. Where cold and flu viruses centre on the cells in the respiratory tract, haemorrhagic viruses – such as the infamous Ebola virus – damage the cells that make up the blood vessels in the lungs causing bleeding. In many cases the bleeding is catastrophic and the victim dies.

Developing immunity

It is very difficult to generalize about the effects of viruses – different viruses are spread in different ways and they affect and damage different parts of the human body. Most viruses have a host animal (although the natural host for Ebola has not been found) and in that animal the virus may cause little or no harm, or perhaps cause only mild illness, but when a virus jumps the species barrier – and the flu virus is particularly good at this – the species in which it now appears for the first time will usually have no immunity and the effects are likely to be catastrophic until, in time, the virus mutates into a milder form, or the newly infected species begins to develop immunity.

The classic case is myxomatosis in rabbits. Myxomatosis is endemic in Brazilian rabbits. They suffer little or no harm by carrying the virus because over thousands of rabbit generations they have developed immunity and have learned to tolerate the presence of a virus that no longer kills them. When the myxomatosis virus was released in Britain, probably in the 1950s and almost certainly deliberately as an attempt to eliminate rabbits, which were a serious agricultural pest, the result was that more than 98 per cent of the rabbit population was wiped out.

However, a very few rabbits (that surviving two per cent) had a slight genetic variation in their make-up which meant they were not killed by the virus. Since they and only they survived to breed, all their offspring shared the same resistance to myxomatosis – a classic example of Darwinism in action. The rabbits had a genetic advantage over other rabbits, so they succeeded in breeding where the other rabbits failed because they did not have that advantage and died out. Within a few years rabbit populations – all descended from the few that survived the first release of myxomatosis – were back at the number that had existed before myxomatosis was ever released. Though they suffer periodic outbreaks of myxomatosis still, the British rabbit population will never again be controllable using this virus. The same is true in Australia, where myxomatosis was used in the same way and with precisely the same short- and long-term effects.

Between man and other animals and the viruses that infect them there is and has always been a kind of arms race. As viruses mutate – and they mutate at a relatively rapid rate (compared to humans) because they reproduce so quickly – they are able to infect those who do not have immunity to the new, mutated form of the virus. Being immune to the older form of the virus may impart partial immunity, but if the virus is very different that older immunity will be useless. But assuming a death rate below 100 per cent the human body slowly catches up and becomes immune or at least partly immune, which means the virus is in danger of being wiped out.

By this time, however, new victims without any immunity will often have been infected or the virus will change again to keep ahead of the body's defences, and the body's immune system is once again left behind. Extremely virulent viruses such as

Ebola, though terrifying, are so deadly that any outbreak is likely to remain local because it kills or incapacitates so quickly that it soon exhausts the available supply of victims. In other words, these first victims die before they have had the chance to spread the disease further afield.

As we can see, one of the main problems with viruses is that there may be many different yet closely related viruses. Being immune to one of these will not protect you from all the others. One of the most interesting of all viruses from this point of view is the common cold.

The common cold

It took until the 1950s to grow the virus that causes the common cold. Scientists had long tried to infect study groups with the agent that causes the cold, but had failed. It took the work of David Tyreell in the late 1950s to come up with an answer. He changed the temperature of the culture in which scientists were trying to grow the cold virus so that it matched not the temperature of the body but the temperature of the nasal passages where the cold virus has, as it were, its home. Instantly he was able to culture the virus but he discovered that the newly isolated virus – which was named rhinovirus (*rhino* is Greek for nose) – was only one of many. We have since discovered that there are as many as 150 cold viruses, and immunity from one gives little or no immunity to the others. This explains why, typically, the average human is infected once or twice a year by one or other of the rhinoviruses and experiences the typical cold symptoms. The curious and as yet unexplained part of this is that humans should so regularly be infected with these and other respiratory infections – dogs, cats and monkeys, for example, do not suffer in the same way.

The situation is made even more difficult because there is an additional group of viruses that cause cold-like symptoms. There is no cure for the common cold nor is there likely to be; there is currently no chance of developing a vaccine that would be effective against that vast array of different viruses. We must be grateful that none of the cold viruses causes anything more than discomfort. If they were more serious – even life threatening – there would be little we could do to protect ourselves.

Ebola

Far more serious than the common cold is the Ebola virus, which first came to the attention of the public in the developed world after an outbreak in the African state of Zaire in the mid-1970s. Within a short time of the first case being identified more than 300 people had contracted the virus and some 280 died. Ebola virus is a haemorrhagic fever. That is, it attacks the cells that line the blood vessels and capilliaries, particularly those that affect the respiratory system. As the cells are destroyed blood begins to leak into the lungs and other organs until the victim drowns in his or her own blood. Ebola did not spread beyond Zaire partly through luck and partly through the fact that it is too efficient at killing for its own good – those who catch the disease usually die so quickly (it is roughly 90 per cent fatal) that they do not have time to infect large numbers of other people before they succumb.

Like other viruses such as hanta and HIV, Ebola seems to have come from nowhere to wreak havoc among human populations, but it is almost certainly the case that this and other newly arrived viruses have reached us via animal hosts; it is generally agreed that HIV came to us from one of our closest primate relatives, though how it made the jump from species to species and then mutated sufficiently so that it could be passed from human to human (rather than in each case from animal to human) is not fully understood.

The arrival of HIV and Ebola (not to mention avian flu) in human populations is something of a new development and it may be that we are simply encroaching too much and too often into parts of the world and among populations of animals with which previously we have had little contact. When we catch a virus to which we have no historical immunity – the classic example is HIV – the effects are likely to be deadly. Yellow fever is another example; it exists in monkeys and does them no harm, but when it infects man the mortality rate is very high. Like malaria, yellow fever – which causes bleeding, nausea, vomiting and finally jaundice – is carried by a species of mosquito.

A breakthrough – the electron microscope

By the early 20th century scientists still did not know that influenza and the common cold were caused by viruses, but they did know that certain illnesses were caused by an agent that could not be filtered – it was too small to be trapped as bacteria were trapped using dense porous devices made from, say, porcelain.

It was also clear that the agent that caused influenza and other diseases could not be grown or cultured. However, a number of scientists correctly guessed, despite the lack of clear evidence, that they were dealing with a bacteria-like agent that was simply too small to be detected under a conventional light microscope or trapped in the filters then in use. The invention of the electron microscope in 1938 changed all that – for the first time viruses could be seen. At last their precise nature could at least begin to be analyzed and recorded.

Surrounding the genetic material in each virus is a capsid – that is, a protein shell. Within this the tiny particle of DNA contains a code for the virus to reproduce itself. Viruses reproduce at an astonishing rate, but, as we have seen, they cannot do it on their own since they do not have the necessary molecular equipment. What they do have is the ability to make other living cells do the work of reproduction for them. Within hours of finding a new victim a virus, having entered a cell, will have (usually) destroyed that cell and turned it into a factory producing thousands of new viruses.

Doctors had long known that there were diseases such as tuberculosis that were caused by an agent they could see and grow; then there were others, such as yellow fever, measles, smallpox and influenza that seemed similar to diseases caused by bacteria, but no bacteria could ever be found or grown from those infected by the diseases. These pathogens became known as 'invisible microbes'. Even when the electron microscope became available and viruses could at last be seen, it still took until the early 1950s for the deep structure of viruses to be understood, because the structure of DNA itself (the famous double helix) was not understood until Watson and Crick's pioneering work in the 1950s.

How viruses spread

As we have seen viruses – like bacteria – have been with us as long as any life form and the most likely explanation for their origin (though scientists are by no means fully agreed on this) is that they somehow managed to break away from chromosomes to become independent and able to reproduce independently as parasites.

Like all living things they are programmed to survive and to do so by reproducing. Once inside a host cell the virus begins this process and new viruses from that first cell factory will quickly infect other cells. But if the virus kills its host too quickly it will not have time to allow the host to spread it to other suitable hosts and it will die in the original host; this is why victims of influenza are contagious before they show any signs of illness themselves. The influenza virus can survive outside a host for a couple of days at most, but it is supremely successful at survival where large numbers of people are gathered together. Influenza is spread by droplet infection (when we sneeze, for example, tens of thousands of microscopic droplets are propelled into the air), but if you touch a doorknob or any other surface that has fresh virus on it and then touch your mouth or nose you are likely to become infected. In isolated and small groups of humans the flu virus would quickly run out of new victims, which would endanger its own survival unless, like some other viruses, it was able to lie dormant for many years (like HIV) without killing or seriously harming its host.

Yellow fever works in a different way – because it is carried between victims by mosquito it doesn't matter if it incapacitates each victim. In fact, in evolutionary terms incapacitating the host is a good idea for yellow fever because it means that the victim is in bed and therefore more likely to be bitten by the mosquito that carries the disease far and wide. Cleverly, yellow fever does not harm the mosquito at all; again, in evolutionary terms, this is a smart move. Killing the creature that carries a disease to a new host would make no sense.

The virus replicates itself in vast quantities; these copies pour out of each infected cell and infect other cells around the body. Within hours the body is mobilizing its counter attack with a formidable array of weapons. Assuming the victim of infection isn't quickly killed, he or she will gradually begin to fight back as the immune system mobilizes and destroys the virus – that is why it is essential for the virus's long-term survival that it should reproduce and then move on before it is overwhelmed by the body's defences. It doesn't matter if the viruses in a particular victim are eventually all killed, either by the immune system or the death of the victim, as long as some of the virus is passed on to a new host in whom the cycle continues and the virus's long-term survival is guaranteed.

Viruses cannot swim or fly to another victim, so they are carried by droplet, insect, water or faeces. In faeces and water some viruses can survive for extended periods before a new host presents itself.

Infecting the host

The biggest problem for the virus is gaining entry to the host in the first place. The human body is covered with skin cells, the outer layer of which is dead and inert and therefore perfect for keeping out viruses, which cannot penetrate unaided. The genito-urinary tract and respiratory tract are potential weakspots, however. Here the mucous membrane may be only one cell layer deep, and though the mucous itself makes life difficult for the invading virus – because it is highly acid, as are the vaginal and oral secretions – weaker individuals or those whose immune system is less well developed or compromised in some way may give the virus a chance. The respiratory tract has a remarkable layer of cells covered in miniscule hairs, which move in a synchronized fashion to push any invading foreign items up and out of the body – they are extremely effective (along with the secretions that line the tract) at keeping invaders out. As a result of this extraordinary feat of bio-engineering, the lungs in a normal healthy person are usually sterile. But, despite the best efforts of our defences, viruses and bugs still get through. How do they do it?

The easiest way into the body is, of course, through damage to the otherwise impregnable layer of dead skin — a simple cut is all it takes. The cut may be all but invisible to the person who gets infected, but viruses seek and exploit every opportunity. If there is no cut already a virus may employ an insect to make the cut and deliver the virus — an example is the mosquito that delivers the yellow-fever parasite.

So far we have only been able to control mosquitoes effectively using chemicals, such as DDT, which are extremely damaging to the environment, but genetic science is rapidly opening up new opportunities for control. For example, scientists are working on genetically modified strains of mosquito, which it is hoped will be able to reproduce faster and more effectively than wild mosquitoes. The new mosquitoes have a protein in their gut that kills the malaria parasite. If these new mosquitoes come to dominate mosquito populations and are unable to carry malaria or the yellow-fever virus, millions of lives would be saved each year without the huge damage to the environment caused by DDT.

So, we have a range of viral attackers each capable of infiltrating particular cells and reproducing rapidly at the expense of the host. Once they have got through the formidable defences of mucus, secretions and skin, the big question remains: exactly how do they penetrate the cell that is vital to their reproductive success? The answer encapsulates one of the key aspects of viral behaviour — as we have seen, each virus is perfectly matched to a particular type of cell that it is able chemically to unlock.

Human cells are surrounded by chemicals but only certain chemicals, growth hormone, for example, can enter certain cells; the chemical molecules of growth hormones match the receptors on the surface of the cell that needs that growth hormone. When a particular chemical needed by a particular cell encounters that cell there is a match between chemical receptor and chemical key, and the chemical is allowed to enter the cell. Anything that perfectly mimics that chemical key will therefore fool the cell into allowing it to enter. It is through this ability perfectly to imitate these chemical keys that viruses are able to gain entry to cells. To the appropriate cell the mimicking virus looks like the sort of chemical that should be allowed to enter. Once inside, the virus shuts down the cell's normal activity and harnesses its power to produce more viruses. If the cell is in the walls of a blood vessel, bleeding will result and in the case of Ebola and other haemorrhagic fevers the bleeding may be so extensive as to kill the victim.

Initially, during the first stages of infection the body is taken unawares. The virus usually spreads quickly, infecting increasing numbers of cells, but sooner or later the body's defensive mechanisms kick in — a massive arsenal of powerful weaponry is brought into play to fight the infection. The power of the immune response can be judged by the fact that during the Spanish Flu pandemic of 1918 it was in many cases younger, healthy people who died – as we will see this was precisely because their immune response was so strong. Astonishingly it was so strong that it helped kill the very organism (the human involved) it was designed to protect.

The process of massing the troops of the immune system and sending them into action against the virus is fascinating, and with the benefits of modern science we are now nearer to understanding how it works.

The immune response

The immune response begins when a virus penetrates beyond the first barriers (skin, mucous membranes etc). It then faces being caught and destroyed by macrophages – cells that travel continuously around the body looking for foreign cells. As soon as they detect a foreign cell they destroy it and then send a chemical signal to other immune system cells – B and T lymphocytes – which then concentrate their attentions on the part of the body where the invading cell was first spotted and destroyed by the macrophage.

B and T lymphocytes travel continually through the circulating blood. We produce tens of millions of both B and T lymphocytes each and every day of our lives. Most do absolutely nothing, but every now and then a B or T cell will encounter a viral or bacterial invader with which it matches. It immediately starts rapidly to produce clones of itself and these clones produce antibodies that attack and kill the recognized foreign invader.

In the case of flu, the clones of T cells that recognize the flu virus will kill cells that have been infected by the flu virus. B-cell clones that recognize flu virus also produce antibodies that stick to each flu virus and prevent it invading any further cells. The difficulty is that it takes about a week or perhaps a little longer for the B- and T-cell clones to get up to speed, and in that time the virus has been reproducing at a phenomenal rate.

If you catch measles your B and T cells will usually gradually win the battle, though you will suffer the symptoms of illness while the battle takes place. The extraordinary thing is that the B and T cells that helped you fight the disease – whether it be measles or influenza – stay with you, alive, well and highly effective, for the rest of your life. Because they are there permanently ready and waiting, any measles virus with which you come into contact in the future has no chance of infecting you at all – it will be destroyed before it has the chance. This is how immunity works.

The reason immunity isn't the complete answer in all cases is that in, for example, the case of the common cold there are so many different viruses (probably well over 200 in total) that cause the same feelings of discomfort that you would have to catch them *all* in order to establish the immune defences that work so well in the case of measles, which is caused by just one viral invader. Cold viruses, like influenza viruses, also have the unfortunate habit of mutating rapidly so that your defence against one flu or cold virus type will not protect you – or will only partly protect you – if that type changes.

Mutations are in themselves extraordinary. The process of DNA copying is incredibly accurate and mistakes, or mutations, occur only very rarely – perhaps only once every million times a code is copied. From a human point of view – and inevitably we tend to see things from the scale of single human lifetimes – that appears like an innocuous rate of copying error, but in the vast distances of time spanned by evolution it is actually quite a fast rate of mutation. As we have seen, most of the mistakes in DNA copying will turn out to be disadvantageous to the organism that finds itself saddled with them, and it will find that it is less well able to survive than fellow organisms that don't have the mistake. But every now and then a mistake in DNA copying gives the organism an advantage over its fellows. For example, the rabbits that were immune to myxomatosis suddenly found that their particular genetic make-up – though only fractionally different or mutated from their fellows' genetic make-up – gave them the huge advantage of being able to withstand the killer disease. That slight advantage meant that all rabbits that now survive in the UK are descendants of the small number that had that genetic advantage.

Historic immunity

The situation is complicated too by the fact that, after the initial devastating onslaught of a new virus, it looks as if the afflicted populations of animals, whether human or rabbit, gradually (over generations) become used to the virus at the same time that the virus itself becomes less virulent. This is why Europeans were usually able to survive outbreaks of smallpox when that disease was still endemic. Smallpox returned regularly but humans had built up immunity over generations, which meant that although a percentage of those who caught the disease still died that percentage was relatively small. In the New World the indigenous human population had never encountered smallpox, so when it was released deliberately by the Spanish and the English in the 16th and 17th centuries it killed up to 90 per cent of the indigenous population instead of only the approximate 20 per cent among populations with an historic immunity to the disease.

When the Spanish attempted to settle Hispaniola for sugar-cane plantation in 1509, for example, they introduced smallpox to a population with no historic immunity whatsoever. By 1518 every single one of the estimated 2.5 million aboriginals had been killed by the disease. The Spanish then began to bring in African slaves.

If our relationship with HIV were ancient rather than comparatively recent we might not be suffering the current pandemic. Only the sophistication of modern drugs prevents the already huge HIV death toll being even greater – in the west at least. In Africa and Asia the situation is far worse because HIV continues to infect (almost unchallenged) millions, and millions have already died.

The main reason for the particular virulence of HIV is that HIV infection among humans dates back only to the 1930s; humankind has no historic immunity and HIV is a particularly clever, rapidly mutating virus. HIV kills CD4 positive cells, which are vital to the human immune system. If the virus spread cannot be halted more immune system cells are destroyed until so many have gone that the person infected is prey to a host of other diseases that would otherwise not be harmful. When your defences are destroyed almost anything can kill you.

But, as with myxomatosis in rabbits, there is some suggestion that a tiny number of humans may have a slight genetic difference in their make-up that means, despite repeated exposure to HIV, they do not become infected. Among Kenyan sex workers there is a small number of women who appear to be in this category. Despite the fact that by any reasonable estimation they should be infected with HIV the fact is that they are not. As a result they are now the subjects of intense study by scientists trying to find a way to stop the disease or eliminate it completely. This is obviously preferable to the continuation of the current regime of drugs that does not eliminate the virus but only keeps it under control.

Despite stories in the press that suggest otherwise, HIV is not easily transmittable between humans – at least not when compared to influenza or the common cold. Ebola is similar in this respect – it is not spread by droplet infection or mosquito but only via direct contact. And even direct sexual contact with an HIV sufferer will not guarantee infection. Ebola rapidly incapacitates and usually kills, which means that it causes intensive localized outbreaks that die out almost as quickly as they arise. The virus kills its victims so quickly that they usually do not have time to pass it on to others – something for which we should be very grateful indeed. HIV, by contrast, lies dormant for years before developing into full-blown AIDS. The victim may have no idea he or she is infected and may – as has so often happened – continue to infect others for years.

Animal hosts

Most viruses have an original host animal, and through mutation the virus spreads to humans. In most cases we know the identity of the animal host of a virus, whether it be rabbits or mosquitoes. In the case of HIV, the generally agreed host is probably one or other of the primate species with which humans in West Africa have long had close contact. Monkeys and apes harbour various strains of simian immunodeficiency virus (SIV), some of which are very similar to the HIV virus that now infects humans. The most likely scenario is that a bite or a scratch enabled the virus that causes the monkey form of the disease to infect humans. This may have happened several or many times before the virus suddenly changed – mutated – from a virus that humans could only contract from monkeys to a virus that humans could contract from each other.

This kind of thing may happen with other viruses and the prospect, as we will see in the last part of this book, is terrifying. It is bad enough to find a new disease infecting humans but that disease takes on a whole new dynamic when, instead of each individual case being caused by direct contact with the host animal, it is caused by human-to-human contact. Once that shift has happened the potential for a devastating pandemic increases dramatically. This is the great fear with avian flu – if it became a virus that could be transmitted between humans (rather than from bird to human in each case) the speed of human communication via aircraft and shipping would ensure it was carried quickly round the world.

Smallpox – a success story

This brief journey through the world of viruses has not included many fascinating and deadly viruses including hanta, polio and yellow fever, but smallpox deserves a mention as it is one of the few viral infections that has been totally eliminated.

Smallpox was once endemic in European towns and cities returning regularly to re-infect new generations. It killed up to 25 per cent of those infected and left survivors with unpleasant disfiguring marks.

In England it was said that no man (or woman) could call a child his or her own until it had suffered smallpox and survived. In the New World it played a major part in the defeat and destruction of indigenous peoples at the hands of the British and Spanish, as William MacNeill concludes in his book *Plagues and Peoples* (1977):

> ...on the night when the Aztecs drove Cortez and his men out of Mexico
> City, killing many of them, an epidemic of smallpox was raging in the city.
> The man who had organized the assault on the Spaniards was among those

who died on that 'noche trista' [sad night], as the Spaniards later called it. The paralyzing effect of a lethal epidemic goes far to explain why the Aztecs did not pursue the defeated and demoralized Spaniards, giving them time and opportunity to rest and regroup, gather Indian allies and set siege to the city, and so achieve their eventual victory.

Moreover, it is worth considering the psychological implications of a disease that killed only Indians and left Spaniards unharmed. Such partiality could only be explained supernaturally, and there could be no doubt about which side of the struggle enjoyed divine favor. The religions, priesthoods, and way of life built around the old Indian gods could not survive such a demonstration of the superior power of the God the Spaniards worshipped. Little wonder, then, that the Indians accepted Christianity and submitted to Spanish control so meekly. God had shown Himself on their side, and each new outbreak of infectious disease imported from Europe (and soon from Africa as well) renewed the lesson.

Smallpox was once greatly feared but with concerted worldwide effort it was, against all the odds, eradicated. With flu the situation is more complicated, but there may be lessons for us here, nonetheless.

For centuries smallpox was a simple fact of life for Europeans, particularly city dwellers. The magic of the immune system meant of course that those who survived thereafter enjoyed a lifetime of immunity from the disease. Survivors suffered a number of serious complications for the rest of their lives, however: scarring of the skin with deep pock marks, eyes would sometimes lose their eyelashes, some victims were left blind, others infertile. The effects were determined, as with all viruses, by the particular strain of smallpox and the level of historic immunity enjoyed by the afflicted population. Smallpox was endemic well into the 20th century and literature is filled with its horrors – famously in Charles Dickens' *Bleak House* the heroine Esther Summerson is left deeply scarred by the disease. Though Esther does marry, the implication is that this was a rarity for women who suffered smallpox scarring.

Various forms of smallpox caused varying degrees of illness, which explains the wide variation in the levels of fatality. Europe was lucky to some extent as the dominant strain in this part of the world was known as *variola minor*. It was less virulent than the *variola major* form of the disease, which was endemic in South Asia.

Variola major was the haemorrhagic type – up to 50 per cent of those infected died, and in addition to fever and scarring, symptoms included an appalling smell, cardiovascular collapse and internal bleeding. By contrast, among those affected by *variola minor* the death rate was sometimes as low as one to five per cent.

Where cholera, typhoid and other terrifying afflictions of the past in Europe were seen as more likely to affect the poor and undernourished, smallpox terrified everyone from the highest to the lowest as it was no respecter of class or position.

The years following World War I saw the earliest international efforts to get to grips with major diseases – the attack on malaria began and continues to this day, but so far with only limited success. The United Nations (UN) and World Health Organization (WHO) spearheaded this work and in 1958 they lobbied for a concerted effort to eradicate smallpox completely from the world.

What followed was a remarkable example of nations working together in a way that would have seemed impossible in any earlier period. Partly the effort resulted from a sense that the devastation of two world wars needed to be redressed – the lack of international co-operation had led to a war that cost the lives of more than 75 million people – and medical science at least was going to try to show that something more positive than the usual bickering could emerge from the disaster of world war.

Governments across the world drew up national smallpox-eradication programmes, which were then coordinated by the World Health Organization. The WHO also provided technical assistance, but despite all these efforts the success of the eradication programmes was initially uneven – in Asia, for example, lack of funds caused problems and progress was very slow. Success in India was crucial, and though it took longer than expected (the original plan was eradication within three to five years) the final case – in Somalia – was reported in 1980. Since then there have been no reported cases anywhere in the world.

Antigenic drift and genetic shift

Through the manner of its eradication smallpox provides both an insight into the difficulties of dealing with influenza and perhaps some hope for the future. Smallpox was easier to defeat than influenza because though it existed in two main forms it did not have a natural animal host in which it could constantly mutate, nor did it have influenza's incredibly rapid rate of mutation. *Antigenic drift* is a characteristic of many viruses, including influenza. The genetic make-up of influenza changes over time until various human populations begin to lose their immunity as their immune systems fail to recognize the attacker.

Each year scientists across the world try to predict the latest strain of influenza and prepare a vaccine for it to be given to those who are particularly vulnerable – the young and very elderly, for example. But there is a limit to the number of flu strains that can be included in a vaccine (usually three) and a vaccine that works one year will almost certainly not work the next.

Worse still, influenza is prone to a phenomenon known as *genetic shift*. There are three types of influenza, known as A, B and C. C-type influenza causes mild illness and only sporadic outbreaks. B-type influenza is far more serious and causes epidemics, but the most deadly is the A type, which causes pandemics. Genetic shift occurs when the influenza A-type virus infects an animal that is also susceptible to human A-type influenza. Within that animal the genes of the two types of influenza virus may be 'reassorted' – to use the technical jargon – to produce a new virus to which human populations will have no immunity. So as well as gradually changing (antigenic drift, see above), influenza can make a sudden leap and human populations find themselves, in the worse-case scenario, facing a virus to which they have no immunity at all. The risk then is of massive worldwide pandemic and huge numbers of deaths, precisely the situation that the world faced, as we will see, in 1918–19.

Pandemics, then, are caused by world populations faced with a new strain to which few if any enjoy immunity. Estimates vary, but it is generally agreed that pandemics occur with depressing regularity; since influenza was first recorded pandemic outbreaks have hit us at intervals of roughly 11 to 42 years.

In the 20th century there were pandemics in 1957–58 and 1968–69, as well as the worst pandemic ever – the Spanish flu of 1918–19. The great fear during all pandemics is that large numbers will die and that support services may collapse as doctors and nurses become ill – this is precisely what happened in 1918–19.

The complexity of the situation can be judged by the fact that two influenza-A subtypes currently circulate globally in humans, known as H1N1 and H3N2. The H represents hemagglutinin (also abbreviated to HA) and the N represents neuraminidase (also abbreviated to NA); both hemagglutinin and neuraminidase are surface proteins and H and N refer to the subtype classification of influenza viruses. In wildfowl, at least 16 distinct antigenic subtypes of HA (H1 to H16) and nine of NA (N1 to N9) have been identified. Only A viruses (i.e. not Influenza B and C viruses) are classified by subtype, using HA and NA. Knowledge of the viral surface proteins is vital for researchers since the chemical nature of these proteins may hold the key to attempts to combat the virus.

Genetic shift is unique to influenza-A viruses and it was influenza-A viruses that caused the three pandemics experienced in the 20th century; the combination of antigenic drift and genetic shift gives the A-type virus a superb reproductive advantage because it ensures a constant supply of susceptible hosts.

The reason most pandemic influenzas are believed to originate in southern China is that here is the world's greatest concentration of waterfowl – influenza's natural host – living in close proximity to enormous numbers of human beings.

Recent outbreaks of bird flu have probably been caused exclusively by human-to-animal interaction. If avian flu were to mutate or be reassorted within, say, a pig, then a strain could arise that could be passed from human to human. That is the ultimate nightmare scenario and is explored in more depth in Chapter 7.

It is easy to become confused – baffled even – by the technical jargon and the mass of varying influenza types, subtypes and strains. The important point to remember, however, is that human influenza has a seemingly endless capacity to vary itself in ways that even scientists are sometimes hard put to classify. The notation used by scientists simply reflects that variation.

The race to keep pace with the ever changing nature of flu costs the world billions of dollars each year and as the research becomes more complex costs rise disproportionately. However, this is seen as a necessary evil since the costs of failing to keep pace with antigenic drift and genetic shift would be far higher than the cost of keeping up, which is why first world nations at least are committed politically, socially and financially to ongoing and expensive research.

CHAPTER 2

The Age of Superstition – From Ancient Times to the 17th Century

The earliest reference to influenza occurs in Italy where the word was probably coined in the late 15th or early 16th centuries, although the exact date varies widely according to which historian one consults. The *Oxford English Dictionary* offers the following explanation:

> Influenza. Literally influence. Medieval Latin *influentia*. Influenza has the various senses of English influence but has besides developed (from the notion of occult or astral influence) that of visitation or outbreak of any epidemic disease which assails many people at the same time and place (e.g. *influenzo di catarro*) a sense known as early as 1504. In 1743 applied specifically to 'the epidemic' (called also *la grippe*) which then raged in Italy and spread over Europe generally and for which their Italian word (anglicized in pronounciation) became the English specific name.

Other sources are equally precise but vary widely – one gives the date as 1580. Two 17th-century Italian historians – Domenico and Pietro Buoninsegni, who wrote a history of Florence up to 1460 – are said to have recognized the distinct symptoms of the disease and to have blamed its mysterious arrival on the malevolent position of the stars at certain times.

But the exact year in which the word was coined is ultimately irrelevant as the disease had clearly been around long before its general effects were sufficiently defined in order for it to be given a specific name. Before that date (whenever that was) fevers and colds would have been common, and without the scientific tools that have only become available to the world in the past few decades, it was always going to be difficult to know where a bad cold became a mild dose of flu or where some other fever differed from influenza in the extent to which it made the patient ache and sneeze and cough.

Influenza was no doubt a good catch-all term for a severe cough attended by fever and aches and pains and one which could, moreover, strike down whole villages and towns and then vanish as mysteriously as it had come. Once the word influenza had been coined it quickly gained currency and passed into other languages.

The problem of historical diagnosis

In an age in which diseases were not easily categorized medically, let alone understood, nicknames were inevitable and in England influenza may well have been the disease described – under an entirely different name – by one of Mary Queen of Scots' courtiers in a letter written towards the end of the 16th century. The letter was addressed to William Cecil, Elizabeth I's chief advisor, and it describes a disease sweeping through the court and the town of Edinburgh:

> Immediately upon the Queen's arrival here she fell acquainted with a
> new disease that is common in this town called here the new
> aquaintance which passed also through her whole court sparing neither
> lords, ladies nor damosels not so much as either French or English. It is a
> plague in their heades that have it and a soreness in their stomakes with a
> greate cough that remaineth with some longer with others shorter tyme
> as it finde apt bodies for the nature of the disease. There was no
> appearance of danger nor manie that died of the disease except some
> olde folkes.

That reference to a 'plague in their heads' and the fact that the disease tended to be fatal only among the elderly strongly indicates that this was indeed influenza. It was clearly highly contagious which is, again, characteristic of the disease. Influenza, or something very like it, was also known in both England and America in earlier centuries as the 'gentle correction' or the 'jolly rant'.

Discovering the first certain account of the disease is exceptionally difficult. According to Kenneth Kiple in *The Cambridge World History of Human Disease*:

> The origins of influenza are unknown. It is not an infection of our
> primate relations and so it is probably not a very old human disease.
> It has so far as we know no latent state and it does create a usually
> effective though short-lived immunity and so it was unlikely to have
> been common among our paleolithic ancestors or those of our herd

animals before the advent of agriculture, cities and concentrated populations of humans and domestic animals. In small populations it would have burnt itself out quickly by killing or immunizing all available victims quickly. But because the immunity engendered is ephemeral it does not require the large populations that measles and smallpox do to maintain itself.

That is a neat summary of the currently accepted view of the origins of influenza. It is certain that well within the period of recorded history influenza or something very like it was beginning to attack settled communities.

As birds, particularly waterfowl, are the natural hosts of the various flu viruses, it may be that flu only began to infect humans in the medieval period, coinciding with an increase in the practice of keeping poultry and waterfowl in increasingly large numbers and in greater density. But there are no hard and fast answers here. Influenza may have been with us since the dawn of civilization or earlier, or it may only have begun to infect humans as late as the 15th century.

The 'sweating sickness' which is first recorded in England in 1485 may have been flu – but contemporary descriptions of the symptoms are vague, and some experts believe that the sweating sickness may actually have been hanta virus, a serious respiratory disease usually contracted from rodents.

What we do know is that shortly after Henry Tudor defeated Richard III at the battle of Bosworth Field in mid-summer 1485 (the battle took place on August 22) his army was suddenly afflicted with 'The English Sweat'. Commentators at the time described the disease as hitherto unknown. What were the symptoms? We know that those who succumbed either died within a few hours or recovered within a few days, but only after experiencing severe symptoms of sweating, coughing and weakness. Painful joints were described, as well as thirst, headaches, very high fever and vomiting. The disease spread quickly through the army and though Henry was crowned king on the battlefield, his formal coronation in London had to be postponed until late October, such was the chaos caused by the disease among his soldiers and noblemen. Then, as quickly as it had arrived, the disease vanished.

Was this influenza? At this distance in time it is impossible to say for certain but there are strong indications that it was either flu or something very like it. A number of ancient epidemics had strong affinities with what we know of influenza and it is therefore worth looking at what evidence there is to suggest the connection.

The ancient world

As far back as the 4th century BC the great Greek physician Hippocrates (who lived roughly from 460–370BC) described the symptoms of many diseases, but fitting a modern diagnosis around his sometimes vague descriptions is very difficult indeed. Take the following from his book *Of the Epidemics*, which seems to describe a disease similar to flu:

> In most instances these fevers were prolonged under the Pleiades
> [a constellation] and till winter. Many persons, and more especially
> children, had convulsions from the commencement; and they had fever,
> and the convulsions supervened upon the fevers; in most cases they were
> protracted, but free from danger, unless in those who were in a deadly state
> from other complaints. Those fevers which were continual in the main, and
> with no intermissions, but having exacerbations in the tertian form, there
> being remissions the one day and exacerbations the next, were the most
> violent of all those which occurred at that time, and the most protracted,
> and occurring with the greatest pains, beginning mildly, always on the
> whole increasing, and being exacerbated, and always turning worse, having
> small remissions, and after an abatement having more violent paroxysms,
> and growing worse, for the most part, on the critical days.

Hippocrates, whose oath doctors still abide by today, is infuriatingly vague in the above passage, but a little later in the same work he seems to describe something rather closer to influenza:

> Coughs attended these fevers, but I cannot state that any harm or good
> ever resulted from the cough. The most of these were protracted and
> troublesome, went on in a very disorderly and irregular form, and, for the
> most part, did not end in a crisis, either in the fatal cases or in the others;
> for if it left some of them for a season it soon returned again. In a few
> instances the fever terminated with a crisis.

Like all early physicians, Hippocrates based his diagnosis and remedies for various diseases on the idea of bodily 'humours' – a concept that endured in medicine well into the Renaissance and beyond. The key to health, according to the theory of humours, was that there should be a balance between the choleric, sanguine, melancholic and phlegmatic humours. Choleric was hot and dry, sanguine moist and cold. Hippocrates' advice to his fellow doctors doesn't sound convincing to modern ears:

> The physician must be able to tell the antecedents, know the present, and
> foretell the future – must meditate these things, and have two special
> objects in view with regard to diseases, namely, to do good or to do no
> harm. The art consists in three things – the disease, the patient, and the
> physician. The physician is the servant of the art, and the patient must
> combat the disease along with the physician.

A little before the time of Hippocrates, sometime during the Peloponnesian war (431–404BC) which saw the great city state of Athens pitted against Sparta, the Athenians were suddenly afflicted by a mysterious disease that bears some of the hallmarks of flu, although it could have been smallpox.

The Greek historian Thucydides survived the disease that first struck in 430BC. He writes about the great orator Pericles' (495–429BC) speech about Athenian democracy and follows this immediately with an account of the disease that hit the city in 430BC. The Athenians were crowded together within the walls and unable to tend their nearby farms because of the invasion of Attica by the Spartans. This no doubt contributed to the rapid spread of the disease, but there are hints that it may well have been spreading throughout the eastern Mediterranean anyway. People in Athens died in large numbers – perhaps between a quarter and a third of the population according to some estimates – and Pericles himself may have been one of the victims.

Thucydides describes the symptoms of the disease in some detail and it has been suggested that it was bubonic plague or measles, typhus or influenza. If it was influenza then it must have been influenza with secondary infections of various kinds. The case for typhus is strong, as the disease is characterized by fever and a rash, gangrene of the extremities and extreme thirst. But other symptoms suggest it may have been something else; it may even have been a disease – as A. J. Holladay and J.C. F. Poole have argued (in *Classical Quarterly* 29, 1979) – that no longer exists.

But back to Thucydides. His description may not be accurate by modern standards but it is certainly vivid:

> People in good health were all of a sudden attacked by violent heats in the
> head, and redness and inflammation in the eyes, the inward parts, such as
> the throat or tongue, becoming bloody and emitting an unnatural and
> fetid breath.

This was followed by sneezing, coughing, diarrhoea, vomiting and violent spasms. Extreme thirst was experienced and sufferers developed pustules and ulceration. Some simply died of exhaustion but many survived, we are told, and enjoyed immunity for the rest of their lives. Thucydides tells us that the disease was first noticed in Ethiopia, before spreading up through Egypt and Libya and then into the Greek world. In four years almost a third of the Athenian population died.

Then, in AD165 another devastating epidemic tore across the ancient world. Roman troops returning from campaigns in the east of the empire brought back a disease that killed an estimated five million people. The Greek physician and writer Galen (AD129–216) described some of the symptoms of what was known as the Antonine Plague, after Marcus Aurelius Antoninus, one of two Roman emperors who died from the disease. Galen mentions fever, diarrhoea and inflammation of the pharynx, but the tell-tale pustular eruptions of the skin he describes suggest that the disease was probably smallpox.

Bubonic plague was a constant epidemic enemy at this time. In the 6th century AD, under the reign of the Byzantine Emperor Justinian I, a plague hit the city of Constantinople, modern Istanbul. In little more than a year – from AD541–542 – it killed 40 per cent of Constantinople's population and spread from North Africa into Europe and then right across the Mediterranean. This was almost certainly the same plague that eight hundred years later was to devastate Europe's population.

The 16th century

From the end of the Roman Empire through the so-called Dark Ages and right up until the early medieval period it is impossible to detect any signs of influenza in surviving written records. It may well be that influenza was peculiarly adapted to the settled and organized societies created by ancient Greeks and Romans and not suited to the more nomadic lives led by the Germanic tribes – Goths and Visigoths – whose incursions led to the fall of Rome.

Bubonic plague – the Black Death – was the great affliction of the Middle Ages, eclipsing all other natural disasters. Between 1347 and 1350 plague probably killed about a quarter of Europe's population – perhaps 25 million people in total. (But if these early pandemics were massive killers they pale into insignificance, as we will see, when compared to the influenza pandemic that swept across the world in 1918.)

Smallpox and bubonic plague are relatively easy to identify from contemporary descriptions of the disease, but flu is more difficult. In his book *A General Chronological History of the Air, Weather, Seasons, Meteors Etc.*, published in 1749,

Dr Thomas Short describes an epidemic that hit Britain in 1510:

> The disease called Coccoluche, or Coccolucio, (because the sick wore a
> cap or covering close all over their heads) came from the island of Melite
> in Africa, into Sicily; so into Spain and Italy, from that over the Alps into
> Portugal, Hungary, and a great part of Germany, even to the Baltic Sea;
> every month shifting its situation with the wind from East to West, so into
> France, Britain. It attacked at once, and raged all over Europe, not missing
> a family, and scarce a person. A grievous pain of the head, heaviness,
> difficulty of breathing, hoarseness, loss of strength and appetite, restlessness,
> watchings, from a terrible taring cough. Presently, succeeded a chilness, and
> so a violent cough, that many were in danger of suffocation. The first days
> it was without spitting; but about the seventh or eighth day, much viscid
> phlegm was spit up. Others (though fewer) spit only water and froth. When
> they began to spit, cough and shortness of breath were easier. None died,
> except some children. In some, it went off with a looseness; in others, by
> sweating. Bleeding and purging did hurt.

We don't know Short's sources for this description but it is fascinating and far more
detailed than many later reports. The tell-tale heaviness, breathing difficulty and loss
of strength and appetite suggests this may well have been influenza. It's worth noting
too that severe attacks of influenza can produce bizarre symptoms that make even
expert physicians doubt their diagnosis – many of the world's top scientists were
convinced in 1918, for example, that Spanish flu wasn't flu at all. They were fooled
by the ferocity of the disease and the speed with which it incapacitated and killed.
Like earlier doctors those 1918 practitioners were still largely in the dark since they
could not identify the pathogen that caused the disease (and would not do so until
1938). Like all doctors they relied on characteristic symptoms. When the symptoms
seemed uncharacteristic they were sometimes deceived. And if it was difficult in
1918 it was far more difficult in earlier centuries, both for doctors and those who
wrote about disease.

We know that in the first three decades after Columbus landed in the Americas
in 1492 – and therefore only a little earlier than the 1510 outbreak described above
– the populations of native peoples in the Antilles were almost completely wiped
out. Smallpox has usually been blamed, but recent evidence suggests that smallpox
arrived only in 1518 by which time much of the damage had already been done.
The most likely explanation is that the Spaniards carried influenza, a disease then

unknown in the New World and to which, inevitably, the indigenous population had no immunity. The effects of infection were therefore almost always lethal.

In his book *A Short Account of the Destruction of the Indies* published in 1545 Bartolome de las Cases described the astonishingly high levels of mortality suffered by the Indians when infected by European diseases, including what was almost certainly influenza. De las Cases was, incidentally, one of the very few Europeans to accept that the Spanish conquest of the Americas was both unchristian and deeply immoral.

In 1513 the great humanist scholar Erasmus (1466–1536) described in some detail the 'sweating sickness' or 'English disease' as it was sometimes known, in a letter to his friend Juan Luis Vives. What makes Erasmus's account so interesting is that it describes some of the habits of the English that he believed led to infections:

> I often grieve and wonder how it happens, that Britain has now, for so many years, been afflicted with a continual Plague, and chiefly with the Sweating-sickness, which is a malady that seems almost peculiar to the country. We have read of a state being delivered from a long-continued pestilence by changing the style of building, upon the advice of a philosopher. If I am not deceived, England may be freed in a similar manner. In the first place, the English have no regard to what quarter of the Heavens their windows or doors are turned; in the next, their sitting-rooms are generally so constructed, as to be incapable of being ventilated, which is a thing that Galen particularly recommends. Furthermore, a great part of the wall is made transparent by glass plates (or squares), which admit the light, but exclude the wind: and yet, through the small crevices, they admit the air to be strained, which becomes somewhat more pestilent by staying there a long time. The streets, too, are, generally covered with clay and rushes, which are so seldom renewed, that the covering sometimes remains twenty years, concealing beneath a mass of all descriptions of filth, not fit to mention. Hence, upon a change in the atmosphere, a certain vapour is exhaled, in my opinion, not at all wholesome for the human body. Added to this, England is not only surrounded by the sea on every side, but it is also, in many places, marshy, and intersected by salt streams, to say nothing at present of the salt food, of which the common people are amazingly fond.
>
> It is my firm opinion, that the island would become much more wholesome, if the spreading of rushes on the ground were not used, and if

the chambers were so built as to be exposed to the Heavens on two or
three sides, the windows of glass being so made as to open altogether, and
close in the same way, and to shut so as not to admit noxious winds
through the crevices. Since, as it is sometimes wholesome to admit the air,
so it is sometimes as much so to keep it out. The common people laugh, if
a person complain of the cloudy sky. If, even twenty years ago, I had
entered into a chamber which had been uninhabited for some months,
I was immediately seized with a fever. It would contribute to this object
(to render the island more healthy), if more sparing diet could be more
generally recommended, and a more moderate use of salt provisions; and if
certain public officers were commissioned to keep the roads more free
from nuisances. Those parts, too, should be looked to more particularly,
which are in the neighbourhood of a town. You will laugh at my having
time to trouble myself about these matters. I love the country which has
for so long a time given me an hospitable abode, and in it, should
circumstances allow, I would willingly spend what remains of life.

I have no doubt from your character for wisdom, that you know these
matters better than myself; I resolved, however, to mention them to you,
that you may, if my opinion coincides with yours, recommend these hints
to the notice of the great. For, in former days, kings were wont to interest
themselves in such things.

Dr Short's account of the 1510 epidemic is followed by his description of a similar
outbreak of influenza in 1557. In his account of this epidemic he looks at England
but also the effect of the disease as far afield as Spain and beyond. Smallpox could
strike at any time, while bubonic plague was always at its worst during hot
summers. Influenza usually attacked and arrived with the first cold winds of
autumn and winter:

In the end of September, came a very strong cold North wind; presently
after were many Catarrhs, quickly followed by a most severe cough, pain of
the side, difficulty of breathing, and a fever. The pain was neither violent
nor pricking, but mild. The third day they expectorated freely. The sixth,
seventh, or, at the farthest, the eighth day, all who had that pain of the side
died; but such as were blooded the first or second day, recovered on the
fourth or fifth; but bleeding on the last two days, did no service. Slippery,
thickening linctuses, were found of most service. Broths, or spoon-meats,

or moist foods, were good. But where the season continued still rainy, the case was very different; for at Mantua Carpentaria, three miles from Madrid, the epidemic began in August, and bleeding or purging was so dangerous, that in the small town 2,000 were let blood of, and all died. There it began with a roughness of the jaws, small cough, then a strong fever, with a pain of the head, back, and legs; some felt as though they were corded over the breast, and had a weight at the stomach; all which continued to the third day at farthest; then the fever went off with a sweat, or bleeding at the nose. In some few, it turned to a pleurisy, or fatal peripneumony.

At Alcmaria, this year in October, raged such an epidemic, as seized whole families at once. In that small place, died in three weeks 200 persons of this mortal peripneumony. It attacked like a catarrh, with a very slow and malignant fever, bringing, as it were, a sudden suffocation along with it; then seized the breast with so great a difficulty of breathing, that the sick seemed dying. Presently it laid hold of the precordia and stomach, and with a violent cough, which either caused abortion, or killed gravid women. Some, but very few, had continual fevers along with it; many had double tertians [fevers]; others simple slight intermittents. All were worse by night than by day; such as recovered were long valetudinary... This disease seized most countries very suddenly when it entered, catching thousands the same moment.

Thick, ill-smelling fogs preceded it some days. In some places, few recovered who had it accompanied with a violent fever. If intermittent fevers accompanied the pain of the throat (which was neither a quinzy, nor scarce a slight inflammation) they were better off, even without bleeding. But if the fever supervened, and was not well managed, it was often fatal. Gentle bleeding the first day was useful. For the throat, gargles of plantin, scabious, and red rose waters, quinces, mulberries, and sealed earth, were used. For the cough and hoarseness, pectoral and oyly mixtures. Scarification with cupping succeeded better than bleeding. The year 1555 had been most excessively rainy, and 1556, as great a drought. After a great scarcity of corn, not from famine, but the rich cornmongers had bought and hoarded it up till it was spoiled, which forced the poor to eat oxes' and swine's dung.

This year, the season was mostly wet, but in some countries dry. The Influenza set in about the time when a cold north wind succeeded intense heat. In the previous year was an eruption of Etna.

That reference to Etna erupting fits with the prevailing idea that influenza was caused by a malign supernatural or environmental influence – volcanic eruptions were clearly likely to accompany outbreaks of the flu since they too were caused by some deeply rooted astrological circumstance. Short describes, too, the common remedies that were in use in the early 16th century. None of these – whether bleeding or venesection as it was known – nor rosewater, nor the use of quince is questioned by Short: these were remedies still in use for influenza when he was writing in 1749.

Other commentators noted the connection between turbulent weather and natural disasters of one sort or another and the sudden appearance of influenza or other diseases. But in making these and similar links they were not reporting what they knew but rather making assumptions based on received wisdom.

A supposed epidemic of influenza in 1578 was thus described by the great historian of London John Stow, 20 years later:

> In 1578, and on April the 6th, this year, and May the 12th, were general Earthquakes over all England. October the 10th, a Comet in the South rushing toward the East; it continued from October to January, full two months. The weather for some years past having been extraordinary moist, wet, and rainy, wind South, at the rising of the Dog star came a cold, dry North wind. From the middle of August to the end of September, raged a malignant epidemic Catarrh; it began with a pain of the head, and feverish heat: some were disposed to sleep, others to watching: presently followed a dry cough, pain of the breast, harshness and roughness of the throat, weakness of the stomach; at last, a terrible panting for breath, like dying persons. Though the cough lasted not long, yet the panting for breath continued to the fourteenth day; some sweated, such recovered the thirtieth or fortieth day; they did not expectorate much. With some the disease went off by stool, in others by urine. Though all had it, few died in these countries, except such as were let blood of, or had unsound viscera. Of the first, died in Rome at this time 2,000. The cure consisted in repeated lenitives, cooling inciders, and pectorals [pain and fever relievers]. In other places it appeared somewhat different, according to the varying constitution of the season.

Even allowing for an occasional inability to resist rather colourful language, Short is impressively detailed in his account of the symptoms of the disease, which seems to have spread rapidly between most of Britain's larger centres of population. But given that communications were slow and difficult during the 16th century it is hardly surprising that many smaller, remote communities were spared. So long as they remained isolated and there were no infected visitors from bigger cities, villages and even smaller towns often escaped infection. But those characteristic symptoms – weariness and coughing, aching limbs and fever – are strong indicators that once again the country was hit by influenza.

Dr Short describes another epidemic of 1580:

> In sundry places it begun with a weariness, heaviness, and painful
> sensation; heat and horrours seized the whole body, chiefly the breast and
> head, with a dry cough, hoarseness, roughness of the jaws, difficulty of
> breathing, weakness and languor of the stomach, vomiting green bile, like
> juice of leeks; which symptoms increased with the disease, as the fever,
> cough, weight and pain of the head, pricking pain of the extremes,
> watching, dryness and roughness of the tongue, and shortness of breath. At
> the start of the disease all these were heightened, catarrh, cough, spitting.
> Some had swellings on the glands of the throat. In some it went off by
> stool; in others by urine or sweat, or bleeding at the nose. Some had spots.
> All recovered very slowly. This disease raged over all Europe at least, and
> prevailed for six weeks. Yet, if in any place it was preceded by a drought,
> bleeding gave the speediest and greatest relief; as at Montpelier, so as not
> one of a thousand died of it. The same epidemic returned in October and
> November that year; then bleeding even in these places was hurtful, except
> when a spitting of blood, pleurisy, or peripneumony attended it. At the
> same time a Fever of the same kind prevailed… all over the world; and was
> the same with that of 1551, as the catarrh and disorders of the breast were
> the same with those of 1510, 1591, 1597, 1610, &c., over all Europe, with a
> rheum and distillation from the head, either with or without a fever, pain
> of the head, heaviness, hoarseness, weakness. To those symptoms this year
> were joined a cough, pain of the jaws and neck.
>
> After a prodigious plague of Insects in April and May, the like epidemic
> broke out and strangled many; but where proper means were used, all re-
> covered. It began with a fever and cough, then followed again a pain of the
> head, and loins; then the fever intermitted a few days, and returned with
> fresh vigour. Some had no rest, but the heat increasing, they died; as some
> did of a phrenzy, and others of a consumption; but speedy proper means

secured them, viz., bleeding, laxatives, and pectorals, cuppings, cooling clysters, cordial opiates, and epithems.

We now know that none of these supposed remedies to which Short refers would have had any influence at all on the progress of the disease in individual patients. Bleeding may well have made the situation far worse, and the reference to the use of laxatives simply shows that ancient remedies – laxatives were recommended for almost every ailment by Hippocrates – were still being recommended simply because there was nothing else to suggest.

It is impossible to be sure at this distance in time if the epidemic of 1580 was as serious as Short suggests. If it really did travel all over Europe and the world as Short indicates then it almost certainly should be considered a pandemic.

The disease of 1580 seems to have returned in a slightly different form in 1581. According to Dr Short, in the north of England the arrival of influenza was preceded in April 1581 by 'an Earthquake not far from York, which in some places shook the stones out of the buildings, and made the church bells jangle'. Short also mentions late 16th-century reports that in Kent 'the next night the earth trembled once or twice, as it did also May the 1st following'.

Short describes how in Kent and the marshes of Essex, there was:

> …a sore plague of strange Mice suddenly covering the earth, and gnawing the grass roots; this poisoned all field herbage, for it raised the plague of murrain among cattle grazing on it. No wit nor art of man could destroy these mice, till another strange flight of Owls came, and killed them all.
>
> In April and May a prodigious number of insects, supposed to rise out of the earth, obscured the air, and were crushed by millions on the roads. Birds felt the influence of the bad air, for they abandoned the countries where the epidemic appeared. Birds of passage migrated before the usual time, and those accustomed to build on trees and in elevated localities, rested during the night in low situations, and on the ground. Even animals which feed on herbs and leaves, took a dislike to their pastures, which were apparently influenced by some virus in the air.

This extraordinary picture of a natural world gone mad fits the long-held belief that somehow influenza or catarrhal fever as it was sometimes known was caused by 'miasma'; by poisonous air or some general disturbance in nature.

The 17th century

Between 1581 and 1658, influenza seems scarcely to have been mentioned in diaries, letters, medical reports and other written evidence. This is almost certainly because during the first half of the 17th century the great fear was that the plague would return, which it did periodically until the 1660s when one of the worst outbreaks of bubonic plague took place in London and elsewhere. Indeed, it was only the Great Fire a year later in 1666 that helped bring that particular outbreak of the plague under control, at least in London.

Influenza is said to have prevailed throughout Europe in 1610 but it sounds as if this was the sort of flu that had high morbidity (that is, a very large number of people were infected) but low mortality; with this exception, influenza is scarcely noticed by authors between 1580 and 1658.

The difficulty of analyzing exactly what happened in the past is compounded by the fact that early authors emphasize, as we have seen, plagues of mice, changes in the direction of the wind, comets and other natural phenomena and do not necessarily provide the sort of evidence modern scientists need. We have to try to put ourselves back into the minds of people who simply could not have conceived that disease was caused by an invisible living entity.

The year 1658 marks the arrival of the next serious attack of flu that was so widespread as to be noticed by many writers and commentators, not just physicians. The following symptoms were described by Dr Willis in his account of the 1658 outbreak, published in *Practice of Physic: Being the Whole Works of that Renowned and Famous Physician*:

> An equally intense frost followed, the next Winter, the immoderate heat of the foregoing Summer, so that no one living could remember such a year, for either excess both of heat and cold. From the ides of December, almost to the vernal equinox, the earth was covered with snow, and the north wind constantly blowing, all things without doors were frozen; also, afterwards, from the beginning of the Spring, almost to the beginning of June, the same wind still blowing, the season was more like Winter than Spring; unless now and then a hot day came between. During the Winter among our countrymen, there was a moderate state of health, and freedom from all popular diseases. The Spring coming on, an intermitting fever (as used to do every year before) fell upon some. About the end of April, suddenly a Distemper arose, as if sent by some blast of the stars, which laid

hold on very many together: that in some towns, in the space of a week, above a thousand people fell sick together. The particular symptom of this disease, and which first invaded the sick, was a troublesome cough, with great spitting, also a Catarrh falling down on the palate, throat, and nostrils; also it was accompanied with a feaverish distemper, joyned with heat and thirst, want of appetite, a spontaneous weariness, and a grievous pain in the back and limbs: which feaver, however, was more remiss in some, that they could go abroad, and follow their affairs in the time of their sickness, but complaining, in the mean time, of want of strength and of languishing, a loathing of food, a cough, and a catarrh. But in some a very hot distemper plainly appeared, that being thrown into bed they were troubled with burning thirst, waking, hoarseness, and coughing, almost continual; sometimes there came upon this a bleeding at the nose, and in some a bloody spittle, and frequently a bloody flux; such as were indued with an infirm body, or men of a more declining age, that were taken with this disease, not a few died of it; but the more strong, and almost all of an healthful constitution, recovered: those who falling sick of this disease, and died, for the most part died by reason of the strength being leisurely wasted, and a serous heap more and more gathered together in the breast, with the feaver being increased, and a difficulty of breath, like those sick of an hectic feaver. Concerning this disease, we are to inquire, what procatartic cause it had, that it should arise in the middle of the Spring suddenly, and that the third part of mankind, almost, should be distempered with the same, in the space of a month: then the signs and symptoms being carefully collated, the formal reason of this disease, also its crisis and way of cure, ought to be assigned.

The observation that only the elderly were killed strongly suggests that this was influenza, but that commentators and physicians were baffled can be judged by Dr Willis's account. The very high levels of infection referred to and the 'difficulty of breath' and exhaustion are key symptoms of the most serious influenza attacks. The vast array of potential explanations and influences, and the confusion that surrounded attempts to understand precisely what was happening can be judged by Dr Willis when he says of the arrival of influenza:

That the Northern Wind is most apt to produce Catarrhs, besides the testimony of Hippocrates common experience doth make known: but why catarrhs did not spread, at least in some peculiar places, all the Winter and Spring, but only in one month's space, and then joyned with a feaver, this distemper should become epidemical, doth not so plainly appear.

I know many deduce the cause from the unequal temper of the Air, at that time; which, although for the most part very cold, yet the North wind sometimes lessening, there would be a day or two very hot between: wherefore, from this occasion, as from cold taken after the heat, men should commonly fall sick. But indeed, for the exciting the distemper, so suddenly rising, and commonly spreading, there is required, besides such an occasion, a great foregoing cause or predisposition, though the other might suffice, perhaps, for an evident cause for to distemper them with this sickness; for we ought to suppose, that almost all men were prone to the receiving this disease, otherwise no evident cause could have exercised its power so potently on so many, wherefore, it seems very likely, that this disease had its origine from the intemperance and great inordination of the year: and as the Autumnal Intermitting Feaver before described, was the product of the preceding immoderate heat, so this Catarrhal Feaver depended altogether upon the following part of the year, being so extremely cold; for the blood being now thoroughly roasted by the very hot Summer, and prone to the feaver before described, then being made more sourish by the Autumn urging it, and apt for a Quartan Feaver, afterwards being a little ventilated by reason of the strong cold of the Winter, and hindred from its due perspiration, retained yet its dyscrasie or evil disposition, and readily broke forth on the first occasion given: wherefore, when the blood, in the middle of the Spring (as the juice of vegetables), being made more lively, and also begun to flower and grow rank, by reason of the stoppage being still continued, was strained in its circulation, and easily made prone to a feaverish effervescency: and as the serous water redounding in the blood, could not evaporate outwardly, because of the pores being still straitned by the cold, restagnating within, and chiefly falling upon the lungs, (where it might be moved about, instead of an outward breathing forth,) excited the so frequent and trouble-some cough.

The only accurate part of this extraordinary document – by modern standards – is the tendency for flu to affect populations in the colder winter weather. The idea that 'rank blood' and water in the blood being unable to evaporate should have anything to do with flu will strike any modern reader as bizarre. The reference to Hippocrates is characteristic of all early writing about disease, because it was seen as more important to know what ancient and revered writers had said than to question their judgement or try to establish the facts for oneself. But the writer was clearly a knowledgeable and experienced physician by the standards of the time. He goes on to describe the problem of what he calls effervescent blood and compares this with wine that has been stored at too high a temperature.

Dr Willis is more convincing when he explains the symptoms of influenza and crucially describes those who are more likely to be killed by the disease. His description matches the progress of influenza when it is not in its most virulent form:

> The prognostick of this disease, concerning private persons, is, for the most part, easie, that one may deliver the event from the first assault; for if this sickness be excited in a strong body, and healthful before, and that the feaverish distemper be moderate, and without any grievous and horrid symptom, the business is free from danger, and the distemper is to be accounted but of light moment, as that commonly is of catching cold, neither needs a physician be consulted, nor remedies, unless trivial and ordinary, be administered. But if this distemper happens in a weak and sickly body, with an evil provision, or that the feaver being carried into a putrid feaver, or the cough growing grievous, induces difficult breathing, and as it were a rabid or consumptive disposition, the event of the disease is much to be suspected, and often terminates in death.

According to Dr Thomas Sydenham the year 1675 saw a serious though probably not pandemic outbreak of flu:

> In the year 1675, warm and mild weather (indeed Summer weather) lasted longer than usual, even to the end of October. However, it was succeeded by weather very different, viz., sudden cold and moisture. Then it was that coughs prevailed in greater number than at any other time within my remembrance. No one escaped them, whatever might be his age or temperament; and they ran through whole families at once. Nor were they only remarkable for their frequency; this being the case every winter. They were remarkable on account of the accidental dangers which they brought

upon those they affected. The constitution of both the present time, and the whole of the previous autumn, exerted itself to the utmost in the production of the epidemic fever already described; and besides this, there was no other epidemic disease by the antagonism whereof the activity of the present one might be traversed in even the least degree. Hence the coughs paved the way to fever, and passed, without difficulty, into it. Meanwhile, just as the coughs helped the constitution in producing the fever, so also was the fever determined by the cough to the lungs and pleura. These it attacked, just as a week before, it had attacked the head. This sudden change inclined the unthinking to consider the fever as either an essential pleurisy, or an essential peripneumony. Yet it was neither more nor less than what it had been throughout. Now, as before, it attacked with pain in the head, back, and limbs; and this was the symptom of the fever of the constitution.

Dr Sydenham's regime for curing the disease was as ineffectual as all those that had preceded it, but we know that belief in a particular cure (the placebo effect) can be powerful enough to have enormous beneficial effects. This must explain why doctors using what to modern ears sound like hopeless treatments enjoyed enough success to stay in business. Sydenham writes:

> I treated my patients as follows: If the cough had not yet brought on the usually concomitant fever, I was satisfied with forbidding animal food, and fermented liquors. I recommended moderate exercise, fresh air, and occasional draughts of a cooling pectoral balm. This was sufficient for checking the cough and anticipating the fever. The abstinence from meat and wine, and the refrigerant draught, tempered the blood, and made it less ready for the febrile impressions, whilst the exercise opened the pores of the skin, and supplied the natural and genuine passage for the exhalations. These were dispersed, and the patient was the better for their dispersion.
>
> As to the allaying of the cough, the application of narcotics and anodynes was not wholly safe. And just as dangerous was the use of spirituous liquors and hot cordials. Both modes acted alike. They entangled and hardened the matter of the cough, so that those exhalations which, by departing quietly and gradually from the blood, should vanish into the atmosphere at large, were now denied an exit, corked up in the mass of the blood, and became, thereby, sources of fever.

Although doctors' accounts of the symptoms, spread and possible cures for influenza are reasonably common – at least from the 17th century onwards – far rarer is an account of the experience of individual patients. The following is an anonymous account of the treatment of a particular patient towards the end of the 17th century:

> In the November of the aforesaid year, I attended Mr Thomas Windham,
> the eldest son of Sir Francis Windham, knight. The patient was sick of the
> fever in question, and complained of pain in the side, and the other
> symptoms of the malady. I bled once (and no oftener), blistered the nape of
> the neck, threw up daily clysters, ordered, one day, balm and refrigerant
> emulsions, another milk and water (sometimes thin small beer), and
> recommended him to be out of bed a few hours every day. This set him up
> within a few days, and after a free purge he was thoroughly cured.

Most of the recorded early outbreaks of influenza were probably epidemic rather than pandemic in extent. There are some rather sketchy records of infection spreading across Europe and beyond, but they may be sketchy because the spread across these distances was not recorded adequately at a time when communications across national and international borders were either very slow or non-existent. In other words, absence of evidence is not evidence of absence.

CHAPTER 3

The Age of Reason – The 18th Century

The first pandemic explosion that is recorded with any real accuracy was probably the 1580 outbreak, which was reported to have swept across Europe, Africa and Asia. There is almost no evidence that earlier epidemics shifted up a gear to become worldwide pandemics.

The 18th century was the first century of reasonably well-recorded pandemic, although as we have seen flu on an epidemic scale has been with us since the middle ages and earlier; certainly flu has returned with unfailing regularity to affect human populations ever since. At most we have probably only escaped its ravages for a decade or two since the closing of the Middle Ages.

Greater accuracy in diagnosis

By the end of the 17th century in England at least descriptions of flu or flu-like diseases begin to have a more detailed and convincing feel to them. The general vagueness of diagnosis and cure begins to change as we reach the 18th century and the so-called Age of Enlightenment. A more scientific language evolved during this century, particularly in England, and English doctors' ability carefully to delineate symptoms of all diseases helped define influenza.

Improved communications also meant that the spread of certain diseases across national and sometimes international boundaries could be properly tracked. In 1782 a Dr Haygarth described how improvements in coach travel had brought disease to the north of England. 'The gentleman who brought the distemper into Chester in 1782, from London, travelled with it at the rate of 182 miles in 27 hours. Such facts explain in a satisfactory way why it spread through the whole island in such a short time.'

We know that after the 1580 pandemic (see Chapter 2) a century and more appears to have passed without influenza outbreaks of a pandemic nature – certainly, as we have seen, there were regular epidemics and their regional spread is reasonably well attested. Their international spread is not.

It is notable that the spread and virulence of influenza increased dramatically as human travel became easier and more frequent for larger numbers of people. So far as Europe is concerned, trade with the east had increased considerably by the middle decades of the 18th century and after a relatively influenza-free period during the 17th century the 18th century saw at least three major influenza pandemics and two epidemics on such a scale that they have sometimes been re-classified as pandemics. The influenza pandemics and epidemics of the 18th century are, without question, directly related to increased trade between east and west, and improvements in the speed of communication between hitherto far-flung regions of the world.

The pandemic of 1729–30 was described in detail by a number of contemporary writers, doctors and even politicians. One of the best accounts of this pandemic appears in John Huxham's *Observations on the Air and Epidemical Diseases* published in London in 1758, more than 20 years after the pandemic, but Huxham was writing from experience and observation.

> About this time a disease invaded these parts, which was the most compleatly epidemic of any I remember to have met with; not a house was free from it; the beggar's hut, and the nobleman's palace were alike subject to its attacks; scarce a person escaping either in town or country: old and young, strong and infirm, shared the same fate. Finding it to prevail so much and with so great force, insomuch that sooner or later it had spread almost all over the country, I resolved to commit a succinct history of the disease and its appearances to writing, with which I now present the reader.
>
> This distemper had raged in Cornwall and the Western parts of Devonshire, from the first coming in of this month (February); but did not reach us at Plymouth till about the 10th, which was on a Saturday, and that day numbers were suddenly seized: the day afterwards they fell down in multitudes, and by the 18th or 20th of March scarce any one had escaped it.
>
> The disorder began at first with a slight shivering; this was presently followed by a transient erratic heat, an headache, and a violent and troublesome sneezing; then the back and lungs were seized with flying pains, which sometimes attacked the breast likewise, and though they did not long remain there, yet were very troublesome, being greatly irritated by the violent cough which accompanied the disorder; in the fits, of which a great quantity of a thin sharp mucus was thrown out from the nose and mouth. These complaints were like those arising from what is called

catching cold, but presently a slight fever came on, which afterwards grew more violent; the pulse was now very quick, but not in the least hard and tense like that in a pleurisy; nor was the urine remarkably red, but very thick and inclining to a whitish colour; the tongue instead of being dry was thick covered with a whitish mucus or slime: there was an universal complaint of want of rest, and a great giddiness. Several likewise were seized with a most racking pain in the head, often accompanied with a slight delirium. Many were troubled with a tinnitus aurium, or singing in the ears; and numbers suffered from violent earaches or pains in the meatus auditorius, which in some turned to an abscess; exulcerations and swellings of the lances were likewise very common. The sick were in general very much given to sweat, which, when it broke out of its own accord, was very plentiful, and continued without striking in again, did often in the space of two or three days wholly carry off the fever; the urine depositing a copious, whitish, or yellowish coloured sediment, but very seldom a reddish one; numbers, however, had great difficulty in making water, whether from their blisters, or from their profuse sweats, I will not take upon me to determine. The disorder often terminated with a discharge of bilious matter by stool, and sometimes by the breaking forth of fiery pimples. You have here a description of this epidemic disease such as it prevailed hereabouts attacking everyone more or less; but still, considering the great multitude that were seized by it, it was fatal to but few, and that chiefly infants and consumptive old people.

It generally went off about the fourth day, leaving behind a troublesome cough, which was very often of long duration; and such a dejection of strength as one would hardly have suspected from the shortness of the time; but this chiefly happened where there had been an imprudent and untimely use of the lancet. Bleeding was of the most benefit to such as laboured under a great pain and weight at the breast, and that at the beginning, not decline of the fever. In all, the blood taken away was covered with a thin whitish pellicle, but not very tough; unless in those where bloodletting had been too long neglected, and the fever had thereby turned to a pleurisy and peripneumony, which was the case with not a few, especially where there had been a preposterous use of hot volatiles and cordial medicines.

A nausea or vomiting indicated a gentle emetic, which always remarkably relieved the sickness of the stomach and weight of the breast;

and did likewise in some sort excite a diaphoresis, to promote which it was absolutely necessary to pour down quantities of warm diluting drinks, whether drought required them or not. White-wine whey drank a little warm was in general found the best diluter, and such quantities of it were used at this time, that the country round could scarce supply milk enough to make it.

Blisters to the back and behind the ears were of eminent service in this disorder, nor were they on any account to be omitted, for they were a certain relief to the violent pains of the head, as well as to the exulceration and swelling of the jaws; add to this, that by diverting the course of the acrid humours they prevented its falling upon the lungs.

The medicines I used to prescribe were chiefly these: sperm whale oil, dissolved in some water, or else very weak milk-whey, which generally eased the cough, and promoted the salutary sweats. If the difficulty of breathing and expectoration remained after the bleeding, I generally found it necessary to give a solution of gum ammoniac; for the disease was much in the nature of a peripneumonia, and seemed to require the same method of cure, such as the sharper pectorals, to cut the tough, viscid phlegm, blisters to the legs, and sometimes emetics, or the more lenient cathartics.

The cough was very violent during the whole course of the disease, insomuch that it was often a hard matter to keep it under, even by the use of anodynes; nay, after the fever was gone off, this symptom would sometimes remain so extraordinarily vehement, that it threw several into consumptions, which carried them off within a month or two, especially such as had been formerly subject to disorders of the breast and lungs. Having frequently observed, that if a looseness came on, the cough was commonly carried off by it, following nature as the best guide, I used to give rhubarb, manna, tartar, &c., about the decline of the fever, and generally found a happy effect from it; for the appetite, which had, during the whole course of the disease, been greatly impaired, if not wholly destroyed, was by this method happily restored.

On the whole, this disorder was rarely mortal, unless by some very great error arising in the treatment of it; however, this very circumstance proved fatal to some, who, making too slight of it, either on account of its being so common, or not thinking it very dangerous, often found asthmas, hectics, or even consumptions themselves, the forfeitures of their inconsiderate rashness.

This careful description of the disease and its symptoms has a local and convincing air to it. Doctor Huxham worked throughout his career in the Plymouth area and knew his broad spectrum of patients well. It is difficult to doubt that the disease he describes was a particularly virulent form of flu – despite very high morbidity, this particular pandemic does not seem to have had a particularly high level of mortality. Like most commonly circulating strains of flu it tended to be fatal only in the very young, the elderly or those with weakened immune systems.

Descriptions of the spread of the disease over a much wider area are, as we have seen, rare in early accounts, because information was difficult to get and very difficult to analyze. An exception to this rule is Dr John Arbuthnott who published his *An Essay Concerning the Effects of Air on Human Bodies* in 1751. Here he describes the progress of influenza across Britain and Europe:

> There have been of late two remarkable instances of the influence of the air in producing an epidemical disease, perhaps over the greatest part of the surface of the earth; the first happened in the year 1728, the last in the latter end of the year 1732 and beginning of 1733, which, being the more recent and remarkable, I shall give a short description of it, till a more particular one can be procured from the collected memoirs of the several countries which it invaded, of which I have seen only a few.
>
> The previous constitution of the air was, in England and in the greatest part of Europe, a great drought, which may be inferred from the failure of the springs, in the abatement of the fresh water in all its usual currents and reservoirs, which are the best measure of the quantity of moisture falling from the clouds. What is most generally taken notice of, in the accounts I have seen from Germany, France, and some other places, was, that the air in the beginning of winter, especially in November, was more than usually filled with thick and frequent fogs, the matter of which was not precipitated upon the earth in rain, snow, or any other fruits of the air. Fogs are so usual in this country in November, that there was nothing particular observed about them that I know. But there was hardly anything fell from the clouds during the month of November, except a very small quantity of snow, attended with a frost of no long duration; and this was all the winter we had. In the northern parts of France, there was a very small quantity of snow, which lasted from their 15th and our 4th of November, till after Christmas. This was succeeded by southerly winds and stinking fogs, during which there was observed, by some chirurgeons,

a great disposition in wounds to mortify. Both before and during the
continuance of the disease in England, the air was warm, beyond the usual
temper of the season, with great quantities of sulphurous vapours,
producing great storms of wind from the south-west, and some-times
lightening without thunder.

As to the time of invasion of the disease, they were different in different
countries. It invaded Saxony and the neighbouring countries in Germany
about the 15th of November, and lasted in its vigour till the 29th of the
same month. It was earlier in Holland than in England; earlier in
Edinburgh than in London. It was in New England before it attacked
Britain; in London before it reached some other places west-ward, as
Oxford, Bath, &c.; and, as far as I can collect from accounts, it invaded the
northerly parts of Europe before the southerly. It lasted in its vigour in
London from about the middle of January, 1732–3, for about three weeks;
the bill of mortality, from Tuesday the 23rd to Tuesday the 30th of January,
contained in all 1,588 names being higher than any time since the plague.
It began in Paris about the beginning of their February, or the 21st of our
January, and lasted till the beginning of their April, or the 21st of our
March; and I think its duration was longest in the southerly countries. It
raged in Naples and the southern parts of Italy in our March. The disease,
in travelling from place to place, did not observe the direction, but went
often contrary to the course of the winds.

The uniformity of the symptoms of the disease in every place was
most remarkable. A small rigor or chilliness, succeeded with a fever, of a
duration (in such as recovered) seldom above three days. This fever was
attended with a headache, sometimes pains in the back, thirst in no great
degree, a catarrh or thin defluxion, occasioning sneezing, a coryza, or
running at the nose; a cough with thin expectoration at first, and
afterwards of a viscous matter, in which, if there was observed a clear oily
matter, it proved generally the case to be mortal. These were the most
common symptoms; but a great many, during that season, were affected
with spitting of blood, pleurisies, and inflammations of the lungs,
dangerous and often mortal; in some places, particularly in France, the
fever, after six or seven days, ended in death; in Holland, often in
imposthumations of the throat; in all, the blood was thick; and everywhere
the disease was particularly fatal to aged people. What was observable was,
that the fever left a debility and dejection of appetite and spirits, much

more than in proportion to its strength or duration; and the cough outlasted the fever in some more than six weeks or two months.

There was, during the whole season, a great run of hysterical, hypochondriacal, and nervous distempers; in short, all the symptoms of relaxation. These symptoms were so high in some, as to produce a sort of fatuity or madness, in which, for some hours together, they would be seized with a wandering of their senses, mistaking their common affairs; at the same time, they had not any great degree of fever to confine them to their beds; but in several who were thus affected, the urine was observed often to change from pale to turbid, alternately, so that there was some fever; though I did not observe nor hear that the bark was effectual, but the saline febrifuge draughts had generally a most surprising good effect. Since this disease has been over, the air has continued to be particularly noxious in diseases which affect the lungs, and, for that reason, occasioning a great and unusual mortality of the measles, at the rate of 40 in a week, from which one has reason to expect some specialities in the diseases of the succeeding season.

The remedies commonly successful in this epidemical catarrhous fever were bleeding, sweating, promoted by watery diaphoretics, blisters, and the common pectoral medicines, and what I observed before, draughts of salt of worm-wood, juice of lemon, &c. I have not particulars enough to enable me to enter into the etiology of this distemper.

It was matter of fact, that there was a previous ill constitution of the air, noxious to animal bodies. In autumn, and long afterwards, a madness among dogs; the horses were seized with the catarrh before mankind; and a gentleman averred to me, that some birds, particularly the sparrows, left the place where he was during the sickness.

The previous great drought, as has been observed before, must have been particularly hurtful to mankind. Great droughts exert their effects after the surface of the earth is again opened by moisture, and the perspiration of the ground, which was long suppressed, is suddenly restored. It is probable that the earth then emits several new effluvia, hurtful to human bodies; that this appeared to be the case by the thick and stinking fogs which preceded the rain that had fallen before. It is likewise evident, that these effluvia were not of any particular or mineral nature, because they were of a substance that was common to every part of the surface of the earth; and therefore one may conclude that they were watery exhalations, or at least such mixed with other exhalable substances that are common to every spot of ground.

Lastly, it is agreeable to experience, that watery effluvia are hurtful to the glands of the windpipe and the lungs, and productive of catarrhs.

This lengthy extract shows how the new medicine, as it has been called, was beginning to attempt really detailed descriptions of disease. But is is still mixed with the older sense that illness is somehow linked to fogs and winds and a generally malevolent influence in the air.

If we move to the other end of the country from Doctor Arbuthnott's home in London – to Scotland – we can see that the strain of influenza described (if indeed it was influenza) was killing at a significant rate. The following is taken from the proceedings of the Edinburgh Medical Society for 1732.

The tertian agues, which were mentioned in the close of our preceding year, continued likewise through June and part of July, 1732. Towards the end of June, this disease did not form into regular paroxysms and perfect intermissions, but appeared more in the shape of a remitting fever. During the remissions, the pulse was much sunk; but as the sweat came on, the pulse became fuller and stronger. When the sweat did not break out, the patients became delirious, and some continued quite deaf for some days. The urine was pale, and without sediment, till the disease was going off.

Some were cured of this disease after two or three paroxysms, after a vomit or two; but with others, the disease lasted much longer. Bleeding was not found of use, although some symptoms seemed to require it; but vomiting and blistering succeeded much better, either of them bringing out the sweat when untimely stopped or prevented.

In July, some few fevers remained; they were then more regular and gentle than before. Towards the end of this month, the cholera began to appear, but it was neither very frequent nor violent.

In August, many among the poorer sort of people in the suburbs and villages near Edinburgh were taken with slow fevers, generally attended with a violent headache and ravings; some with a diarrhoea; others with pains of the rheumatic kind all over the body. As few of the sick had access to timely assistance, several died in this distemper.

The same fever continued among the poorer people through September and October, and proved mortal the eighth or ninth day.

Besides the symptoms before mentioned, many complained of great weight
of their heads and drowsiness, loathing and vomiting; others had pains of
the breast, and difficult breathing. Children in this fever, beside the
headache and drowsiness, had pain and tense swelling of the belly.

The professionalization of medicine

The Edinburgh Medical Society was part of an increasingly sophisticated network
of communication between doctors, who shared information despite the slowness
of the penny post and the difficulties of printing and distributing magazines and
books in the 18th century.

Jenny Uglow has brilliantly chronicled the rise of scientific societies in the 18th
century in her book *The Lunar Men*. In fact rise is probably too mild a word for
what almost amounted to an explosion of such societies. They appeared all over
Britain in major cities and provincial towns and reflected the enthusiasm for
discovery and thirst for knowledge that gripped what justly came to be known as
the Age of Enlightenment. Rather than accepting inherited modes of thinking and
ways of behaving, these 18th-century pioneers concentrated entirely on the new
and their discoveries and researches covered an extraordinary range of disciplines
from the magnificent beam engines created by James Watt to the revolutionary
pottery designs of Josiah Wedgwood. Both were members of the Lunar Society
(it was so called because meetings were held on moonlit nights so that travel to the
meeting place was easier). Erasmus Darwin, grandfather of the famous naturalist
Charles Darwin and another Lunar man, is generally agreed to be one of the greatest of all English polymaths, but he was first and foremost a doctor. His medical
reputation was unparalleled for the simple reason that, typically of the new age, he
trusted only to tried and tested cures.

The Edinburgh Medical Society report cited above continues with an excellent
description of the peculiarities of the effects and the spread of influenza during the
pandemic of 1732–3:

This disease was not of itself mortal, but it swept away a great many Poor,
old and consumptive people, and of those who were much wasted by other
distempers. As a proof on whom it fell heaviest, we may remark, that,
though the number of burials in the Grayfriars churchyard (where all the
dead of Edinburgh are buried) was double of what it used to be in the
month of January, yet the number of those who were buried at the public

charge was so great, that the fees of the burials scarce did amount to the sum commonly received in any other month.

It was very remarkable, that, notwithstanding this disease was so universal here, the people in our prison, and the boys, who are numerous, in Heriot's Hospital, which is contiguous to the west side of the Grayfriars churchyard, and the inhabitants of the houses near to that hospital, escaped this fever and cough.

This epidemic disease, which was felt sooner at Edinburgh than any other part of this island, spread itself gradually over all Scotland. It did not reach the most northern and western parts till about fifteen days after the time above mentioned, of its attacking this city. The ship *Anne and Agnes*, David Littlejohn master, having made a voyage to Holland, with one sick sailor on board, returned with the other ten in perfect good health, till they made Flamborough Head, where, on the 15th of January, six sailors were taken ill; next day, two more were in the same condition; and the day thereafter, one more fell sick; so that, when the vessel came to the road of Leith, none on board were in health, except one, who was seized the day after he came on shore with the same disease which his comrades had, whose symptoms were the common ones of the raging epidemic distemper.

We believe it will not be improper here to mention, the horses in and about this place being universally attacked with a running of the nose and coughs, towards the end of October and beginning of November, before the appearance of this fever of cold among men.

This epidemic distemper, above described, spread itself over all Europe, and also infested the inhabitants of America; so that it was, perhaps, the most universal disease upon record. The first accounts we have of anything like it this last year in Europe, was in the middle of November, from Saxony, Hanover, and other neighbouring countries in Germany. It raged at one time in Edinburgh, and Basle in Switzerland. It appeared in London and Flanders after the first week in January; toward the middle of which it reached Paris; and, about the end of the same month, Ireland began to suffer. In the middle of February, Leghorn was attacked; and near the end of it, the people of Naples and Madrid were seized with it. In America, it began in New England about the middle of October, and travelled southward to Barbados, Jamaica, Peru, and Mexico, much at the same rate as it did in Europe.

Personal recollections of the disease are very rare from this period but at least one survives. Sir John Pringle caught the disease in 1733. He wrote:

> The species that I had of the Influenza was a sore throat, with fever and shooting pains through the back part of my head; but, these symptoms were never followed by a cough. I heard of several others who, like me, had never been troubled with a cough, and only with this inflammatory angina.
>
> The 28th of October was the first day on which the late epidemic cold seized upon me. The violence of this distemper usually began to abate in five or six days.
>
> It began with a sickness and perpetual vomiting, sneezing, and a copious de-fluxion from the nose and eyes. I complained of a hoarseness and sore throat, and of a tightness, oppression, and heat, and of feeling pains in various parts, particularly in my head, sides, and back. I was afflicted with a racking cough; with a sense of coldness, frequently returning; with a failure of appetite and of sleep, and with a languor and weakness much greater than might have been expected from the effects of any of the other symptoms.

In York the epidemic of 1775 was significant enough to have been widely commented on – high levels of morbidity were combined with relatively low levels of mortality. One of the best accounts is that of Dr White who wrote from York on 22 December of that year:

> This epidemic disease seems to have appeared rather earlier with us than in London: it was observed before the end of October, became general in the beginning of November, at which time many whole families were indisposed. Not one dwelling house escaped. I was myself seized with it on the 2nd of that month; and in a very short time, it became the most universal disease that hath been remembered with us. It was much abated by the first week of December, and seems now to have entirely left us.
>
> The attack was generally sudden, with a sense of severe coldness, especially in the back and lower extremities. This, in many, was attended with a giddiness; in a few with nausea and abhorrence of food, generally uneasiness, great anxiety and weariness. The pulse small and contracted, from ten to twenty above the natural rate; urine pale; body generally

costive. Some had more or less soreness in the throat, and what is called a stuffing in the head, and sneezing violently; all had a very bad tickling cough, which soon caused stitches and soreness in the breast.

These symptoms, as they were more or less violent, were sooner or later followed by feverish heat, but seldom to any high degree; remarkable soreness all over the body, and slight pains in the head, limbs, loins, and breast. The urine, now seldom high-coloured, forming a cloud when cold; a diarrhoea uncommon here, the contrary state common. Pulse in most one hundred in a minute, in several much quicker, seldom full or strong. Tongue whitish, but moist; little remarkable thirst; a complaint of a bad taste in the mouth was general, and the breath offensive.

No regular crisis was observable; the fever was of the remittent kind, and gradually subsided in general. All became much worse in the afternoon, and so continued till three or four o' clock the following morning, about which time a moderate sweating relieved the patient, who, after a few hours of quiet sleep, awoke much easier. The disease thus went on several days, without any intervening cold fit. For four days together my pulse was 90 (15 above the natural rate) in the morning; in the evening 115: the same I observed in several others.

In all, the nervous system was much disordered; various affections of the spasmodic kind occurred, and the anxiety, despondency, and restlessness were much more remarkable than the general mildness of the vascular irritation gave room to expect.

Regarding the prognosis – a quick recovery followed such urine as quickly turned milky after making, soon after depositing a copious sediment; it was always attended with moist skin, an abatement of the cough, the quickness of the pulse, and anxiety. Some had more considerable sweats; I saw no crisis by a spontaneous diarrhoea, nor any recovery without the urine above mentioned.

This epidemic was, with us in general, so mild, as seldom to engage the attention of a physician: yet it brought some aged asthmatics, and young people of a consumptive habit, into imminent danger. Of such, a few died in this city, especially the former.

As to the curative part, it was seldom necessary here to take away blood: some were relieved by it, but, in general, it did hurt by depressing the patients. An ingenious apothecary, who, from his extensive practice, had a very great number of the sick under his care, informed me that this evacuation seemed to relieve some immediately, but that he never saw in any other disease so many bad symptoms follow bleeding as in this epidemic.

The pandemic of 1781–2

If the epidemics and near pandemics of the early 18th century were dramatic in their effects – and clearly they were – the worst was yet to come. It is generally agreed by historians that the influenza pandemic of 1781–2 was among the greatest manifestations of disease in all history. At this distance in time it is impossible to know precisely why this pandemic was to prove so devastating and even now it it hard to assess it in relation to other pandemics – in particular the pandemic of 1918 – simply because evidence from the 18th century is lacking. We cannot now rediscover and study the genetic make-up of the precise virus that spread across the world at that time.

It is easy to speculate on whether it was an avian influenza virus or a human influenza virus that had drifted so far genetically that it left human populations with little or no immunity, but the truth is we simply don't know. What we do know is that the effects of the disease were widespread and devastating and the pain and suffering, not to mention social disruption, it caused is recorded in many contemporaneous documents. Dr Edward Gray in *An Account of the Epidemic Catarrh of 1782*, which was compiled at the request of the Society for Promoting Medical Knowledge and published in 1784 wrote:

> In the account of an epidemic disease, it may be expected that it should be
> compared with those of the same species, which have already been
> described…they who may be inclined to do so will find a very ample
> catalogue of them, ranged in chronological order, in Dr. Cullen's *Synopsis
> Nosologiae Methodicae*, under the article 'Catarrhus a Contagio', to which
> species the late influenza belongs; and when the various forms, which in
> different persons and places it put on, are taken into consideration, it will,
> no doubt, be found, that some of them were the same as some of those in
> which it formerly appeared; but, when the more general character of it be
> considered, it will probably appear to have differed, in some respects, from
> all the former disorders of the same species; and with regard to the number
> of persons affected by it, and the great space of the earth over which it
> spread its influence, to have been equalled by few of them, perhaps
> exceeded by none. In particular places, indeed, some of the former

epidemics may have been more general; in one place that of 1775 was
thought to have been so, but upon the whole there will perhaps be found
no reason to alter the above opinion.

This is one of the earliest observations of how influenza varies in its effects and takes
slightly different forms as time passes — an observation that reflects what we now
know is the tendency for flu to change rapidly via genetic shift (see Chapter 1). Dr
Gray next looks at how the disease spread rapidly:

> Very little authentic information has been procured, respecting the history
> of the disorder, before the time of its appearance in London; all that can
> upon good authority be related, is, that it prevailed at Moscow, in the
> months of December 1781 and January 1782, and at St Petersburgh in
> February 1782; it was traced from Tobolski, to which place it was supposed
> to have been brought from China.
>
> In confirmation of this opinion it may be observed, that several
> accounts from different parts of the East Indies, mention that a disorder,
> similar in its symptoms, prevailed in those parts in the months of October
> and November 1781. It was in Denmark, the latter end of April, or the
> beginning of May; and many people were said to have died of it at
> Copenhagen, before the 11th of May. It is not easy to determine with
> precision the time of its first appearance in London; that it was here the
> second week in May, seems very certain; and though it was thought by
> some to have been here long before that time, the more general opinion
> is, that the cases then observed did not belong to the disorder in
> question. But whatever difference of sentiment there may be respecting
> the time of its arrival in this metropolis, the fourth week in May is very
> well known to have been the period of its most universal prevalence here,
> which circumstance may surely be considered as a strong argument that
> the cases observed so early as March, or even April, were common
> catarrhs; for it seems very improbable that a disorder, which in every
> other place reached its highest pitch of general prevalence in a week or
> two after its appearance, should in London be two months before it
> arrived at that period.
>
> According to the accounts received from the different parts of
> England, it seems that in most of them the influenza did not begin to
> appear until after its prevalence in London, as in every letter, except two,

its appearance is dated either from the latter end of May or the beginning of June. In Scotland and in Ireland it seems to have been rather later. It prevailed in France in the months of June and July; in Italy, in July and August; and in Portugal and Spain, in August and September. It is said that it was afterwards observed in America; but no authentic information on that head having been obtained, it is mentioned only as common report.

But still there were difficulties with precise diagnosis:

It must here be remarked, that a complaint, similar to the influenza, was taken notice of in some parts of the kingdom several months before that disorder made its progress through it. Mr Mortimer, surgeon to the North Devonshire regiment of militia, was seized on the 24th of March (1781), at Great Torrington, with a disorder, the symptoms of which were perfectly similar to those of the influenza; after him his family had it, and it then became general in that town. It did not extend to the neighbouring villages, nor could Mr Mortimer, upon enquiry, find that any such disorder had been observed at any other place in that part of England. At Barnstaple, which is only twelve miles from Torrington, the influenza was common in the beginning of June, when it went through that part of Devonshire; but the inhabitants of Torrington were not then affected by it. This last circumstance seems to show, that the disorder observed in March was of the same species with the influenza; but admitting it to have been so, it is very extraordinary that its activity should, at that time, have been confined to so small a space.

The fact that having spread rapidly the disease can then just as quickly vanish is recorded in London during the same epidemic:

The fourth week in May was (as is before mentioned) the period at which the disease prevailed most generally in London. From that time it began to decline, and in the space of two or three weeks ceased to exist as a general disorder. It did not, however, leave the City till the month of September. A family from Portugal landed at Harwich in the beginning of that month, and came directly to London; the day after their arrival there, the lady, two children, and two maid servants, were seized with evident

and unquestionable symptoms of the influenza. No certain instance of it
in London, after that time, can be adduced.

In other parts of the country the disease seems to have lingered through until August
and September, but it is a tribute to the growing organization and professionalism
of the medical profession that the views and reports of doctors from widely different
parts of the country were collected together to give a picture of the general progress
of the disease.

The *London Medical Journal* records that:

> …the *Convert* and *Lizard* ships-of-war, upon their arrival at Gravesend, from
> the West Indies, in the beginning of September, had three Custom-house
> officers put on board them, and in a few hours after, the crews of both
> ships, till then in good health, were seized with symptoms of the influenza;
> hardly a man in either ship escaped, and some had it very severely.

Most of the accounts received from various parts of the country simply reported the
numbers afflicted with influenza:

> At Dover Castle, 390 privates of the 59th regiment; and at Dublin, upwards
> of 700 of the 36th and 77th regiments of foot, were ill of it at the same time.
>
> At London it was also very general; and though a want of proper
> observation on that head renders it impossible to determine the proportion
> of persons affected by the disease, it may be safely asserted, that the number
> of those attacked by it was much greater than that of those who escaped it.
> With respect to sex, there seemed little or no difference; though in some
> places it was thought, that the number of men affected by it was greater
> than that of women.

Dr Simmons observed, that of 96 patients who were admitted under his care at the
Westminster Dispensary, on account of the influenza, 50 were females, and 46 males.
But though, upon the whole, it seemed to show no distinction between the sexes it
was more disturbing in its effects on various age groups. 'Old persons were certainly
less subject to the disorder than those of a middle age; but when attacked, they
generally had it very violently.'

In France the *Journal de Medecine* records a lucky escape for the children in a
Parisian orphanage:

Children were still less subject to it than old persons, and infants considerably less than either. In the Hospice de Vaugirard, near Paris, where there were upwards of forty children, all under two years of age, it was observed that not one of them was affected, though the epidemic was common in the village.

Back in England the picture was occasionally rather different at least so far as children were concerned. Dr Simmons continued his report:

Of the ninety-six persons above mentioned, who applied to the Westminster Dispensary, thirteen were under the age of twenty, sixty-three between twenty and forty, and twenty above forty years of age. But notwithstanding young persons were less liable to the disorder than adults, and when affected, commonly had it in a less degree, yet even infants were not entirely exempt from it, and some of them had it very severely.

Because nothing precise was known at this time about the immune system or the method of transmission of viral and bacterial disease, doctors could express only their bafflement when the effects of the disease seemed rather random:

General as it was in London, some whole families escaped it; one for instance, residing near Red Lion Square, which at that time (including children and servants) consisted of thirteen persons, remained entirely free from its attack. It was also remarked, that many persons who escaped the epidemic of 1775, were affected by that of 1782, and many who escaped the latter were affected by the former.

By this time, however, doctors were far better at observing and recording the precise progress of the disease and its symptoms:

Chilliness and shivering, sometimes succeeded by a hot fit, and alternating with it for some hours; languor and lassitude; sneezing; discharge from the nose and eyes; pain in the head (particularly between or over the eyes); cough, sometimes dry, sometimes accompanied with expectoration; inflammation of one or both eyes; oppression and tightness about the precordia; difficulty of breathing; pain in the breast or side; pain in the loins, neck, shoulders, or limbs; sense of heat and soreness in the throat and

trachea; hoarseness; bleeding from the nose; spitting of blood; loss of smell
or taste; nausea; flatulence.

In the spectacularly devastating influenza pandemic of 1918 (see Chapter 5) one of
the most striking features was that those attacked later during the pandemic were
generally far worse affected than those afflicted early. The currently accepted explanation is that those attacked initially were hit by a less virulent strain and, having
survived that, they were immune to some extent from the effects of the second wave
of attack. Their survival was all the more remarkable because as the virus mutated it
became far more dangerous. Something similar seems to have happened in the late
18th century. As Dr Gray reports:

> It was also remarked that those who were attacked later from the time of
> the appearance of the disorder, commonly had it more severely and were
> longer ill. But this remark must not be applied to those who suffered
> relapses; as in that case it was frequently observed that the latter attacks
> were milder than the former ones... it seems probable that the same cause
> which renders the constitution not disposed to receive it a second time
> should also render the second attack less severe.

Another similarity between 1918 and a century and a half earlier was the use of
some opium-derived medicines. Even today similar opium-derived medicines are
used to suppress the coughing reflex in severe cases:

> Opiates were a common remedy with most physicians and they all agree in
> testifying their great use, particularly in mitigating the cough which was in
> many cases the most troublesome and tedious symptom of the disease. On
> account of the great debility which seldom failed to accompany or to
> follow the disorder bark and cordials were frequently necessary especially
> towards the close of it.

The outcomes of disease were typically varied, as a number of doctors testified in
reports published later:

> The terminations or consequences of this disorder were like every part of
> it extremely various. In many places not one instance of fatal termination
> was observed; in others the number of deaths caused by it was not small. In

general a great weakness remained after the disease and the cough was sometimes troublesome for some weeks.

A better understanding

As we move towards the end of the 18th century – into an age in which scientific discovery and the Industrial Revolution were already well underway – the mysterious origins of the disease still played upon the minds of commentators, historians and doctors alike. Some, like Dr Gray, came very close to understanding how the disease was transmitted using common sense and logic:

> Different opinions have been entertained respecting the manner in which this disease was produced and propagated. Some physicians thought it arose solely from the state of the weather; in other words, that it was a common catarrh, occasioned, as that complaint frequently is, by changes in the sensible qualities of the atmosphere, such as the increase of cold, or moisture; and consequently, they supposed it unconnected with any disorder that had prevailed, or did at that time prevail, in any other part. Others, admitted its cause to be a particular and specific contagion, totally different from, and independent of, the sensible qualities of the atmosphere, yet thought that cause was conveyed by, and resided in the air. But the greatest number concurred in opinion, that the influenza was contagious, in the common acceptation of that word; that is to say, that it was conveyed and propagated by the contact, or at least by the sufficiently near approach, of an infected person.

Despite endless floundering with the possible causes of the disease, doctors such as Gray sometimes came close to the truth. Dr Gray hits the nail on the head when he remarks: 'If the common and general progress of the influenza be taken into consideration, it will certainly be found to favour the opinion that the disease was propagated by personal intercourse.'

At last the idea that influenza emerged from mists and foul marsh airs was being dispelled. Gray is largely discounting the commonly held view – though he does not dismiss it entirely – that certain types of weather caused the disease. Dr Houlston writing from Liverpool confirms Gray's insightful analysis. Houlston points out that, 'Many reasons combine to make us think it is propagated by contagion.' Yet more impressive is a letter sent to London by a Dr MacQueen who was working in Great Yarmouth in the 1780s:

I am inclined to believe, that the late influenza was communicated by human effluvia, and not by any matter generated in the atmosphere alone. What I have myself seen of the disorder, the whole tenor of the reports I had from others, and the analogy it bears to other contagious disorders, all lead to this conclusion – not to mention the difficulty of accounting for such a peculiarity in the atmosphere – its occurring ten or twelve times in the course of a century, at no regular or certain periods; and that no naturalist has yet been able to ascertain in what this atmospheric matter consists. I would not, however, be understood to speak with confidence on the subject, nor do I deny that a certain condition of the atmosphere may not possibly favour the propagation of the effluvia from their first source: the extensive progress of the disease over so large a portion of the globe will be thought to favour such an opinion. I only assert, that the analogy between the symptoms of the influenza and those produced by contagious effluvia, is, in every respect, uniform and complete.

Another remark occurs to me on the subject of contagion, which I do not remember to have met with in medical writers. It is this: that contagious effluvia have a natural tendency to lodge in the mucous membrane of the body, and exert their greatest force in those parts. I do not venture this as an universal position, but I have no doubt of its being very general. Besides its application to the influenza, the measles, whooping cough, malignant sore throat, dysentery in all its forms, cholera, and perhaps the smallpox, are all strong confirmations of it; even the slow, nervous, and putrid fevers are often accompanied with affections of the throat and lungs; and a cough and expectoration are frequent symptoms towards the crisis of such disorders.

The dissemination of medical knowledge

The development and organization of 18th-century medicine is impressive. As we have seen in the preceding pages, doctors were increasingly sharing their observations and theories in accounts published in an increasing number of journals. As the century wore on links were established between hospitals across the country and indeed Europe and beyond, so that the levels of practical efficiency we find in medicine in 1800 is very different indeed from that which prevailed just half a century earlier. It would be misleading to imagine that ignorant doctors worked alone in remote areas using guesswork and old wives tales to try to cure their patients. In fact they corresponded across wide distances in England and abroad and they tried to keep up to date with the latest thinking in their subject.

As an example of this, the Dr MacQueen whose perceptive remarks we have already discussed, reported to the Royal Society in 1782 on the effects of colds and influenza on the tiny island of St Kilda in the Hebrides:

> Amongst the islands on the western coast of Scotland, there is one very remote from all the rest, named St Kilda. It rises like a rock in the ocean, about 16 or 18 leagues west of the Lewes islands. This place is inhabited by 20 or 30 poor families, who subsist chiefly on the flesh and eggs of sea fowls which they have in prodigious quantities. They have, besides, a small quantity of barley, and a considerable number of sheep. The open and boisterous sea around them, together with their distance from every other land, exclude these poor islanders from the rest of their species; and they scarcely ever see a human being, except once in a year, when they are visited by the steward, who receives the rent in feathers, wool, and mutton.
>
> St Kilda being an appendage to that part of the Lewes called Harris, and the property of Mr Macleod, the steward always resides in the latter place. He makes his annual voyage to St Kilda in the month of June, when the day is longest and the season most temperate. His retinue consists of ten or a dozen men, sufficient to manage a large open boat, such as are in common use in these islands. The inhabitants meet him on the beach, and prompted by a desire of intelligence, as well as a respect for his person, all assemble round the strangers. But behold the consequence! The next day the steward has hardly a St Kilda man at his levee. They are universally seized with a catarrh or cold, as they call it, which rages so fast, that in twenty-four hours every individual on the island is generally laid low. The symptoms are a cough, heachache, sneezing. This is so invariably the case that it is considered as the natural and infallible consequence of the steward's visit and the poor people are prepared accordingly.

Such hints and guesses that the infectious agent was spread by human contact were confirmed in many other places. Dr Hamilton writing to the *London Medical Journal* in 1783 remembered:

> One of Lord Bute's labourers, living on the banks of the River at Luton, happened to receive a compound fracture of his thigh about the

beginning of April, a month at least before the influenza appeared there. When the rest of the family were seized with the disease though he had never been from his bed since the accident yet he caught the disease, and suffered considerably. Here was no exposure to the viccissitudes of the weather.

Merchant ships had only to put in to port for the disease to reach them – this was a source of continuous surprise to early 18th-century doctors, who clearly believed that continual contact rather than occasional contact should be necessary for the disease to be transmitted. Dr Hamilton, again writing in 1783, discusses the fate of the naval ship *The Fly*.

> The captain affirmed that forty of his men fell ill in less than eight hours; several of whom he declared dropped down at the wheel as they steered the vessel. The circumstance obliged him to put back and stand again for the Yarmouth Roads, which he had only left a few hours before with all hands apparently well merely for want of hands to navigate her. The infection must have been received from shore.

A scarcity of effective remedies

Careful observation was beginning to give some clues as to the nature of the disease and the means by which it was spread, but the range of remedies on offer remained as they had been for a century and more past. Central to attempts to relieve the symptoms was venesection or blood letting. Dr Fothergill, writing in 1790, explains that taking eight ounces of blood from a patient is recommended when influenza has caused 'considerable inflammation of internal parts'. He insists that bleeding should not be used, on the other hand, where a patient complains of pain in the thorax. He does not explain the thinking behind the different approaches.

Apart from opiates – presumably laudanum – and bleeding, there were few practical remedies available to 18th-century doctors. One or two sensibly recommended keeping the patient in bed and giving plenty of liquids and food when the patient felt able to eat – advice that holds good for the treatment of flu to this day. Another popular remedy that has long vanished from the medical scene was blistering or cupping. It was thought to increase the pulse rate and remove congestion.

Flu Stateside

A major outbreak of influenza in the United States in 1789–90 was seen by many as being the same disease that had caused the European pandemic back in 1782. We now believe that this is unlikely given the speed at which the flu virus mutates, but like all flu viruses the virus responsible for the 1789–90 epidemic in America was probably related to the virus that caused the pandemic of 1782. Thomas Joseph Pettigrew gives a good account of the spread of influenza across America:

> The influenza, well known in Europe, invaded the whole of the United States in the course of the last autumn. The symptoms with which it was attended were much the same with those described by Dr Fothergill in his work, and by Dr Hamilton in his letter, contained in the memoirs of the Med. Soc. of London, as attendant on the epidemic of 1782. Similar methods of treatment, with those therein recommended, were generally found successful. It prevailed here in November and December, at Georgia; the most southern state in the Union, in September; and in the British government of Nova Scotia in December. The present spring, with us, has been remarkable for an epidemic, almost as universally prevalent as that in the fall. The symptoms, however, were extremely different, as far at least as they have fallen under my own observation. In the latter the affection was almost entirely confined to the nasal passages, insomuch that though the same disease has undoubtedly frequently made its appearance in this country before, yet from its assuming the form of a catarrhal fever, it has never been noticed under any other denomination. In the former this mucus membrane in the nasal passages was seldom diseased. The attack was for the most part sudden and violent generally, without any cough at this period, and without those pungent pains (so remarkable in the influenza), about the frontal sinuses.
>
> The predominant complaint at the seizure was violent pain in the back and limbs, sometimes with headache, often without, and rarely preceded by very severe rigor. The pulse frequent, seldom very full, sometimes however hard; the tongue oftener dry than in the epidemic of the fall; but, like that, covered with but little foulness.
>
> In this stage an emetic generally removed all the complaint in thirty-six or forty-eight hours, except the debility. This was attended with loss of appetite, and frequently continued for several days afterwards. Small doses of emetic tartar, combined with an opiate preparation, were

sometimes necessary to determine to the skin, promote expectoration and relieve a slight cough, with which some were afflicted. Those who did not take the emetic in the beginning were not so completely relieved by it afterwards, and the cure was often protracted to the term of two or three weeks. In no disease do I recollect ever to have met with such immediate and sensible success from medicines of this class, as in that which I am describing; and this I may remark was by no means in proportion to the quantity of matter evacuated from the stomach, for the relief was as complete when nothing was discharged, but the substances just taken down, as when large quantities of biles were ejected. The efficacy of the emetic seems to have depended upon reaction in the act of vomiting, produced by the contraction of the diaphragm and of the abdominal muscles.

I must, however, remark that the sweats with which this disease terminated were by no means so profuse as in the autumnal epidemic; they were rather a moderate and universal diaphoresis; children under eight years of age commonly escaped it as they did also that of the fall. Few adults were exempt from its ravages, and I cannot find that the aged were less subject to it than others; most who died were of the latter class, yet the bills of mortality were remarkably enlarged in all ages at the epidemic period. It began about the middle of last month in this town, and spread as universally through the country as through the metropolis, and that with such astonishing rapidity that it was scarcely possible to notice any circumstances that might lead to the ascertaining the degree of its contagion. It is now about three weeks since it ceased in the capital, and we have not yet obtained any accurate histories of its progress in the country. The first appearance of it is said to have been earlier than here, pretty high up upon the Hudson River; thence it is said to have proceeded down Connecticut River, and to have bent its course hither, after which we heard of it at Portsmouth, sixty miles eastward, before it appeared at Salem, which is forty miles on this side the capital of New Hampshire. At New York, as far as I can learn, its appearance was somewhat later than here, and our beloved President Washington is but now on the recovery from a very severe and dangerous attack of it in that city. From all accounts I have been able to collect, bleeding was sometimes but seldom had recourse to; blistering, very commonly and almost always with success, especially in cases where the disease assumed the form, as it was often observed to do, of a rheumatic affection. Whether this is a variety of influenza, or a new disease with us, I am at a loss to determine. The first stage of it appears very dissimilar from it, but the last approaches nearer to a likeness. I have not met with any account of it under this form, and can scarcely believe that the difference of season is sufficient to explain the variation of symptoms.

Though, as we have seen, medicine had taken great strides forward since the beginning of the 18th century, there was still confusion among doctors as to what exactly influenza really was and what should be done about it. One or two doctors, through a careful analysis of symptoms and an equally careful analysis of the spread of the disease, were making astute and helpful observations. As the Industrial Revolution took hold in the 19th century, particularly in Britain, medical improvements accelerated but not at a pace, as we will see in the next chapter, to inspire confidence that the next pandemic could be kept at bay.

CHAPTER 4

A Shrinking World – The 19th Century

It may not be entirely accurate to describe the influenza outbreak of 1803 as a pandemic since it is difficult to obtain accurate information from contemporary accounts of exactly how it spread across various countries. We know that it travelled rapidly across England, Wales and Scotland, and a number of reports written within 20 years of the outbreak suggest that the flu that hit England in 1803 was the same flu that was first noted in Paris in the latter part of 1802 before moving to Holland and finally reaching the east coast of England – almost certainly via an infected ship plying its trade between Rotterdam and Harwich.

Town to town, person to person

An East Anglian doctor describes the progress of the disease:

> It seems to have been first observed in London early in January, and to have occupied nearly three months in its diffusion over the kingdom, advancing northwards before it raged to any considerable extent in the west of England, but to this statement there are some remarkable exceptions. For example, it appeared in Taunton as early as the 15th of January, and did not reach Chester till the 30th of that month.
>
> The disorder did not proceed by orderly and successive steps, but rather alighted at various and distant points with seeming capriciousness. It reached Portsea, Hull, and East Retford, nearly on the same day; but it existed at Doncaster two weeks, and at Newark three weeks earlier, although these places were respectively only eighteen and twenty miles distant from Retford. Six or seven months elapsed between the time of its first appearance in the country and its cessation; and, as a general rule, although the duration of its virulence might not materially vary, yet it was longest in disappearing at the places where it was first harboured.

Despite knowing nothing about the pathogen that caused the disease, early 19th-century observers – with their passion for keeping meticulous records – were careful to describe at least what they saw with their own eyes, although the deductions they made from their observations were often wildly inaccurate.

In Ireland, Dr Callaman noted in the spring of 1803 that the disease was prevalent in cities and towns before reaching neighbouring villages, and that when they were infected country people generally seemed harder hit than townsfolk. This shrewd observation would later be confirmed as a general feature of flu pandemics during the world's worst pandemic in 1918–19, and is almost certainly attributable to the greater immunity afforded to town-dwellers by their constant exposure to a range of infectious diseases. Dr Callaman also noted the approximate duration of the epidemic and that by the time it reached the countryside it had often done its worst in the town:

> I remember our being free from it in town by the time it had reached the
> remote parts of the country, even the difference of a week, at a distance of
> less than twelve miles, where the communication with town was not so
> frequent as in the late epidemic, when the playhouse and assizes brought
> town and country more in contact.

Until well into the 19th century it was still widely believed that influenza was connected with changes in the weather but this explanation seems to have been proffered as much out of habit as anything else. On the ground, doctors noted far more practical issues – the way for example it was probably passed from person to person. From Bridgwater in Somerset, on 9 April 1803, Dr Symes wrote to a colleague in London about the influenza epidemic that had raged in the town throughout February: 'There are many places in this neighbourhood, with which the inhabitants of the town have no intercourse, where the influenza has not made its appearance.' Instinctively Dr Symes realized that isolation – or quarantine – was a protection against influenza despite the persistent fear among the populace that it was carried and spread by winds and miasmas.

In the same vein Dr Symes goes on to consider the spread of the disease in the north of England:

> The epidemic appeared at Manchester at an earlier date than in the
> neighbouring towns. An interval of about ten days elapsed from its spread
> here to the time of its reaching Bolton, and some other populous places
> situated at about twelve miles distance. It seemed to diverge from

Manchester, as from a centre, to the surrounding country, but certainly appeared in the more crowded and populous towns, placed at the extremities of the circle, than in the intermediate space, which contains a thinner and more scattered population. This may be explained from the greater intercourse subsisting between the larger manufacturing towns and Manchester; and likewise from the consideration that in towns where the inhabitants are crowded together, the propagation of contagion is much more favoured than in the less populous country villages and detached dwellings.

Like so many doctors at the time, one Dr Faulkner wrestled continually with the various explanations given for the nature of influenza and the means by which it caused infection:

It is a matter of doubt with some, if this epidemic catarrh be a contagious disorder; or propagated from one person to another by infection, as the smallpox or measles; or whether it be owing to a general cause, as a particular disposition, or, as it was formerly called, constitution of air affecting a large number of persons at the same time, which is the correct sense in which the word epidemical is used.

I have no doubt myself that it is contagious, in the strictest sense of the word. It has scarcely ever appeared without spreading to a vast extent; and has affected equally countries in the greatest variety, both in point of climate, and in the manners, diet, and habits of life of the inhabitants. But still there has always been a perceptible and, indeed, sufficiently marked interval between its appearance in one country and another; and it has never appeared in all parts at once, as it would have done, had it been produced in each individual by some generally operating cause.

This practical, no-nonsense approach to understanding the progress of the disease typifies the increasing reliance doctors placed on observation and experience rather than on accepted wisdom. As the 1803 epidemic gathered momentum this does not mean that all doctors were in agreement. As in all professions there were conservatives and reactionaries as well as more enlightened thinkers. Even on the ground experiences and observations differed and led to different conclusions – hardly surprising given the maddeningly mysterious nature of the disease as it was seen more than a century before science identified the real influenza pathogen.

Dr Woodford, who worked in and around the English Midland towns of Shrewsbury and Ashbourne, had a slightly different take on the spread of the disease, noting that: 'The disease must naturally attract attention, first in the metropolis and other cities, from their corresponding population and greater number of the sick. This circumstance seems to have given rise to a precipitate conclusion, that these were the places first attacked, and that from these it was diffused progressively through all the others.'

Most doctors at this time were concerned to record the progress of influenza – and any other epidemic for that matter – among the more affluent from whom they inevitably earned their fees. Dr Woodford is unusual in that he gives us a rare insight into the effects of the epidemic on the poorest sections of society – villagers, farm workers' schoolchildren and even the inhabitants of the local workhouse:

> The influenza first appeared at Brompton, near Rochester, in the evening
> of the 25th of February, when it seized 28 of Mr Hulet's scholars. In the
> house of industry at Worcester, containing about 160 persons, nearly one
> half of whom are children, not more than 5 or 6 were affected, and those
> slightly. In a school for young ladies, consisting of 33 residing in the house,
> not one was indisposed; the day scholars were not equally exempt. In a
> second school of the same nature, consisting with the family of 48, more
> than 20 suffered, but here only one of the pupils had the disorder with any
> considerable degree of violence, though the grown-up individuals of the
> family had it with that degree of severity which more generally prevailed.

A few other commentators tried to tease out significant trends in the progress of the disease and in the manner in which it affected various groups and individuals, but much of the evidence was anecdotal or based on hearsay. One doctor saw significance where there can have been none. He wrote: 'In a workhouse at Ryegate, Yorkshire, wherein there are 200 people employed in a blanket manufactory wherein oil is used, no decided instance of the influenza occurred!' He clearly felt that the oil used in the manufacturing process somehow protected the inhabitants from infection. It is easy for us now to smile at the naivety of such an idea, but as late as 1919 similarly bizarre ideas were still current even among the world's most eminent doctors.

The anonymous doctor describing the situation at Ryegate goes on to look at other groups who escaped infection: 'Within four miles of Pontefract, there is a pottery consisting of upwards of 300 souls; they have daily intercourse with the town and every part of the country, yet not a single person of them has suffered from the disease. The lunatics in the Hereford Asylum were not affected.' The doctor may have felt that the psychiatric afflictions of the inmates of the Hereford asylum played a part in their apparent immunity to the disease, but it is far more likely that in truth they escaped as a result of their relative isolation from the surrounding community.

Some prisons were similarly favoured as Dr Woodford, again writing from the West Midlands, explains:

> The city gaol at Worcester, including the governor's family, contained on
> an average 23, all of whom escaped. The county gaol contained men
> debtors 11, and 1 woman debtor. Men felons 24, women ditto 15, with 3
> children. The governor's family 7, in all 61; of these only the governor and
> his daughter had the complaint, and they very severely. The house of
> correction contained men 18, women 7, 3 children, and the governor's
> family 2, in all 30. Of these only the governor had it, and he also very
> severely.

Among a wide range of reports from across the country there were bound to be curious anomalies. For no apparent reason many areas seemed to escape the flu entirely. From Burton-on-Trent, in the heart of the industrial Midlands and then as now a busy industrial centre, a Mr Whateley, reported: 'I feel satisfied the disorder, which was so prevalent in most parts of the kingdom early in the year, was never met with in this place or its immediate vicinity.'

Old ideas about the mysterious nature of illness provided imaginative doctors with ready-made explanations for things they could not otherwise explain. Fogs and foul airs were still blamed for the arrival of influenza in some areas, but at least one doctor found a new twist on this – he thought the misty rain-swept and water-logged nature of the area in which he lived (the Fens) actually helped prevent flu! This must have seemed a novel idea at the time as the Fens were regarded as noto-riously unhealthy because they were so low-lying and damp. But the damp and water, from being sources of infection, apparently became a godsend when it came to flu, as the good doctor explains:

> The town of Wisbech had a circumvallum of health, none of the
> neighbouring villages had been visited by influenza, and many parts of

England have not been visited by influenza. How is this to be accounted for? Not surely by saying they had no communication with the diseased. I have seen the disease in the most sequestered situations. It may be worth while to inform you a little as to the country I now inhabit; it is a country *sui generis*. We have a few inconsiderable rivers moving sluggishly to the sea, but every four or five acres for twenty miles around me, is surrounded by a ditch with stagnated water. When these ditches are filled with water, the people are healthy, and in proportion as water diminishes, our epidemic diseases increase. We had very little rain here during the Winter and Spring, but much dry weather and unusual warmth in the Spring months. These are the reasons, in my opinion, why influenza was complicated with our endemics; and they lead me also to believe, that influenza is a weed of our own growth, that is, that it would have appeared here without communication with any other place.

Already by this time such views would have seemed decidedly old-fashioned – particularly the idea that the disease 'is a weed of our own growth'. Too many doctors had noted the apparent spread of the disease from person to person, although even this was complicated by the fact that those infected with influenza were able to pass the disease on before they themselves appeared to be ill.

The symptoms of the 1803 epidemic

But what of the symptoms of this first widespread outbreak of flu in the 19th century? These appear to have been classic and unmistakable in the main. Various doctors and other commentators from the West Country to the far north-east noted the 'spontaneous weariness and languor, succeeded by slight shiverings, with alternate flushings of heat'. A doctor from Newcastle-on-Tyne then goes on to describe the situation of a typical patient:

He then complains of a deep-seated pain in the course of the frontal sinuses, accompanied, for the most part, with sneezing, and a profuse discharge of lymph from the nose and eyes. In the space of an hour, acute, darting pain in the muscles subservient to respiration, attended with a tickling cough, and hoarseness, frequently occur; as the disease advances, the patient complains of dull, aching pains in the back and knee-joints, and of great debility, languor, and depression of spirits. The pulse is small and quick, seldom if ever hard and full; the tongue is covered with an extremely white mucus, and has the appearance of having been suffused with milk. The tongue being moist, little or no complaint is made of thirst. The appetite is not only entirely lost, but a fixed loathing of any solid food is expressed: on the third day, and sometimes as late as the fourth, the disease seems to have attained its acme.

The anonymous doctor was astute enough to notice, too, one of the key difficulties of influenza and its treatment – that its symptoms varied widely from individual to individual and from outbreak to outbreak; the latter we now know is typical of a virus that mutates so quickly. The doctor continues:

The above description is only intended to apply to the genuine unmixed form of the epidemic. Modified by age, sex, and temperament, and (admitting it to be contagious) by the circumstances under which contagion was communicated, it exhibited a remarkable diversity in its effects, upon different subjects; yet in every case some degree of resemblance might be observed. Its distinctive character was never completely lost. In most delicate females, either sickness or diarrhoea, with transient shiverings and debility, unaccompanied with any catarrhal affection, formed the prominent symptoms of the disease.

In some the mucous membrane was but slightly inflamed; in others, great pain and difficulty of breathing, with a sense of rawness and soreness of the trachea and chest, indicated more extensive inflammation. Members of the same family were differently afflicted — some were solely affected with the almost pathognomonic symptoms of intense pain in the head and general debility; others chiefly suffered from the catarrhal affection, attended with unusual languor, and derangement of the stomach and bowels.

For all their newfound ability to describe and accurately identify the disease doctors were still prone to confuse the issue by drawing into their descriptions many confusing and irrelevant facts. Having described very accurately influenza as it afflicted his patients one doctor then noted that:

At the time the human species became a prey to the influenza, the dogs and horses were evidently affected; many dogs were killed as mad dogs which were not hydrophobic. During its prevalence the cattle were unhealthy, cows and sheep in particular, and the farmers lost a great number of lambs. Cats also were affected, many of which died. A disease among cats and cows was noticed at Gosport, Hants, four or five months before the outbreak of influenza at that place. At Dublin dogs had sore eyes, whilst influenza prevailed. At Garstang, in the month of February, two months before the appearance of influenza in that place, a very fatal epidemic was predominant among the swine; in the town and neighbourhood whole herds were swept off by the disease.

Interestingly, while dragging in all sorts of animal problems that were clearly not related to human influenza, the writer has hit on one of the few animal species that is implicated in the appearance of new and particularly deadly strains of influenza – the pig. Pigs as we will see in a later chapter are almost certainly the means by which avian and swine flu are able to mix with human flu to create new and deadly strains of the virus.

But wild speculation based on hearsay was never easily forsaken, as we can see from this anonymous letter to the Medical and Physical Journal:

It has been often observed during the prevalence or previous to these epidemics, that various animals and birds have been affected and destroyed; and, if I am not much mistaken, even an impression on the vegetable creation has been some-where mentioned. I have just learnt, and I have no doubt the information is perfectly correct, that several horses died in this neighbourhood very suddenly during the time the late influenza was at the worst with us. That during the close of the last year and the early months of this, horses were everywhere unusually diseased, that very many died.

It is rare, as we have seen, before the 1803 pandemic to find systematic descriptions of the disease and its effects on individuals, particularly where those individual's movements are recorded prior to their becoming infected. A doctor from Brentwood writing in 1803 is a notable exception. Rather than generalize he mentions a specific case, even giving us the man's profession:

The first case of well-marked influenza I saw, I believe was on the 5th of March; it happened to be a robust and healthy farmer, who the week before, on a journey into Essex, passed twice through London: he lives in a village about five miles from hence, where, at that period, the influenza had not appeared, but was then universal in London. Many cases come now daily before me, for it very much prevails at this time in this town, and in the neighbouring village.

Two ladies of this place spent a few days at Exeter, and slept at a friend's house, where the family had been ill of the influenza (and indeed some part of it then laboured under the complaint); one of them was seized as she was returning, and the other two days after; and the whole family, where they lodged, had the complaint within ten days. About the same time, a person coming from Plymouth Dock, where the influenza was very prevalent, was seized at a friend's house at a different part of the town from the ladies just mentioned. The family of this house, likewise, soon became infected. These were the first instances of the complaint in this town, but it soon became general.

One large family in the country, and who had little communication with others, escaped the disease till June. They thought they caught it from their music-master. Seven persons, who attended in succession a lady who had it severely, were attacked with it. Her daughters, who were kept away from her, escaped.

The detail of this description is remarkable for the period, but he is still recording the effects of something fundamentally mysterious to him. In the north of England a Dr Morrison recorded similar individual experiences:

Mr M Donald, with his wife, his son, and his daughter, were in London in the beginning of 1803; they left London on the 3rd of February, at which time the influenza was very prevalent there; but they did not know of their having been in any house where there were individuals subjected to that disease. When they set out on their journey they were all in perfect health. They arrived at Berwick-upon-Tweed on the 8th of February, and were there in a house where there were several persons subjected to influenza. They arrived at Powder Hall, situated within a mile of Edinburgh on the 9th of February. The next day Mr McDonald himself was attacked with severe febrile symptoms, attended with uncommon prostration of strength, and all the other appearances which most frequently occur in influenza. Soon after Mr McDonald was attacked with this disease, almost every other person in his family, amounting to near a dozen, were attacked in succession; but its progress, as far as I could learn, was not immediately afterwards very rapid in the city of Edinburgh, and I did not myself attend any case where the disease was distinctly marked till the 23rd of February, when I was called to a gentleman dangerously ill of the disease, several of whose family had before been affected with it in a much slighter manner.

Had they but known it there was no way our early 19th-century ancestors could have countered influenza given the state of medical science at that time. But in many ways they were closer to an understanding of what flu really was (and how it was transmitted) than they realized.

The lessons of Jenner and smallpox

Decades earlier Edward Jenner had discovered almost by chance that immunity to that most deadly 18th-century disease, smallpox, could be induced if an individual were deliberately infected (via a tiny scratch) with a minuscule amount of material known to be infected with cow pox. It was a very hit-and-miss affair but the idea behind it was sound. Jenner had noticed that milkmaids infected with cowpox developed sores from the cowpox but never thereafter seemed to catch the far more dangerous smallpox. The reason – though Jenner did not know this – was that cowpox was sufficiently similar to smallpox to confer immunity to anyone infected first with the bovine version of the disease. Jenner recognized the significance of his observations but he did not understand the mechanism behind it.

Influenza, though caused by a virus – like smallpox – was unfortunately not treatable in the same way because the influenza virus mutates too quickly and there are too many different varieties of the influenza virus. Inoculation against one type of influenza would not protect against a particularly virulent new type of influenza. The unique speed of the virus's ability to mutate is in-built, but is also due to its ability to reassort its genes (see chapter 2) in its natural host animal – birds. Smallpox does not have a natural host animal.

Doctors active during the 1803 epidemic realized that influenza protection was not as straightforward as protection against smallpox. One country doctor noted in his diary: 'The contagion of influenza is not indeed conveyed on the point of a lancet to be intentionally communicated like small-pox.' The same doctor was perceptive enough to realize that flu had far more to do with person-to-person contact than with fogs and foul airs. His realization was part of a growing conviction that the medical orthodoxy of the past was not providing the right answers.

From all that I have been able to learn of the history of this disease, as recorded by eminent writers for many centuries past, from all that I have seen of it during former epidemics, from its progress during the present epidemic, with very different states of the atmosphere when passed from Paris to London, and from London to Edinburgh, &c from its progress in Edinburgh after it appeared in this city; and, finally, from its progress in my own family, after its introduction into my house; I have no more doubt of its contagious nature.

Contemporary reports of the progress of the disease continue through those terrible early months of 1803 and though the disease continued to kill, its strength and virulence was beginning to wane. Morbidity levels were still high, but death rates began to fall. The rate of spread can be judged by this account from a Mr Hugo:

During the Lent Assizes the influenza was exceedingly prevalent in Shrewsbury: most of the country gentlemen, composing the grand-jury, came to town in health, but very few returned without taking the disease along with them. At these Assizes a case was tried from Clun, twenty-seven miles south-west of Shrewsbury. Most of those who came here on that account were taken ill of the disease on their return, and spread it all over that little retired town.

The first case which came under my observation, was on the 22nd of March, in the family of a gentleman who resides about three miles west of this town. He had been attending, with his lady, the Assizes at Exeter the whole of the preceding week, at which time the influenza was very general there. They came home both ill of the disease. On the next day the servant who returned with them was seized with it, and by the 25th, it had been communicated to every other person in the house. Some labourers who resided at an adjoining farm, were affected about the same time; but a woman who had been employed at Exeter was the first attacked by it. It appeared very soon afterwards in the town of Crediton; and here, also, the first case I visited was a gentleman who had been attending at the Assize. It spread very rapidly, and in a short time became general in the town and adjoining villages.

The same correspondent noted – like so many of his contemporaries – how isolation seemed to be the only protection against the disease:

In some country-places, isolated and detached from any adjacent dwelling,
I have known the whole family continue exempt from the influenza, until
one of them happened to come to town, bring it home, and, after a few
days' confinement, communicate it to the remainder. Though this epidemic
diffused itself very extensively through all ranks and descriptions of people,
I have notwithstanding known many entire families to escape that must
have been constantly exposed to infection, supposing it to exist; nay, I have
remarked, that some who acted in the quality of nurse-tenders in the
family-way did not take it; but these were few indeed when compared
with the immense numbers who caught it by their attendance of the sick.

The explanation for immunity – or apparent immunity among some of those caring
for the sick, may well be that, as in 1918 and in many other pandemics, they would
have been hit by an early wave of the disease when it existed in its milder form.
Having been infected with this and recovered they were largely immune to the
disease when it returned in a more virulent form later on during the same outbreak.

Doctors and town officials may have been unable to halt the spread of infection
but they never gave up trying, as the assiduous Mr Hugo explains:

> Fumigating is employed to purify the air in the Salop infirmary, and the
> floors are mopped with lime water some hours previous to the first
> process; it did not, however, prevent the introduction of the influenza:
> indeed how should it, when the friends of the sick are perpetually visiting
> them from the town?

The belief in the contagiousness of the disease, although increasing at this time was
by no means universal. The view that person-to-person contact was not responsible was supported by published accounts of the disease that were at best confusing
and at worst downright misleading. The following was published in 1810, many
years after the pandemic of 1803. The writer placed undue importance on his
anecdotal evidence. He had found a number of instances that did not fit the
prevailing thinking and seems to have believed that they were sufficient in
number to overturn the theory – which was to prove correct but was then only
beginning to be accepted.

> Many individuals have taken the disorder without any intercourse with
> the sick. I have seen some instances of one individual in a full family ill of

the disease, and all the rest escaped. I have known wives sleep with their disordered husbands without being infected, and husbands sleep with their sick wives with equal impunity. I cannot say that any sickened by immediate contagion or intercourse with the sick, but as they happened to be constitutionally predisposed, and incurred, or were exposed to the exciting cause, which, when closely investigated, could in general be traced up to some evident cause, as exposure to cold air, change of bed, laying aside heavy cloathes and putting on lighter, overheating and getting cold afterwards, fatigue, a wetting, or some such cause. The hurtful impression of cold, however incurred, was the most general occasional cause both of the primary disease and subsequent relapse. I cannot say that human effluvia had any effect in propagating or multiplying the epidemic. Many more of the inhabitants of the most remote and thinly peopled parts of the country, in proportion to their number, were ill of the epidemic, and suffered much more.

Ironically he is right in some particulars. Influenza does not rely entirely on droplet infection caused by contact with someone already infected – the virus can survive for up to 48 hours on a door handle or in a handkerchief for example. Someone who touched the handle and then touched his or her mouth could well become infected despite not having come into direct contact with an infected individual. The author is also right in part about the more damaging effects on those in rural areas that were hit by the disease. City dwellers – having generally come in contact with more diseases than country people – were and are likely to resist the worst effects of flu better than their country cousins.

Treatments – Bloodletting, vomiting and cupping

What of cures? Whatever their failings – and these certainly were due more to ignorance than incompetence, doctors across Europe and America never gave up their search for a cure for influenza. Because most people survive even when a pandemic strikes, bizarre or sometimes very simple cures were hailed as a break-through, when in fact the person to whom those cures were administered was simply one of the lucky ones who would have survived anyway.

Remarkably little had changed in the methods available to doctors for the treat-ment of influenza since the 16th century. Central to most physicians' work at this time was the practice of bloodletting. At this remove, of course, bloodletting seems barbaric but it is worth remembering that even at the height of the 1918–19 pandemic bloodletting came back into fashion as attempts to control the disease became ever more desperate.

A Dr Bishop of Leicester, writing to The Sydenham Society in 1820, noted that, 'in those who appeared to labour under phlegmonic inflammation of the chest in whom recourse was had to general bloodletting in the first instance, pulse being hard, frequent, and oppressed, the evacuation was of considerable advantage in relieving the chest, and abating the hardness of the pulse.'

Aside from bloodletting there was a range of measures taken by doctors, many of which seem today like common sense, as Dr Kinglake notes: 'Small, close, hot rooms were always injurious; many received great benefit by opening the windows, or permitting them (the patients) to go out into the air. A cold temperature was highly gratifying and beneficial; I recommend a temperature of from 40–45 degrees of Fahrenheit. The complaint is always aggravated when it rose to 60 degrees.'

Perhaps the most important – certainly the most widely used – of all 19th-century drugs was opium, usually administered in its liquid form as laudanum. For influenza it was widely used and almost certainly did alleviate some of the symptoms. 'Opiates,' says Mr Swan of Lincoln, 'did much good, and were given pretty generally, when no inflammatory or other symptom indicated their use. They quieted the cough, and abated many of the other symptoms.' Dr James Flint of St. Andrew's, was equally enthusiastic: 'it was necessary to command the cough by gentle opiates. I never saw any harm from opiates when properly administered.'

Opium was taken internally in most flu cases but many doctors believed that it worked wonderfully when applied both internally and externally. One Dr Evans of Ketley made up an opium-based embrocation for his flu patients and tells us that, 'when rubbed on to the back and sides of the patient at bedtime, it never fails to procure a comfortable night's sleep.'

However, many other doctors thought opiates were likely to be harmful when used to counter influenza. Dr Longfield from Cork in the south of Ireland, argued that it should never be administered at the beginning of a patient's disease, while Dr Martin Wall of Oxford found that opiates produced confusion of the head and constipation. Dr Wall goes on to say that, 'The most judicious practitioners, for the most part, deferred the use of opiates till after the abatement of any inflammatory symptoms.'

Other medicines considered useful in flu cases included acetate of ammonia, antimonials and ipecacuanha (powerful emetics). None could have done more than perhaps alleviate the symptoms as much perhaps from the placebo effect as from any genuine efficacy. Other long-forgotten medicines recommended by numerous

Georgian doctors include squill (a plant extract used to make cough medicine), combined with ammoniacum, limoniated kali, and pediluvia (all plant extracts designed to alleviate the symptoms of influenza).

Dr Gridlestone reporting from Yarmouth at the height of the pandemic in late 1803 was certainly among the more sensible when he wrote:

> When the disease assumed the intermitting type, recourse was had to red
> bark (plant extract used to control fevers) as soon as the intermission was
> complete; and, if taken to the extent of half an ounce in sixteen hours,
> never failed to prevent the recurrence of the fit. The greatest number of
> children who were under my directions required no other medicine than
> as many oranges as they chose to suck.

Doctors at this time would have noted that eating fresh fruit tended to improve a patient's general health though they did not know precisely why. The clearest need for fresh fruit of some kind was proven by the experience of sailors, whose diet on a long journey lacked anything fresh. They would begin to fall ill and die from scurvy – caused, we now know, by a lack of vitamin C (ascorbic acid). Vitamin C is essential for collagen synthesis; without it the body quickly begins to suffer. Eighteenth-century doctors who recommended fresh fruit would have been aware that at least so far as oranges were concerned only the rich could afford to take the cure, but other fruit was often recommended instead.

A more substantial account of the 1803 pandemic and the attempts by doctors to come to terms with it is recorded in Dr Richard Pearson's *Observations on the Epidemic Catarrhal Fever or Influenza of 1803*. Dr Pearson quickly pinpoints one crucial aspect of influenza that is still a key factor today – the danger of secondary infection, particularly pneumonia. Dr Pearson writes: 'Very few died of the disease in this neighbourhood and of these most if not all seemed to fall victim to the accompanying pneumonia. Several instances occurred to me of pneumonia in its most violent degree, superinduced by the influenza.' Here he is on safe ground but his solution to the problem of secondary infection probably increased the chances that the patient would die:

> The lancet was imperiously called for, and repeatedly employed; twice,
> thrice, and, in one case, five times, with as liberal a hand as in ordinary
> pneumonia, and with as eminent and uniform advantage. The loss of
> blood was borne every bit as well as in other diseases, where bleeding is

indicated. I witnessed the unfortunate termination of several, where the
patients, I am fully persuaded, fell victims to an unfounded terror of
venesection in all cases of the influenza; derived, I suspect, from some
foolish paragraphs in newspapers, which not only materially influenced
the opinion of the public at large, but likewise that of many medical
practitioners.

Clearly public opinion was already beginning to turn against the idea of bloodletting, but having been trained in the procedure doctors like Pearson would have been
reluctant to abandon the practice.

Dr Faulkner, whom we encountered towards the beginning of this chapter,
recorded the effects of influenza on the elderly who, in 1803 at least, tended to die
more often than other age groups:

> But notwithstanding this formidable detail, the mortality that followed was
> not so great as might be apprehended, though greater than was commonly
> imagined. At the general hospital, in this city (Bath), where upwards of 100
> persons had the disease, not one died, though several suffered severely. Four
> persons of those I attended died, and all of them peripneumonic; but one
> of them had been subject to pulmonary complaints, and in a valetudinary
> state for the last six months; another was in the decline of life and
> debilitated by repeated gouty attacks, and had his end hastened by a
> suppression of urine, which, though relieved by the catheter, introduced
> without much trouble by an able surgeon, produced so much distress as to
> contribute in no small degree to his death. All whose cases terminated
> unfortunately were considerably past the meridian of life.

Faulkner goes on to list his favourite remedies and their specific uses and effectiveness. To the modern reader the cures often sound worse than the disease!

> The application of leeches, in cases where the symptoms were pressing,
> I found inadequate to the purpose. They, indeed, when put on in
> considerable numbers (as to eight or ten) seemed to afford a present
> alleviation of the symptoms; but the relief was transitory only; and bleeding
> by the arm was found to be the only means of imparting effectual
> assistance. It should, however, be considered that it is only in cases where
> the symptoms threaten life, that bleeding by the arm is necessary. In

common cases, where the breath is little affected, other remedies supersede its use, or at least render the application of leeches sufficient.

A tradition that went back as far as Hippocrates was that a patient's condition would improve – whatever the disease – if vomiting could be induced. The idea seems to have been based on a conviction that disease meant something alien had got into the body and needed to be purged. Of course in a simplistic sense this is correct so far as influenza and other viral and bacterial infections are concerned: something alien (the pathogen) really *has* got into the body, but no amount of vomiting will expel it. Dr Faulkner, like most of his contemporaries, had other ideas, as he explains:

> Emetics have, in my observation, been found particularly serviceable. If administered at the beginning of the complaint, they served to obviate the peripneumonic symptoms altogether, by throwing off with more ease the profusion of mucus, that in a good measure characterises this disease. But in the advanced state I was sorry to find the use of emetics less successful. When the breathing was greatly oppressed, it was difficult to make them operate upwards; but they were subject to run off by stool – an operation which did not afford the same relief with an emetic, and which, by diminishing the strength, without proportionably relieving the symptoms, seemed rather prejudicial than otherwise.

Perhaps more sensible was Faulkner's advice that:

> …moderate warmth, as that of a bed, is highly necessary; together with the frequent administration of thin diluting liquors. I observed, however, that much heat, either of fires or of bed-clothes, was prejudicial, and prevented rather than encouraged the salutary evacuation. The access of cold sharp air I found essentially necessary to be guarded against, as it immediately aggravated the cough and other morbid symptoms.

Doctors knew that one of the most dangerous aspects of the disease was congestion of the lungs and they worked hard to relieve this using steam and a number of chemical expectorants. Dr Faulkner again:

> The medicines, usually called expectorants, as *lac ammouiacum* [the gum from a flowering plant] and squills [the dried bulb of a Mediterranean

plant], could not in bad cases be employed; and in the slighter attacks, there
was no necessity for their use. The former was too heating and stimulant;
and the latter was apt to run off by stool. I must own, that nothing which
I tried with this intent succeeded to my wishes, except the volatile alkaline,
which, in the proportion of thirty or forty drops of spirits of hartshorn
(ammonium bicarbonate) taken pretty frequently in any warm vehicle,
seemed to be of service. I had some expectation that the steam of warm
water drawn in by the breath, by means of some of the inhalers, might
have answered this purpose, but was deceived. The breath was too short to
admit of its being used effectually in bad cases, and in others it was
superfluous.

Also well known was the 19th-century practice of cupping: glass cups were heated
to create a vacuum within them and then placed on the patient's back or elsewhere
where they would raise blisters. As with so many early medicines there was
absolutely no evidence that this did any good at all – other of course than reassur-
ing the patient that something was being done. Dr Faulkner was not a great believer
in the power of cupping:

> Blisters were, I believe, pretty freely tried; but, in the cases that fell under
> my observation, I cannot say that they were as serviceable as I expected.
> In some bad cases they seemed to give a temporary relief to the difficulty
> of breathing; but, in several instances, no good effect whatever was
> produced by them. I did not however find, except in one instance, that
> they were productive of any mischief. It should, however, be noticed, that
> I speak here of peripneumonic cases; for in those where vertigo was the
> leading symptom, blisters were of great use; and, indeed, I think the
> principal cause of its abatement, even after leeches had been tried with
> little advantage.

An early autopsy on a flu victim

Later flu epidemics and pandemics, particularly that of 1918–19 are well documented so far as records of autopsies are concerned, but to find an autopsy report
on a flu victim prior to the 20th century is unusual. An account of one such case
does survive from 1803, however, and the condition of the victim's lungs as
discerned during autopsy are characteristic of influenza. Dr Broderipp describes
what happened:

I was desired to visit M Ditcher, a young woman, in the 21st year of her age, who was indisposed with the prevailing epidemic disease; it was on the ninth day of her indisposition; and I found her in imminent danger. Upon inquiry into the origin of her complaint, and the symptoms which attended the incipient state of it, she informed me, that she was first seized with cold shivering over the whole body, drowsiness, and frequent chills, passing in the direction of the vertebrae; this was succeeded by feverish heat, a violent pain in her head, principally across her forehead, and immediately above the eyes; throbbing at the temples, an acrid discharge from the nostrils, troublesome cough, and difficulty of breathing. The following day she was troubled with an internal pain, which she described as directly underneath the left mamma; her respiration was more hurried, and she became more thirsty; her urine was very high-coloured, and, after standing a short time, threw down a considerable lateritious sediment; her tongue was much furred; and the phlegm which she attempted to expectorate was so tenacious, that she could not loosen it from the faeces. With remissions in the day, but returning with more violence towards evening, the train of the chief symptoms continued to the day of my seeing her.

When I called, she was sitting in her bed, gasping for breath, and apprehensive. Her cough was incessant, and of a peculiar kind; she expectorated a small quantity of mucus tinged with blood, her pulse was at 140, low, small and tremulous. Her tongue was foul, but not dry; the coating different from what is usual in febrile affections, and more resembling the appearance which we generally find in cases of croup. She complained of unusual pain; but particularly at the back part of the head, and across her chest; in short, her situation presented one of those distressing cases which result from inflammation, protracted from the omission of timely bleeding, &c. Immediately on leaving the room I expressed my concern that she had not applied earlier to the medical gentleman who was then attending her; and submitted to him my opinion of the morbid state in which the thoracic viscera would probably be found, upon dissection, after death.

Soothing and such medicines as appeared to me the best calculated to relieve the pressure of the various symptoms, were administered till the 13th day, when she was suddenly seized with general spasm, and expired. The following day the body was opened by Mr Cam, in the presence of Dr Davis. When the contents of the thorax were exposed to view, the anterior part presented nothing remarkable; but in attempting to take up the long lobe of the left lung, we found that adhesive inflammation had taken place over the whole posterior surface of that lobe. The adhesive exudation was considerable, and had attached that part of the lungs to the corresponding costal pleura.

Just as they would in 1918–19 (see Chapter 5) the doctors had discovered that the poor woman's lungs were massively congested and badly damaged by the disease.

Unlike the 1918–19 pandemic, the disease that raced across Britain and Europe in 1803 did not overly affect the young and fit, notwithstanding the case of the 21 year old described above. We will never know for sure if 1803's outbreak should properly be described as an epidemic or a pandemic – we know it crossed Europe, but there is little evidence that it crossed continents or had the high mortality associated with pandemics generally. But if it should really be described 'merely' as a severe epidemic its effects were nonetheless very serious, more often affecting the young and the very old. In 1918–19 the virus tended far more often to kill the young and the strong.

Efforts by doctors across Britain and Europe almost certainly did alleviate the suffering that the 1803 flu pandemic caused, although some treatments, as we have seen, could have hastened their patients' demise, or at the very least sapped their strength. There is no doubt that the particular strain of the virus that raged at that time was one to which the population seems to have had very little immunity. It was certainly not in the same league as the 1918–19 virus to which general immunity across the world was absolutely minimal, but devastating, nonetheless. It is impossible to calculate the numbers that died as a result of the 1803 epidemic, but it would certainly have been in the hundreds of thousands in Britain alone.

For the next 30 or so years various strains of influenza would have circulated through human populations worldwide, but no one strain seems to have genetically shifted to such an extent that it was seen – at the time – as being especially virulent.

The pandemic of 1831

In 1831 influenza became a serious issue once again. A strain that was unusually lethal began to be noticed across Europe. In France, in 1831, M. Sauvage, in his *Nosologia Methodica*, described how *la grippe* hit Paris:

> It came on about the beginning of Lent, which appears that year to have taken place on the 5th of March, not very different from the season when

the late epidemic came on in this country. Its symptoms were a dry cough, pain of the limbs, fever during the day-time, and headache; but, in young subjects, these symptoms did not continue longer than the fourth day, and were relieved by increase of spitting and expectoration. In old people, these symptoms came on with greater violence; and when accompanied with a hissing noise attending the cough, carried the patients off, about the ninth or the eleventh day. On dissection, the lungs were found either gangrenous, or much charged and distended with blood. In many persons a haemorrhage from the nose had come on before death, and sometimes afterwards, notwithstanding the patient had been bled two or three times. Forty persons died daily of this disease, for some time, in the Hospital of the Invalids at Paris.

Discharge of large quantities of blood from the nose became one of the more terrifying symptoms of the most deadly flu pandemic of all time – the 1918–19 pandemic. In 1831 it was less frequently seen, but pneumonia – a secondary infection – was common, and in those pre-antibiotic days it usually signalled that the patient was beyond hope of recovery. The suggested medical regime for flu patients had changed little since 1803:

> The most successful method of treating this disease was as follows: on the first day, two bleedings; on the second, an emetic or purgative; on the third, bleeding again; and in the evening, an opiate; from the fourth day to the ninth, a medicine was given, composed of three grains of Kermes mineral, with half a drachm of tartar, and the like quantity of diaphoretic antimony. This quantity was divided into six doses, of which one was taken every three hours: about the tenth day the recovery was perfected by the accompanying expectoration.

Such optimism was not always justified, but times were changing and the fashion for bleeding was on the wane. This particular French doctor looked back to the epidemics and pandemics of the previous century to find a useful set of procedures in order to help him deal with the present outbreak of flu:

> This practice [of bloodletting] is now rather out of date. But by the recommendation of repeated bleeding among so many of my colleagues, I am apt to suspect that the late [i.e. most recent] epidemic partook more

of an inflammatory disposition than those in 1775 and 1782. That in 1788, more resembled the late influenza in this respect; but the inflammation of the throat was in that more common and more vehement, and the peripneumonic symptoms less urgent. Bleeding, however, which, in those of 1775 and 1782, had been less necessary, was in that indispensable, as it was in the one with which we have been lately visited.

Dr John Nelson Scott wrote from the Isle of Man in 1831:

> The influenza, permit me, residing in this detached spot of the British empire, to trouble you with my observations on the late epidemic, premising, that the climate of the Isle of Man very much agrees with the description of that of Ireland. Our weather is very vicissitudinous, and our atmosphere exceedingly moist. The latter quality it very peculiarly possessed this last winter. Patients under typhus were in a greater proportion… and we met with some sporadic instances of scarlet fever.
>
> The influenza appeared among us towards the end of March. The first patient I saw was on the 24th, who had received the infection from a gentleman, who, two days before, had arrived from Parkgate, and who had been seized with the complaint in London, and was still labouring under it. In a few days after, one of our Liverpool packets arrived, having many passengers on board under the epidemic. From my inquiries, I have every reason to think that thus it was imported among us.
>
> It was not generally attended with symptoms which shewed an inflammatory tendency; and even much less so, in this respect, than in the epidemic of 1782.
>
> The proportion of pneumonia cases was very small. They amounted to a few, indeed, when compared to the number of other patients. Stout young men, who were exposed to wet, &c., had strong pneumonic symptoms. Pregnant women were also much affected with pain in the side (particularly the left); had great cough, and difficulty of breathing, and, on the whole, suffered much from the complaint. But, except in these two sets of patients, genuine marks of inflammation in the lungs and pleura were seldom to be met with.

That snapshot from a small off-shore island halfway between Britain and Ireland can be contrasted with an anonymous account of the origins of the same epidemic in

China. At the time it may have seemed to many observers that the appearance of flu in China was pure coincidence, but it is now believed that most, if not all, of the world's major flu pandemics have their origins in rural southern China.

> The disease first appeared, as related by Mr Lawson, on board the ship *Inglis*, while at China, on the 25th of January 1830, on which day eight or nine men were suddenly seized; on the following day twenty-four were attacked; on the 27th eight or ten; and on the 28th and 29th six more cases are recorded, after which there were no new cases. The attack was sudden, and the disease, within two hours, as severe as during any time of its continuance. The symptoms were pain in the head, more especially over the frontal sinus. Cough, discharge from the nose, sense of rawness in the throat and chest, rather than severe pain; great prostration of strength; in some of the cases there was pain … across the loins, with severe aching pains in the limbs; pulse frequent, but generally soft. The febrile symptoms in most cases had entirely subsided on the third or fourth day, and the cough, in the majority of instances, in about the space of a week from the commencement.
>
> The disease prevailed again in China during the month of September, and at the same time visited Manilla, and exhibited similar symptoms to those which were presented in China. The crew of the ship *Charles Forbes*, which arrived at Manilla from China, on the 18th of September, was attacked with the epidemic during the voyage.

Our anonymous correspondent continues with a long passage on the state of the weather and its malevolent influence and tendency to promote illness – particularly influenza. From the detail of this account of atmospheric changes it is clear that old ideas – about the arrival of influenza – died hard:

> During the month of May the weather was unusually variable; the barometer rising and falling suddenly, and the thermometer standing one day at 80 degrees Fahrenheit, and a few days afterwards at 32. The wind was prevailing steadily from the north-east. The month commenced with heavy clouds, murky storms, copious precipitations of rain, and remote thunder; the thermometer ranged from 55 to 60 degrees, and the wind blew for a few days from the west, and then shifted round to the north. This condition of atmosphere was succeeded by an overcast sky, with intervals of sunshine; a keen, cutting wind from the north-east, frost, ice,

and snow; the thermometer rapidly sinking to 32 degrees. Greatcoats which had been thrown off were resumed, and the fire-hearth became acceptable. By the middle of the month the weather cleared, and became warmer; the sky brightening, a high blustering wind prevailed from the north-east, drifting before it clouds of the dust from the roads; the thermometer ranging with celerity between 62 and 32 degrees...

And so on for several more pages. Eventually the point of the lengthy weather report becomes clear:

Additional evidence of the unhealthy character of this year is afforded in the following extract from the Statistical Reports on the Health of the Navy for the years 1830... In certain positions within the tropics, or on their confines, little surprise is excited when an unhealthy succeeds a healthy year, or when a series of years in which there is much mortality follows a number in which there had been comparatively little; because we are prepared by experience for the eruption of sweeping epidemics there, which leave no room to question the cause of difference, whatever doubt there may be as to the origin of the epidemic on which the difference evidently depends...the pervading influenza which occasioned increased mortality among the citizens appears to have been extended to the harbours and coasts of these islands, giving to common forms of disease, as on shore, more than ordinary degree of fatal force. During the following year the cause of malignant cholera became operative in many parts of the United Kingdom, with great concentration of power, and proved fatal in a very high proportion of the number attacked. Whether the same, or an altered agency, with less concentration and more diffusion, co-operated with the common causes of disease during the year in question, and endowed them with greater destructive agency, cannot be determined; but looking at all the circumstances, and bearing in mind the peculiar power of endemic, epidemic agency in some other cases, it is reasonable to conclude that it did.

This remarkably prescient comment is one of the earliest acknowledgments of influenza epidemics causing a general increase in the incidence of other, often fatal diseases. It is as if an already weakened immune system becomes prey to diseases that the body would under normal circumstances be able to keep at bay. As our anonymous correspondent puts it:

During the prevalence of influenza many other diseases exhibit more than the ordinary degree of fatality. On the continent, during the year 1830–31, intermittent influenza prevailed, succeeded by remittent and gastric fever. At the beginning of 1831 the prevailing type was again intermittent. In Italy influenza appeared, to be followed in Summer by cholera.

Waves of illness…

Across Europe in 1830–31 influenza moved rapidly and with occasionally devastating effects. It is curious, however, that mortality rates differed widely in different countries. This may well have been a reflection of the flu virus's curious habit of coming in waves – the first wave of a pandemic strain would normally be relatively mild, which meant that when the second, far more virulent wave attacked, those hit by the earlier wave would have some immunity. Dr Lombard writing from Paris in the late 1830s describes some of these patterns of variation:

> There were great variations in the duration and severity of this visitation in different places. Thus, for example, it did not increase the mortality in Paris, but at Berlin was as fatal as cholera. At Berlin it lasted only a few weeks, at Moscow and St Petersburgh two months, but at Paris it hung about for a year.

Dr Lombard noted that the symptoms in Geneva were similar to those in England. Lombard was convinced that in almost every case, influenza sufferers were best treated using emetics – he found them 'so useful that patients often felt cured the day after their employment, the pulse sinking from 100 to 80 or 70, and the headache, whatever its intensity, disappearing as if by enchantment'.

In England it was noted by a number of physicians that widespread outbreaks of influenza were often followed by raging dysentery and cholera. It was argued, too, that the extent to which these diseases followed one another was strongly reminiscent of the pattern of disease that swept across the country during earlier epidemics and pandemics.

But for all their increasing skill at analyzing and recording similar patterns of infection, consistent symptoms, and the real rather than imagined efficacy of various treatments, there were occasional setbacks. Though the insistence on the influence of the weather was less often mentioned by this time, influenza was still often confused with various respiratory diseases known to infect other animals. One doctor wrote of influenza in 1831:

The disease prevailed very extensively amongst horses, affecting the whole system, and often making its attack whilst they were under a medical regimen adapted for its removal. In the months of August, September, and October many horses in the neighbourhood of Chester were affected with dysentery, and the same disease was very widely diffused amongst dogs.

Where disease was noted among chickens our ancestors were on firmer ground, since we now know that birds are the natural hosts for influenza:

In the year 1832 epidemic diseases affected the lower animals. Chickens, in various parts of France, were thirsty, suffered from spasm, sought the sun, and crowded together for warmth, and their blood was darker than natural. Great mortality was also observed amongst fish, especially carp, and their spinal cord was found in a state of great congestion.

The growth of the empirical method

Though they were floundering in many areas in their pursuit of the truth about influenza, the methodology according to which doctors worked and reported their findings was improving all the time. Accuracy in reporting symptoms in a common language was becoming ever more important, and students were continually admonished for their failure to work on the basis of the precise symptoms of individual patients. To a large extent medicine was shifting rapidly now from a discipline that relied on authority to one that relied as far as possible on facts. A good example of this changing attitude is contained in the *London Medical Gazette* of 1833 where a Dr Hingeston wrote:

The passing features of disease are quickly lost and forgotten if we do not pause and depict their aspect while yet they are present. He who has not made the experiment, or who is not accustomed to require rigorous accuracy from himself, will scarcely believe how much a few hours take from certainty of knowledge and distinctness of imagery – how the succession of objects will be broken – how separate parts will be confused – and how many particular features and discriminations will be compressed and conglomerated into one gross and general idea.

Dr Hingeston goes on to provide an example of meticulous reporting:

The following sketch of the influenza, so lately prevalent in London, has been drawn with a rapid pencil from a distinct survey of many cases, and a characteristic outline of the disease is presented as it appeared to one within the circuit of his own recognition.

In the middle of the month of March, several persons were attacked with the affections of the bronchia and larynx common in the spring of the year, but it was not till the 6th of April that the influenza developed its pathognomonic character, and within the city started up widely on a sudden, manifesting itself in three different forms; each of these forms arose in succession, the active preceding the passive, and thus it happened:

1. Bronchitis with acute fever and keen arterial action, which presented itself in single cases towards the end of the month of March, and in the beginning of April. It yielded to ordinary treatment, and ended in a copious expectoration.

2. A catarrh of all the air passages, announced by sneezing, heaviness of the forehead, suffusion of the eyes, running at the nose, and a teazing cough. There were fugitive pains along all the great muscles of the limbs, pain of the hypochondria [the hypochondrium is the upper part of the abdomen, just below the ribs], and loins, and nape of the neck; perspiration and soreness pervaded the skin, but the perspiration was not critical. The bowels were naturally relieved, the tongue was clean, but the urine was scanty. In healthy persons this attack lasted from three to six days, and yielded to salines, nephritics, rest, abstinence, and sudorifics.

3. A dynamic catarrh, announced like the former by sneezing and the usual symptoms of a common cold, but distinguished by deep nervous depression and a subacute fever, running on, in some instances, to twenty-one days. The tongue was foul and loaded, and there was nausea, a complete loss of taste and appetite and smell, a pale languid countenance, torpor of the bowels, praecordial distension, and a deficiency of bile. In some cases there was a sudden and very marked prostration of all the vital powers. The sleep was broken and interrupted, with frightful and fantastic dreams; the

cellular tissue was lax, and the skin humid and universally sore; the
urine was scanty, high coloured, and turbid. In this form of the
disease the thorax was internally sore, with an incessant cough, and a
teazing glutinous expectoration; and occasionally by fits and starts,
there would be a fixed pain in the head or abdomen, simulating
inflammation; the pulse being at the same time quick, and often
accelerated. The patient was cast back on his bed, and appeared
alarmed at his own situation.

This form of the influenza obeyed no simple febrifuge [a medication that
reduces fever], but seemed to run a certain course … It was aggravated by
bleeding … it was alleviated by mild purgations of mercury.

This brilliant description of the disease is rather spoiled for the modern reader by
the reference to mercury – highly toxic, it would have been extremely harmful to
the patient.

A Dr Armstrong, who worked in London throughout the pandemic of 1830–31,
was far less optimistic about the chances of the treatments available to him having
any effect at all on the course of the illness:

As far as my experience has gone, any treatment was fallacious. One
bleeding from the arm was beneficial, but it could not be repeated.
Diffusive stimulants and generous food, when it could be taken, were more
useful than depressants, and the difficulty seemed to lie in making the
kidneys act efficiently. Vomiting was unfavourable, but a spontaneous
purging seemed to be beneficial and decisive. The restlessness and vigilance
could be opposed by opium, only towards convalescence.

These patients might linger for the space of two or three weeks and
then get up well, or they might die in the same number of days. Children
of ten months old were also afflicted with pulmonary disease about this
same period. Now their symptoms were those of pneumonia, and they
looked like little old persons labouring under asthma. Leeches, ipecacuanha
[a plant, the dried roots of which were used to make an emetic], and
mercury specifically, killed them; but relief seemed to be procured by mild
doses of rhubarb, with half-grain doses of Calomel as a purge, and a
combination of Oxymel of Squills with the Acetate of Ammonia. A bland
milk food was the best. Many died.

1833 — a second wave

Although the direct influence of bad weather on the arrival of flu had been largely discounted by this time, doctors were aware that flu epidemics and pandemics tended to arrive during winter when populations were likely to be in a less healthy condition anyway and therefore more likely to be subject to further infection.

In 1833 influenza spread rapidly across Britain and Europe. This was almost certainly a second wave of attack by the same virus that had surfaced in 1831, but it had probably mutated and become far more lethal. One doctor wrote:

> The disease was ushered into London during the prevalence of a bleak wind and a cold vernal atmosphere succeeding to a long, warm, moist winter. Storms of hail, snow, sleet, thunder, and rain, from dark fragments of clouds, were alternated only by currents of gelid air and harsh squalls from the north and north-east. Under these coarse rude flaws of heaven, the pulmonary organs of man, so susceptible of atmospheric changes, were excited and parched or moistened and depressed, and the whole surface of the skin must have suffered universally in its functions. Those persons were the least liable to the influenza who were the most exposed to the outward changes of the weather.

Commentators also noted that the attack of 1833 was:

> attended with greater nervous disturbance and the convalescence was more tardy: nearly four fifths of the inhabitants of Paris were affected. In this city it appeared under three varieties: 1st, the form complicated with Angina, Pleurisy, or Pneumonia; 2dly, with fever and local disturbance; 3dly, with Malaise and hoarseness.

Despite the improvement in disease records, it is still not possible to be certain that we are dealing with influenza in these early references. A commentator in London was clearly confused by the flu that prevailed in the more central areas of the city in 1833:

> In London, concurrently with the prevalence of the disease in man, horses were affected with Influenza; but for some time, whilst those in the low parts suffered, those in the upper and North-West districts

escaped. Not many weeks afterwards, there was not a mews in Marylebone which did not contain some patients, while Westminster was exempt from disease.

A Mr Youatt writing of the same phenomenon confessed that he had known it to be:

> …confined to a district not a furlong square. In one extraordinary case, a fifth part of the horses in a certain mews died, while there was no vestige of disease elsewhere. I recollect that in one of our barracks, the majority of the horses on one side of the yard were attacked by epidemic catarrh, while there was not a sick horse on the other side. These prevalences and these exceptions are altogether unaccountable. The stables and the system of stable management have been most carefully inquired into in the infected and healthy districts, and no satisfactory difference could be ascertained. One very important fact, however, has been established, namely, that the probability of the disease seemed to be in a tenfold ratio with the number of horses inhabiting a stable. Two or three shut up in a comparatively close stable would escape. Out of 30 distributed through 10 or 15 little stables, not one would be affected; but in a stable containing 10 or 12, although proportionably larger and more ventilated, the disease would assuredly appear; and, if it does enter one of the largest stables, almost every horse will be affected.

That idea that cramped conditions exacerbated the spread of influenza is certainly correct, but of course the disease that affected those London horses was certainly not the influenza that killed so many people during the same fateful year.

1837 – a third wave

The year 1837 saw the return of a wave of exceptionally virulent influenza. It is hard to say for sure if it was worse than the outbreaks of 1831–33, but it was clearly bad enough to help lift the British medical profession onto a new level of organization.

After the flu had done its worst – largely during January, February and March of 1837 – the Council of the Provincial Medical Association issued a circular to its members, asking for information on the origin, progress and duration of the epidemic, its symptoms and treatment, the atmospheric phenomena attending and preceding it, 'together with such other particulars as might be necessary for the elucidation of many questions of interest immediately connected with it'. Despite opposition from some of its more reactionary members, the Council of the Provincial Medical Association issued the following list of questions:

- When did the Influenza appear in your neighbourhood? And how long did it prevail there?
- Did it attack a great many individuals at the same time?
- Did it appear partial to any age, sex, or temperament? Or did it appear to attack all indiscriminately?
- Was it milder when it attacked children?
- What age appeared to suffer most from it?
- Was the spread of the distemper very extensive in your neighbourhood?
- What was the proportion of deaths to the number attacked?
- What circumstances predisposed the patients to a fatal termination of the disease?
- What was the ordinary duration of the disease?
- Were relapses common?
- Were persons whose occupations exposed them to the vicissitudes of the weather in the open air, more liable to the distemper than those who were confined chiefly to the house?
- Are you in possession of any proof of its having been communicated from one person to another?
- In persons attacked by the epidemic, who at the time laboured under pulmonary disease, was the former malady found to be aggravated on the subsidence of the Influenza?
- Were there any circumstances that appeared to exempt individuals from an attack of the disease? And, in particular, did the having been attacked during the last similar epidemic of the year 1834, appear to afford any protection?
- What were the usual symptoms of the complaint?
- What unusual symptoms occurred in your practice?
- What was your mode of treating the disease?
- Did any peculiar atmospheric phenomena precede or accompany this epidemic?

Dr Streeten, the man behind this circular, was ahead of his time when he wrote to dismiss, as diplomatically as he could, the last vestiges of the old belief that influenza was caused by malign celestial influences, fogs, miasmas or bad weather. Discussing the 1837 pandemic he wrote:

> This condition – melting snow – was operating at the breaking out of influenza in January, 1837; but did it produce the disease, or did it only co-operate in giving greater effect to other causes? That it did not produce the disease is evident, because this occurred in situations on the continent nearly about the same time, where there was no melting snow, and because the same disease has occurred before, in this and other countries, in summer months. In 1833 it was very general in this country in April and May, and again in June, 1831, partially. Dr Bardsley, speaking of the influenza of 1802, said that the epidemic with which he struggled cannot have originated from any remarkable severity of the weather or sudden changes in the temperature of the atmosphere; no season has been apparently less unfriendly to the human constitution than the whole of the late winter and early part of spring. The epidemic catarrhs of 1762 and 1782 also prevailed during uncommonly warm and steady weather, in the months of May and June. The remarkable epidemic catarrh of 1580 which prevailed across Europe, raged chiefly during the sultry weather of autumn.

Dr Streeten's conclusions are absolutely correct:

> Without uselessly multiplying instances or authorities, it must be evident that the exciting cause of influenza cannot be found in sudden vicissitudes of temperature, great heat or cold, damp weather or melting snow, however much all or any of these circumstances may predispose to the more ordinary catarrhs, eruptive fevers, and other disorders of Spring, Autumn, and Winter.

Trade and empire

The movement of people and goods around the world has been central to the spread of many diseases, but it seems to be particularly implicated in the spread of influenza. (Certainly in 1918–19 it was the movement of troops in their tens of thousands by ship that precipitated the worldwide crisis, as we will see in the next chapter). But almost a century earlier, shipping was heavily implicated in the 1837 influenza pandemic. An anonymous naval correspondent described how influenza spread across the Royal Navy, at that time the biggest and most widely dispersed navy in the world:

During the month of January, 1837, influenza prevailed epidemically in nearly every British vessel of war stationed at the following ports: namely, Sheerness, Portsmouth, Plymouth, and Falmouth. In February it attacked the ships' companies of the vessels employed on the north coast of Spain and at Lisbon. In March it made its appearance on the south coast of Spain, and subsequently attacked the crews of several vessels at Barcelona. In April it reached Gibraltar, and in May, Malta. It appears, however, to have been prevalent also in January at Smyrna and at Trieste. With the exception of the *Thunderer*, there is no evidence of its having broken out in any vessel at sea, unless the crew had been recently exposed in an infected locality. In the above vessel it suddenly made its appearance while she was on her homeward passage from Malta, four days before she arrived in Plymouth. The weather for some time previously had been wet, the wind varying from north-east to north-west. Catarrhal complaints had been for some weeks more than usually numerous amongst the crew, but they did not assume the epidemic form until the 3rd of January. On that day, three unequivocal cases of influenza were placed on the sick list; on the fourth, there were 7; on the fifth, 13; on the sixth, 11; on the seventh, 14; on the eighth, 17.

After this the number of cases occurring daily began to decline until the 11th, when there were two only. On the following day, however, they again began to increase, and continued increasing until the 17th, when they amounted to 44. After this the number of cases gradually diminished, and the disease finally disappeared about the end of the month.

Influenza broke out in the *Sapphire* about the middle of January, shortly after leaving Corfu, and while cruising to the southward, amongst the contiguous islands on the coast of Greece. It was supposed to have been occasioned by cold and moisture. The weather had been previously wet, and the awnings being much worn and defective, the whole of the main deck, and those parts of the lower deck near the hatchways, were almost constantly damp, thus proving a source of much discomfort to the men. Sixty-six cases occurred, all of which were cured on board.

Catarrhal complaints prevailed in an epidemic form, and with an unwonted degree of severity in almost every vessel of war stationed on the coasts of Spain and Portugal. In the majority of the returns these complaints have therefore been denominated influenza. It is first mentioned as having been prevalent at Lisbon, and amongst the merchant shipping, during the latter part of January.

Early in February it appeared in the *Russell* (74 guns), then at anchor in the Tagus, (the disease at that time being prevalent at Lisbon, both in the town and amongst the merchant shipping.) The first man attacked had been exposed the greater part of the day in a boat and on shore. The disease rapidly spread until the cases amounted to 84. The greater number of attacks occurred on the 7th day; namely, on the 23rd. The symptoms for the most part yielded readily to mild cathartics, sudorifics, and warm diluents.

A more detailed description of the effects of flu on the navy is provided by Dr McWilliam who treated the men of HMS *Canopus*. He wrote:

HMS *Canopus*, 84 guns, with a complement of 650 men, after being three years on the Mediterranean station, left Malta on the 1st January, 1837; and having stopped twenty-four hours at Gibraltar and part of a day at Barcelona, arrived in Plymouth Sound on the 1st of February. The following day the ship proceeded into harbour. The weather was cold, rainy, and boisterous, and the influenza prevailed much on shore; yet the crew, although daily exposed in unrigging the ship, in boat duty and at the dockyard, continued in perfect health until the 15th, when the epidemic struck down two thirds of the men in one day. Men in the prime and vigour of life and health, with their spirits in the highest degree elated at the prospect of being paid off, were in an hour or two prostrated in mind and body, as if by some sudden blow, or unexpected reverse of fortune. During the 16th and 17th, upwards of seventeen men were taken to the hospital at Plymouth.

I was labouring under the disease myself; but the surgeon, and the other assistant-surgeon, being worse than I was, I managed to continue on duty, going to bed in the evening, and drinking plentifully of hot negus. Under this system, I got well in a week without confinement.

By the spring of 1837 the pandemic was probably at its height – Barcelona was so badly affected that all public business ceased and every concert hall, theatre and bull ring closed. Ships avoided Spanish ports except where they had no choice, and the crews of those vessels that did dock were quickly overwhelmed by the disease. One report mentioned that in some Spanish and French cities people were collapsing at the rate of three or four every hour, day and night, for almost a week before the disease began to abate.

By now it was generally known that influenza was highly contagious and that there was an incubation period during which the victim felt perfectly well but was actually highly infectious. Dr McWilliam was among a number of enlightened and perceptive doctors who noticed this intriguing time delay:

> On the 4th or 5th of April, it attacked the *Childers*, three or four days after she sailed from Barcelona, where the germs of the disease were undoubtedly contracted. On the 9th of the month it reached its acme, and on the 14th ceased to extend. This vessel arrived at Gibraltar on the 9th, while the disease was at its worst, and anchored near the *Jasseur*, the crew of which was then perfectly healthy. They purposely avoided as long as possible having any communication with the *Childers*; but on the 12th, a signal was made by the latter for assistance, (her crew being, from weakness, unable to weigh the anchor,) when a party of men was sent on board. On the 15th the disease made its appearance in the *Jasseur*, the first man that suffered being one of the party sent to the affected vessel, thus affording evidence of the propagation of the disease by personal communication. The greatest number of attacks took place on the 21st and 22nd; after the 25th, but few cases occurred, and these were of a mild character. The crew of the *Asia* contracted the disease at Salamis, about the 15th of April. It attained the highest point of severity on the 22nd, and ceased on the 29th.

Most contemporary commentators believed that the pandemic of 1837 closely resembled that of 1831–33. Records for 1837 – particularly records that suggest the disease spread across Europe and beyond – are more extensive than for the previous outbreak. But 1837 caused unusually high mortality, certainly higher than in 1831–33. An anonymous correspondent of the *London Medical Gazette* commented that:

> In Berlin, during the month of January 1837, deaths from influenza exceeded births. In Prussia influenza prevailed everywhere and domestic animals, neat cattle, and horses, suffered at the same period from catarrhal and rheumatic affections.
>
> On the continent, the spring equinox of this year (1837) was observed to be like the winter solstice. Cold, heat, dryness, and humidity, alternated previously to the visitation of influenza. When the influenza was about to appear, the ordinary characteristic diseases of the season became

less rife … and soon influenza reigned alone, as if it absorbed all
pathological elements.

Another influenza pandemic of 1889–91 was said to have arrived in Europe via
Russia – it quickly became known as Russian flu – but like most influenza
pandemics it probably originated in southern China. In the same month that it
reached Europe via Russia it also reached the United States – its arrival in America
was attributed to mass immigration and the vast numbers of ships reaching the New
World from the impoverished cities and towns of Europe. The advent of steam ships
reduced dramatically the time it took to travel between the British Isles and the
United States from six to one week – a disaster so far as the spread of disease was
concerned. In America a quarter of a million people probably died from flu in
1889–91, making it a greater killer than cholera.

A fascinating snapshot of the effects of the influenza pandemic of 1889–91 is
provided by one Dr Parsons who wrote:

> The influenza epidemic reached Scotland on 17th December, 1889, when
> a crew from Riga landed at Leith. By the middle of December, cases were
> reported in Inverness and the epidemic later spread to Dingwell and
> Edinburgh, Glasgow, Aberdeen and Dundee. It was present in Dundee
> from the second week in July to the beginning of October when the next
> major epidemic began. In Edinburgh alone, 202 people died between
> November and January. From North America it spread by ship to Japan, to
> Latin America to Asia.

The growth of cities

Throughout the 19th century cities and towns across Europe and beyond grew ever
bigger, but public health measures did not keep pace with the growth of the built
infrastructure and the economies that sustained that growth. The result was numerous outbreaks of cholera, and it is almost certain that weakened urban populations
provided a perfect centre from which influenza could spread.

Large populations suffered most as *The Times* reported in the spring of 1837:

> Geneva was attacked some days before the environs, and Lausanne before
> Morges. In Lyons, the St Just district first. At Geneva, the military were first
> affected; and the gendarmes, who are much exposed to the weather, before
> the artillerymen. The liability was modified by the elevation. In a prison at

PLATE i

An 18th-century Italian engraving shows a family worried about La Grippe getting ready for what was then seen as a cure for almost every ailment – bloodletting or venesection. Bloodletting was practised extensively during all flu outbreaks up to and including the 1918 pandemic.

All outbreaks of flu are frightening and people have tried many bizarre cures and preventatives to outwit a disease that baffled doctors and scientists of the past. These boys, photographed in 1917, are wearing bags of camphor around their necks to ward off the evil influence.

PLATE ii

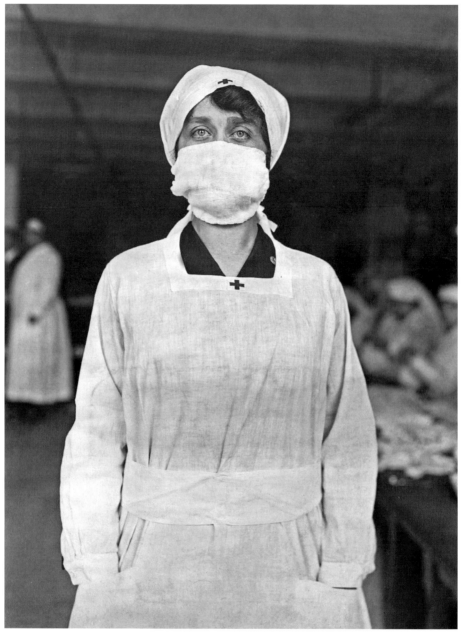

The wearing of masks was made compulsory in some parts of the world during the 1918 pandemic. Here a Red Cross worker models a mask she has just made. In the background other women are busy making similar masks. Unfortunately the masks did little to help.

PLATE iii

During the Spanish flu pandemic of 1918–19 people tried to avoid gathering in enclosed areas and a belief in the efficacy of fresh air led to patients being left out in their beds on hospital roofs and in gardens. Here, in San Francisco, the local court is being held outside.

PLATE iv

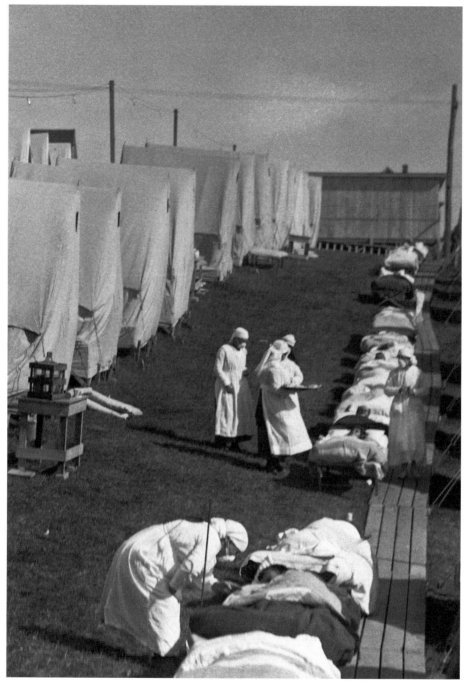

The influenza camp at Lawrence, Maine USA. This photograph, taken on 18 October 1918, shows how doctors were simply grasping at straws in their attempts to combat the deadly Spanish flu pandemic. Patients are being given the fresh air treatment, which probably did as much harm as good.

PLATE V

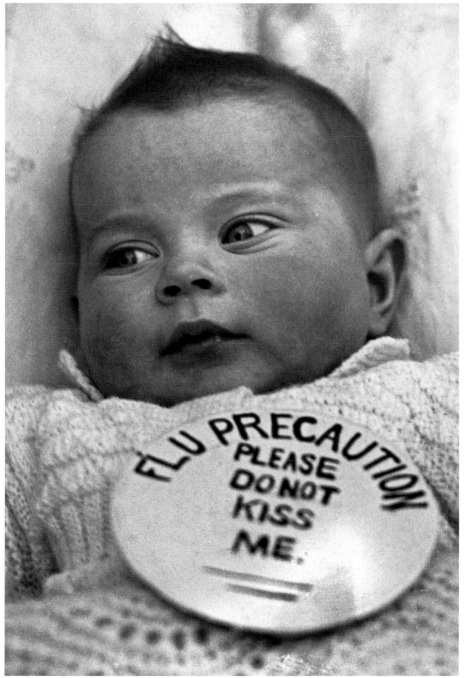

The extraordinary level of public concern about flu infection, even after the virus had been identified, can be judged by this photograph of a baby carrying a health warning.
It was taken in Manchester, UK in 1939.

PLATE vi

Two scientists at work in New York in 1941 using an electron microscope, the first instrument powerful enough to enable viruses to be seen. Having isolated the flu virus doctors were optimistic that a cure could not be far away, but even today that cure still eludes us.

PLATE vii

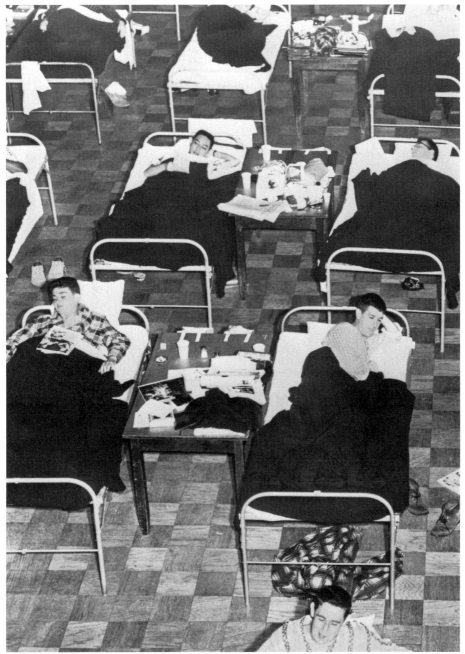

When the Asian flu pandemic of 1957 struck it hit young people as well as the elderly.
Here hundreds of University of Massachusetts students are being treated in an emergency infirmary
– the ballroom of the student union building. The fact that this space had to be used reflects the
pressure on hospital wards.

PLATE viii

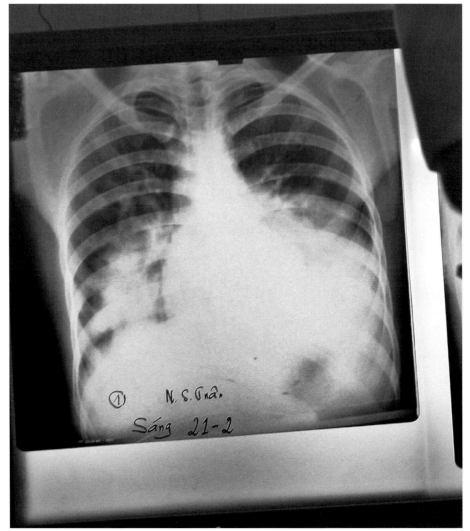

The threat of avian flu spreading freely among human populations has concentrated the minds of scientists worldwide. Until now human to human transmission has been very rare and most cases of avian flu in humans have arisen as a result of bird to human infection. This x-ray shows the lungs of avian flu victim Nguyen Sy Tuan, a 21-year-old man who survived 82 days in a critical condition at the Infectious Disease Department at the Institute for Tropical Disease in Hanoi. The cloudy area shows extensive damage caused to the lungs by the flu virus.
The threat of avian flu is particularly worrying as it is believed that the Spanish flu virus that caused the pandemic of 1918–19 was largely derived from an avian flu strain.

Geneva, in an elevated situation, only 6 out of 35 inmates suffered; in another prison near the water, 23 out of 60.

As late as 1854 celestial occurrences were still occasionally mentioned when influenza appeared: 'Although a superstitious dread of comets no longer exists it would be inexpedient to omit a notice of the fact that these remarkable bodies repeatedly attracted attention about the time of catarrhal epidemics especially near the visitations of 1510, 1557, 1580, 1732, 1737, 1743 and 1762.' But wiser counsels now prevailed almost everywhere. In his book *Epidemics Examined*, of 1850, John Gove wrote:

> If, during some visitations persons most exposed to the atmosphere were most severely affected, in others individuals confined to the house were equally visited and in the year 1836–7 we find the disorder raging at the same time at Capetown and London, the season being midsummer in the one place and mid winter in the other. There can scarcely therefore be any necessary connection between influenza and states of weather, although meteorological disturbances are present in so large a majority of instances as to authorize a strong suspicion that some indirect relation does exist.

It is impossible to estimate the number of deaths worldwide during any of the pandemics and epidemics of the 19th century, but there is no doubt that millions would have been infected and hundreds of thousands at least would have died. The particular circumstances surrounding the 1918–19 pandemic have made it the most lethal pandemic in history, but that should not cause us to forget that these 19th-century outbreaks were also major disasters. Best estimates suggest that more than a million died in Europe and North America as a result of the 'Russian' flu of 1889–91, but this was as nothing when compared to the gathering storm that was to break over the world just three decades later.

CHAPTER 5

The World's Worst Pandemic – the 'Spanish' Flu of 1918

It can be difficult to write about the Spanish flu of 1918, paradoxically because there is both too much and too little information. A number of books have detailed the history of what is generally agreed to be the world's most devastating global outbreak of disease, but estimates of the number of people who died as a result of the pandemic vary wildly – from 20 million to more than 100 million. The current best guess is around 50 million. The strain of flu that caused these deaths has only recently been identified, however, and the origins of that strain are still a matter of debate.

The forgotten millions

One thing is certain, however. The numbers of dead as a result of the Spanish influenza pandemic were extremely high, far higher than the numbers who died in the Great War of 1914–18. There is no question about that, yet our awareness of World War I is far more sharply focused than our perceptions of the pandemic that so quickly followed the cessation of hostilities.

Every village and town in England – almost without exception – still has a memorial to those who died in the trenches between 1914 and 1918, but there are no memorials to the pandemic disease that claimed lives in just as many communities. Around nine million soldiers died during World War I, together with as many as nine million civilians. Most of those deaths occurred in Europe, though of course they included Commonwealth and American soldiers. The 50 million (possibly 80 or 100 million) who died worldwide as a result of flu are hardly remembered at all. The reasons for this are complex.

One is, of course, not comparing like with like. It is not solely the number of fatalities that are at stake, but the significance of those deaths to history. Heroic young men, fighting for their country and suffering mutilation and agonizing deaths in the trenches, in a conflict that the population at large increasingly felt could *and should* have been avoided was a tragic waste. The global political scene was changed for ever as a result of the conflict: political regimes rose and fell, whether via the democratic process or revolution; national boundaries were re-drawn; entire new nations were established; the imperial powers scrambled for more overseas territories; and, in the punitive terms of the Versailles Treaty of 1919, the seeds were in fact laid for World War II, just 20 years later.

The deaths of many more millions of people from influenza, while on individual and humanistic terms every bit as tragic, has not been deemed of comparable historical significance, and thus has received far less attention (perhaps a dozen books have been written about the pandemic of 1918–19 compared with thousands on the Great War). Furthermore, there was at that time no vaccination for flu; the pathogen had not even been identified. Unlike war, sickness and death are a genuinely inevitable part of life – what could one do to prevent it? At that time, and with this particular strain of flu virus, nothing. Thus, rather like an earthquake, tsunami or other natural disaster, the general feeling was that it could *not* be prevented; one had to take one's chances and ride it out as best one could.

The context of war

The fact that this flu pandemic occurred towards the end and immediately after this world conflict had an enormous influence on how the pandemic unfolded. The very unique political, social and psychological context within which it occurred cannot be underestimated. The world was on a war footing, resources were already stretched to the limit, there were other priorities. It is all too easy with the gift of hindsight to say things should have been done differently. Indeed they should have been, and errors in judgement by the governments and political leaders of the time in their reaction – or perhaps non-reaction – to the pandemic had catastrophic consequences. Sadly, this was something people had already come to expect from their leaders.

As the world tried to make sense of the slaughter of war, it found increasingly that it could most easily be understood and accepted if it was seen as the loss of a generation of young men who died because they were obedient, loyal and patriotic. The terrible folly of it all lay not with the ordinary soldier, but with the men who led them. The 'old guard', typified by Earl Haig, were ultimately blamed and the phrase 'lions led by donkeys' came to encapsulate what had gone wrong. Despite any number of books by revisionist historians this view of the war is so deeply embedded that it is unlikely to be eradicated.

But while the Great War was memorialized and society was changing as never before, the havoc caused by pandemic influenza was quickly forgotten. There are few heroic myths attached to the deaths of those countless millions across the world who succumbed so readily to what seemed at first like simple influenza. The lives of the pandemic victims were cut short by an unseen, unknown enemy; there was nothing heroic about it at all – in most cases death was messy and painful, but essentially private. Indeed in many countries – but most notably the USA – the official line throughout even the worst months when tens of thousands were dying daily was that it was nothing to worry about.

This was partly attributable to the influence of American President Woodrow Wilson who would not permit reports about the virulence of the outbreak to be published in case it weakened the war effort. His refusal to accept the seriousness of the situation led to far more deaths than might otherwise have occurred. He refused, for example, to stop troop movements, despite the advice of a number of prominent American doctors that this would lead to a rapid and disastrous spread of the influenza across the country, and beyond. In Europe the situation was similar and governments involved in the war prevented newspapers from reporting the devastating disease then raging in army camps across the war zones.

The fact that the pandemic of 1918–19 was called the 'Spanish' flu at all is a reflection of the political situation of the time and has absolutely no foundation in the real origins of the disease. With the censorship of the press of combatant nations across war-torn Europe the only country that publicly mentioned the new disease was neutral Spain. Because this new virulent kind of flu was first mentioned in Spain it was seen – quite wrongly – as having originated there. Like most, perhaps all pandemic outbreaks of influenza, the disease almost certainly had its origins in southern China. However, there are also strong suggestions that it reached Europe via the United States, where it may even have originated. The balance of opinion among scientists remains, however, that its origin was almost certainly China.

The first reports

It all began in the spring of 1918 when a Madrid-based news agency sent a telegraph to Reuters news agency in London. The message mentioned 'a strange form of disease of epidemic character'. It had appeared in Madrid but the author of the message was optimistic and concluded 'The epidemic is of a mild character.'

In Spain the disease became known as the three-day fever and it spread rapidly across the country affecting as many as eight million Spaniards in total. Transport, commercial premises, factories and offices were forced to close in Madrid and elsewhere, and even the king succumbed to the disease. Though highly infectious, it does seem to have been mild, however. The symptoms were clearly indicative of some form of flu – lack of appetite, headache and pain behind the eyes, high temperature, aching bones and extreme lethargy. Influenza reports began to reach London from across the British Empire and indeed the world. From Scotland to Greece, Norway to India, Russia to China the disease swept all before it.

The Spanish were incensed that they were being blamed for the outbreak and with some justification. Careful study of the dates at which the disease first appeared shows that months before it reached Madrid it was already rife in American military camps, particularly Fort Riley where on a single day in March 1918 more than 1,000 men were struck down by the disease.

Across Europe and America this first wave of the disease was indeed relatively mild – so much so that British army officers are reported to have dosed themselves successfully on champagne. In Spain those who caught the disease retired to bed for three days and usually found that they were fine. But it was not understood at the time that this first wave of attack was caused by a virus that was not yet fully adapted to man. In its first form it could be passed from human to human, but it had not sufficiently mutated to become both highly infectious *and* highly dangerous – for now it was just highly infectious. It merely spread very rapidly causing moderate to severe illness from which the majority of sufferers recovered after a few days.

It is certainly true that the elderly and some of the very young died, as was to be expected from any flu outbreak. But this was a time bomb. This first wave of attack was just a warning of the full horrors to come later that year.

The 1918–19 influenza virus was also singularly blessed by the circumstances of war. Without the massive troop movements caused by the war it probably would not have taken hold to the same extent and the levels of mortality it caused would certainly have been far lower. The virus quickly spread to one of America's largest army camps, and thence, via troopships, to Europe. The emerging pandemic was further exacerbated by the fact that Europe had already been at war for nearly four years and its population was weakened by poor nutrition, poor health care and poor housing. The world's food production system had been massively disrupted by the war and resources that would normally have gone into food, health and housing went instead into armament production. In parts of Italy, France and Germany children were severely malnourished to the point of starvation, and disease of all kinds was far more prevalent as a result of the absence of fruit and fresh vegetables from the diet.

Army camps and troop movements
In the United States the massing of troops in huge army camps caused an enormous number of deaths and probably increased the virus's ability to mutate rapidly into

the killer it became towards the end of the year. The decision to send tens of thousands of troops to Europe (in addition to the small American Expeditionary Force) probably first brought the new strain of flu to Europe. Ironically, it was the allied troops' infection with this first, milder version of the disease that seems to have protected them from the far more virulent second wave of the virus that helped knock out the Germans in the autumn of 1918.

One of the biggest problems for armies throughout history has been disease. Once you bring together tens of thousands of men and cram them together into a small space, disease is almost certain to occur, and when it does its spread is bound to be virtually unstoppable. This was certainly the case before the advent of modern medicines, particularly antibiotics. In the Crimea, the American Civil War, the Boer War – and World War I – many more men died from disease than from their war wounds. In the Boer War it has been estimated that for every soldier who died fighting, ten more died from disease.

In America in 1918 the problem was exacerbated by unprecedented levels of overcrowding. Military camps were crowded at the best of times, but in their haste to do the President's bidding the US Army continued to pull men into camps that were already dangerously overcrowded. Camps designed for 20,000 troops were compelled to accommodate twice that number. While attention was paid to the practical problems of packing that many people together – enough beds were found and barracks were built – almost nothing was done about the soldiers' health. The last part of each camp to be constructed was the hospital, and these were designed to house only a very small number of men at any one time. There existed the tacit belief that putting too much effort into the medical side of a camp would make the men soft.

Measles was the first disease to hit the camps. Few if any can have thought for a moment that flu would be a major problem. The flu that was to become known as the 'Spanish' flu was probably carried from Haskell County Kansas to Camp Funston by a new army recruit in February 1918. How that first soldier contracted the disease is unknown. By the end of March thousands of soldiers in Funston were sick. The disease quickly spread to other camps. More than 20 of America's 36 huge army camps were stricken with the disease, which then spread to major provincial capitals near those infected camps.

By April troop movements between Europe and America had led to a sudden increase in cases of flu among British and French troops. The troop ships had been landing at Brest, which is where the disease first surfaced. Morbidity was high, but generally the troops recovered quickly. It seemed like a normal outbreak of flu:

nothing to worry about. By the end of May almost 40,000 British troops had succumbed to the disease to the degree that they required hospital admittance. The French army was equally badly hit, but few were dying and the disease was regarded as a nuisance encumbering the war effort. As the spring wore on, however, German troops began to fall sick and when the expected German offensive failed to materialize it was widely interpreted as a sign that German troops were simply too sick and demoralized by influenza.

Back in America the huge camps from which soldiers were steadily shipped to Europe began to implode – at Camp Devens near Boston the first few new influenza cases that appeared early in September appeared to be meningitis. Victims who quickly became delirious were struck down at speed, could not tolerate light and were hypersensitive to touch. By the end of September nearly 20 per cent of the 45,000 soldiers in the camp had been hit – and hard – by the disease. After the first few died rapidly and from massive infection with pneumonia, the rate at which they were dying increased quickly to a flood of deaths. We have this vivid first-hand account from a doctor at Camp Devens, writing to a friend:

> Camp Devens, Mass.
> Surgical Ward No 16
> 29 September 1918
> (Base Hospital)

My Dear Burt

It is more than likely that you would be interested in the news of this place, for there is a possibility that you will be assigned here for duty, so having a minute between rounds I will try to tell you a little about the situation here as I have seen it in the last week.

As you know I have not seen much pneumonia in the last few years in Detroit, so when I came here I was somewhat behind in the niceties of the Army way of intricate diagnosis. Also to make it good, I have had for the last week an exacerbation of my old 'Ear Rot' as Artie Ogle calls it, and could not use a Stethoscope at all, but had to get by on my ability to 'spot' 'em thru my general knowledge of pneumonias. I did well enough, and finally found an old phonendoscope that I pieced together, and from then on was all right. You know the Army regulations require very close locations etc.

Camp Devens is near Boston, and has about 50,000 men, or did have before this epidemic broke loose. It also has the Base Hospital for the Div. of the N. East. This epidemic started about four weeks ago, and has developed so rapidly that the camp is demoralized and all ordinary work is held up till it has passed. All assembleges of soldiers taboo.

These men start with what appears to be an ordinary attack of La Grippe or Influenza, and when brought to the Hosp. they very rapidly develop the most viscous type of pneumonia that has ever been seen. Two hours after admission they have the Mahogany spots over the cheek bones, and a few hours later you can begin to see the Cyanosis extending from their ears and spreading all over the face, until it is hard to distinguish the coloured men from the white. It is only a matter of a few hours then until death comes, and it is simply a struggle for air until they suffocate. It is horrible. One can stand it to see one, two or twenty men die, but to see these poor devils dropping like flies sort of gets on your nerves. We have been averaging about 100 deaths per day, and still keeping it up. There is no doubt in my mind that there is a new mixed infection here, but what I don't know. My total time is taken up hunting rales, rales dry or moist, sibilant or crepitant or any other of the hundred things that one may find in the chest, they all mean but one thing here – Pneumonia – and that means in about all cases death.

The normal number of resident Drs. here is about 25 and that has been increased to over 250, all of whom (of course excepting me) have temporary orders – 'Return to your proper Station on completion of work'. Mine says 'Permanent Duty', but I have been in the Army just long enough to learn that it doesn't always mean what it says. So I don't know what will happen to me at the end of this.

We have lost an outrageous number of Nurses and Drs, and the little town of Ayer is a sight. It takes special trains to carry away the dead. For several days there were no coffins and the bodies piled up something fierce, we used to go down to the morgue (which is just back of my ward) and look at the boys laid out in long rows. It beats any sight they ever had in France after a battle. An extra long barracks has been vacated for the use of the Morgue, and it would make any man sit up and take notice to walk down the long lines of dead soldiers all dressed and laid out in double rows. We have no relief here, you get up in the morning at 5.30 and work steady till about 9.30 P.M., sleep, then go at it again. Some of the men of course have been here all the time, and they are TIRED.

If this letter seems somewhat disconnected overlook it, for I have been called away from it a dozen times the last time just now by the Officer of the Day, who came in to tell me that they have not as yet found at any of the autopsies any case beyond the Red. Hepatitis. stage. It kills them before they get that far.

I don't wish you any hard luck Old Man but I do wish you were here for a while at least. Its more comfortable when one has a friend about. The men here are all good fellows, but I get so damned sick of Pneumonia that when I go to eat I want to find some fellow who will not 'Talk Shop' but there ain't none nohow. We eat it live it, sleep it, and dream it, to say nothing of breathing it 16 hours a day. I would be very grateful indeed if you would drop me a line or two once in a while, and I will promise you that if you ever get into a fix like this, I will do the same for you.

Each man here gets a ward with about 150 beds, (mine has 168) and has an Asst. Chief to boss him, and you can imagine what the paper work alone is – fierce – and the Govt. demands all paper work be kept up in good shape. I have only four day nurses and five night nurses (female), a ward-master, and four orderlies. So you can see that we are busy. I write this in piecemeal fashion. It may be a long time before I can get another letter to you, but will try.

This letter will give you an idea of the monthly report which has to be in Monday. I have mine most ready now. My Boss was in just now and gave me a lot more work to do so I will have to close this.

Good Bye old Pal,
'God be with you till we meet again'
Keep the Bouells open.
(Sgd) Roy

As the soldiers died, so too did the doctors and nurses. A camp hospital designed for approximately 1,200 was packed with 6,000 desperately ill men. At Camp Grant the death toll reached more than 500 on a single day.

The bureaucrats and military had rejected the need for a proper medical infrastructure when the camps had been set up following the decision to enter the war. Now they – or rather the soldiers – were paying the price. Corridors and landings, broom cupboards and hallways were filled with beds and mattresses. Those nurses and doctors – now in short supply – who were still well enough to work had to step over the dead and dying. As the sick approached death, blood poured from their noses and sometimes their ears; men were too sick to leave their beds and the hospitals stank of urine and faeces. The nurses, too few in number and working till exhausted, simply could not cope.

In some camps, despite America's 'classless' society, quarantine was instituted for new arrivals, but only those who were ordinary soldiers. Officers were exempt, allowed to come and go as they pleased spreading infection wherever they went. As each camp succumbed to the disease, some attempts were made to limit the damage – disinfectant was sprayed everywhere, roads through camps were sprayed with oil; nothing worked.

Dr William Henry Welch, then one of the world's foremost authorities on pathology, was sent to Camp Devens at the behest of the US government. Hardened by experience though he was, he was appalled at what he found. Thousands of young soldiers were dying before they'd even taken ship for the trenches of Europe. Welch knew when he was beaten. When he saw the bloated, fluid-clogged lungs of the dead in the autopsy room he simply declared that the USA was up against a 'new and terrible plague'. He wasn't even sure that it was flu at all. Welch's contemporary Victor Vaughan who also worked at Camp Devens during the autumn of 1918 wrote of this time in his memoirs:

> I see hundreds of young, stalwart men in the uniform of their country
> coming into the wards of the hospital in groups of ten or more. They are
> placed on the cots until every bed is full and yet others crowd in. The faces
> soon wear a bluish cast; a distressing cough brings up the blood-stained
> sputum. In the morning the dead bodies are stacked about the morgue like
> cord wood. This picture was painted on my memory cells at the division
> hospital, Camp Devens, in 1918, when the deadly influenza demonstrated
> the inferiority of human inventions in the destruction of human life.

The toing and froing of troop ships from that all-important war port in France, Brest, was key to the spread both of the mild spring flu and its deadly autumn manifestation. From Brest, ships came and went creating a melting pot of flu from those who carried it from all parts of the world; ships from Brest carried men and the flu virus to Freetown, Sierra Leone, where they picked up coal, infected dock labourers and then continued on down to Cape Town. From there the virus spread rapidly and devastatingly inland. It was later estimated that as much as six per cent of the African population of Sierra Leone died within a month of the arrival of influenza at the docks. Ships from Brest ferried men to the United States and back again; with each journey the virus was given the ideal conditions in which to claim more victims.

No escape

As the virus spread from the army camps into the general population, the quiet little known area of San Mateo County Coastside, as many places, might have assumed it would be spared any form of disaster, so remote was it in 1918 from large centres of population. The area had if anything declined since the turn of the century, the people mostly living on isolated farms, or in remote villages and small agricultural towns. Despite the best efforts of local inhabitants the Ocean Shore Railroad had failed to open up this lonely but beautiful stretch of farmland and isolated beaches.

Once influenza attacked San Francisco, however, everything changed. The Coastside region became a refuge for those in the big city trying to escape the disease – much as the countryside of Oxfordshire and Gloucestershire had been a refuge for Londoners fleeing the Black Death in the 17th century. The refugees from the big city brought dollars to spend, but also the very disease they were trying to escape.

By September the first cases of influenza were noted by the terrified inhabitants of the district – worse, one of the first victims was the postman who, in travelling widely between houses before he became ill, would have helped to spread the disease. Soon so many were dying that the locals began to move away in their turn – a school teacher, Irmagarde Hazard, was just one of many who decided she would be better off in the city.

The disease raced from Boston to Philadelphia to New Orleans to Chicago, Seattle, San Francisco and beyond. Remote parts of the mid-West were hit too. Whether running from town to country or country to town the scared citizens of America, and soon the whole world, did what they could to outrun the deadly plague. But there was nowhere to run, nowhere to hide.

Cyanosis – the evidence of autopsy

With the onset of autumn the first signs that a very new and very nasty flu virus was doing the rounds became clear – there were reports of otherwise healthy adults suddenly collapsing in the streets. When taken to hospital their symptoms included severe breathing difficulties, a rapid heart beat and palpitations. In many cases they quickly lapsed into unconsciousness and died. Some victims coughed up as much as six pints of pus a day. The most bizarre thing about the latter stages of the new illness was that sufferers' skin began to change colour. In some cases their skin became blue, dark blue or even black. It was terrifying for patients, doctors and nurses alike in the hospitals of London and Paris where these new symptoms were first noted. Nothing like this had been seen before.

The blue colouration, a condition known as cyanosis, was evidence that the patient's infected lungs were unable to transfer adequate amounts of oxygen to the bloodstream. This was to become one the most terrifying key symptoms of the now-mutated and highly dangerous influenza virus – after some hours, during which patients struggled desperately to breathe, they either died from heart attacks brought on by the strain of breathing or other vital organs collapsed as the body began to fail under the enormous strain. As one doctor put it they were being 'asphyxiated in front of our eyes and there was nothing we could do about it'.

Back in 1918 before the invention of super high-powered telescopes and the science of genetics, it was only after death that doctors and scientists were able to gather real hard evidence about the disease. Grim though it sounds, the autopsy table was the doctor's greatest ally during the dreadful autumn and winter of 1918.

Throughout the pandemic, doctors who carried out autopsies on the dead were astonished at what they found – some victims' hearts were double normal size; others' lungs weighed six times their normal weight and were described in some cases as having the consistency of melted redcurrant jelly. During autopsy the lungs were often found to be virtually destroyed. Right down to the tiny alveoli, or air sacs, the lungs were filled with a bloody frothing fluid. There was no space at all for air – a fact that was proved when doctors routinely began to place these lungs into baths of water. Instead of floating as a normal lung would they sank almost immediately. Cyanosis soon became recognized as the clearest sign that still living, but already very weak, patients were going to die.

More alarming symptoms

After the first few cases of cyanosis, other worrying symptoms began to present themselves. Even those who suffered only relatively mild symptoms were bedridden for weeks with severely inflamed eyes, nose and throat, intense headache and cough, great difficulty breathing and overwhelming feelings of tiredness. This was combined with severe aches and pains and high temperatures. In others the heart was found to be damaged or the liver and kidneys.

One of the most shocking symptoms among those hardest hit was the mass of blood that flowed from the nose and sometimes the ears. During autopsy it was found that the whole body cavity was often filled with liquid – a level of devastation associated today only with the Ebola virus. Many doctors said that the only comparable damage they had seen in lungs was caused by deadly mustard gas used in the trenches during the war.

Treating these patients was particularly difficult as there was little consistency in their symptoms. It is true that those who were nearing the point of death did frequently develop cyanosis, but many others had symptoms more usually associated with cholera – burning pains in the stomach, for example; other doctors thought their patients were suffering from typhoid because they were so badly afflicted with aches at the front of the head. Still others thought food poisoning was to blame or scarlet fever, even appendicitis. On one ship where flu had incapacitated more than half the crew the doctor treated each man on the basis that he was suffering from dengue fever.

Pneumonia – the deadly secondary infection

Despite sudden collapse and death, or a more lingering death caused by cyanosis and other complications, the biggest problem was the onset of pneumonia – in an age without antibiotics this was usually deadly. Doctors understood the way pneumonia worked, but when it combined with this new disease they were baffled. The reason? Pneumonia had always been seen as 'the old man's friend' – in other words it was a disease of the weak, elderly and infirm, not of the young and vigorous.

Whereas at the beginning of the year hardly any cases of pneumonia were reported, despite the fact that the virus was so widespread, towards September it became apparent that something strange was beginning to happen– early cases had recovered in a short time, but doctors now found that influenza victims were beginning to die alarmingly quickly.

The new influenza was breaking all the rules. It soon became apparent as the virulence of the flu increased that the young and elderly – the traditional victims of influenza – were actually surviving rather better than those young and vigorous individuals who, in a 'normal' flu epidemic, might have been expected to survive. Those aged between 20 and 40 were far more likely to die in this extraordinary pandemic than young children and those over 60 years of age. And no one understood why.

Going global

By midsummer of 1918 the flu had moved so rapidly across Europe and Asia that governments both local and national had no time to prepare. By May it had reached India, causing havoc in the Balkans, Greece, Turkey and the Middle East on the way. To the north Norway, Sweden and Finland were reporting widespread disruption by June and July. From China it reached Australia and New Zealand.

The shift of the virus into its second deadlier phase can be judged by an exchange in the French parliament early in September 1918. One of the deputies pointed out that in April men in the French armed forces had been dying from flu infection at the rate of five or six a month. Now, in September, they were dying at a rate of five or six a day.

Things were bad enough in Europe and America as the second wave of attack began, but in remote areas of the world the effects of the flu were far more devastating. In the USA it was noted that raw recruits to army camps who arrived from remote rural areas were far more likely to be affected severely by influenza and die. This was because tough inner-city recruits, though less well fed than their rural cousins, had built up tougher immune systems; from the relative isolation of the countryside these rural recruits were immunological innocents and they were cut down in their droves.

This situation was paralleled wherever remote communities were hit by the arrival of disease. Just as the indigenous peoples of the Americas were devastated by the arrival of smallpox and influenza in earlier centuries because their communities had no historic immunity, so too in 1918 were remote island communities particularly hard hit. Eskimo fatalities were far higher than the average in the west, and in the South Pacific some islands lost between a third and half their population. From the Arctic Circle came stories of whole villages dying or being too sick to hunt and their dogs eventually becoming so hungry that they ate the sick and dying.

Only in rare cases was isolation sufficient to keep a community free of disease — it seemed to attack almost every island on the globe, from Pitcairn in the Pacific to Rathlin in the Atlantic off the coast of Ireland; its arrival was often seen as a mystery. In Freetown, Sierra Leone the disease arrived almost certainly via ship, and within days the whole port work force of more than 500 were prostrate. At the other end of the continent in South Africa, mines, shops, theatres and offices were closed. In Tahiti, New Zealand and Cuba the story was the same.

From Norway to Peru, the most frightening aspect of the disease was the sudden collapse — at the worst times people avoided contact with each other and were reluctant to help each other, such was the fear of infection. Stories circulated of bus drivers talking to passengers perfectly normally one minute, then suddenly collapsing with blood streaming from their noses the next. In many cases those who fell were dead before they reached hospital, in some cases before they had hit the floor. Where they survived that first onset of illness and reached home or hospital, they could only be left to fight the disease as best they could. It began to seem that those who were to survive would do so regardless of any treatment they might or might not receive; likewise those who were to die seemed beyond help.

While the death toll mounted in the military camps of England, France and America, it was even higher in the general population – some families were completely wiped out; in others two out of three siblings were killed along with one parent; always the flu hit hardest at the young, strong and healthy. In city hospitals as many as 25 per cent of all flu patients died each and every day as October wore on. It was estimated in Britain and America that half the population was infected; those who fared best seemed to be those who had caught the mild version of the same flu that had spread across Europe back in the spring. They at least had some immunity.

Shortage of doctors

As the disease raced across the world, one of the biggest problems was that it attacked indiscriminately – so many doctors and nurses were ill that there was no one to attend the sick in many areas. In the United States medical students and trainee nurses were released early from their studies, but as quickly as they began work they fell ill. Thousands of doctors and nurses returned to work from retirement, some in their 80s. Even vets were called on across Europe and America to apply their skills.

In Paris at the height of the disease in the autumn of 1918 not one doctor under the age of 65 was still able to work, while in the United Kingdom the ratio of doctors to patients had fallen to one in 5,000. In Eastern Europe – particularly Poland, Hungary and Romania – many rural areas had no access whatsoever to medical help.

The official response

Across the world, influenza, somewhat incredibly, had never been a notifiable disease – that is, a disease that doctors were obliged by law to notify the authorities about should they come across any cases. Nor was it officially a quarantinable disease – all because previous epidemics had lacked the severity of this latest outbreak. Flu was still seen as a nuisance rather than a killer and, besides, the authorities in affected countries were still bickering about whether this really was flu or not.

In the Unites States and Europe there is no doubt too that the war and its aftermath was given far more priority than the fight against flu. Despite the protestations of the medical establishment, Woodrow Wilson refused to stop troop movements in the USA because this would hinder the war effort. So effective was his war propaganda that in some areas men were lynched for making any remark that seemed unpatriotic. He also felt – as generations of military leaders had felt – that soldiers had to be tough and put up with disease and death. Far more American soldiers died from influenza, on American soil, than died in the trenches and on the battlefields of Europe.

But what was happening in Camp Devens was happening in other camps and right across America and with a speed too great to comprehend – it was like a juggernaut out of control. Panic set in but it still took months before a number of cities made influenza a notifiable disease. It was too late and the authorities knew it; they advised people to avoid crowds and to cover their mouths when they coughed but in most cities, theatres, clubs, churches, shops and department stores remained open to military and civilians alike, so the disease continued to spread like wildfire.

In Britain the Chief Medical Officer Sir Arthur Newsholme was as culpable as his American counterparts. When the British Medical Research Council issued a memorandum asking for doctors across the country to forward news of a predicted influenza epidemic, Newsholme didn't even bother to read it. He also blocked plans to reduce overcrowding in factories to try to slow the spread of the disease. Like Britain's political leaders he thought first of the war effort, only then, if at all, of civilian lives.

Some quarantine measures were indeed imposed, but only in some places in some countries, in a half-hearted fashion and with little success. Across the world influential people used their political and social contacts to get round quarantine and other restrictions. When the British ship *Mantua* arrived in Freetown, Sierra Leone, the Colonial Secretary allowed the ship to land despite the fact that it was carrying infected passengers.

In New Zealand the passenger ship *Niagara* arriving from Canada was allowed to dock at Auckland, despite more than 100 members of the crew being stricken with influenza. And the reason? New Zealand Prime Minister Massey and Minister for Health George Russell knew that the ship was filled with VIPs. As a result of the ship being allowed to disembark – and despite the protests of the ship's doctor and captain that it should be quarantined offshore – nearly 7,000 New Zealanders were to die.

In Tahiti the situation was even worse. The island had been entirely free of the disease until French governor Gustave Julien allowed the SS *Navua* into port, despite having been informed that the ship's crew included several men severely ill with flu. Within a week the island was devastated as hundreds of cases were reported each day. Despite the pleas of medical advisors, Julien still refused to act.

Hundreds of Tahitians died. In Bermuda the Governor General's refusal to implement an island-wide quarantine led to the deaths of 200 inhabitants. In Jamaica the British governor refused to quarantine the island; more than 7,000 Jamaicans died as a direct result.

Ignorance of the disease, rather than indifference and deliberate cruelty, lay behind these fateful decisions. In tests and attempts at quarantining both individuals and whole communities, basic facts were misunderstood; that misunderstanding destroyed any effectiveness the measures might otherwise have had. It was assumed, for example, that someone infected with influenza would always be able to infect others. In fact those who have been infected with flu (any flu) are able to infect others only for approximately seven days after they become infected themselves. They will cough and sneeze and appear very ill after the seven days, but they are no longer infectious. The period when an individual is most infectious, in fact, is usually before they show any signs of illness themselves. This was simply not understood in 1918.

Thus thousands of people across the world were allowed on to ships because they seemed healthy, when in fact they were already incubating the disease. Once out at sea they fell ill and infected the rest of the passengers and crew – some ships were so badly affected that not one member of the crew remained at his post. The ships put into ports where they could and passengers and crew were taken to the nearest hospital to further spread the disease. On some ships between five and ten per cent of the crew died.

The medical response

Given the huge range of symptoms described above, the only global consensus seemed to be that this was a new disease, similar in many ways to severe flu, but sufficiently different to leave doctors across the world floundering. Old remedies were tried, both traditional and herbal, including even cupping, bloodletting and opium. Nothing worked. The more astute among the medical profession recommended that patients should simply stay in bed for at least two weeks to give their systems the maximum chance of fighting the infection while not wasting energy trying to work or move about.

With the death toll mounting, and despite the conspicuous lack of support from their respective governments, a number of American and European scientists – most notably the American William Henry Welch, the Louis Pasteur Institute in Paris, and doctors in London's research hospitals – tried against overwhelming odds to find something, anything, that would save the lives of those worst affected by influenza.

Doctors and scientists across the world worked day and night to try to isolate the pathogen that was causing the new disease, but without success – every technique they tried to use to isolate and identify it was doomed to failure simply because no microscope then known could possibly see the virus responsible.

As the autumn wore on desperate measures became commonplace – British doctors treated the sick while smoking big pipes filled with strong tobacco in the hope that the smoke might prevent the transmission of the disease. At the same time doctors insisted that their patients were far more likely to become infected if they drank alcohol even in very small amounts. Opium became popular again as it had been two centuries earlier; quinine and even strychnine were tried, along with steam baths, even regular enemas. Doctors tried placebos – they worked as well as anything else – as well as diphtheria and smallpox serum, tetanus serum: anything and everything on the off chance that it might do some good.

Many families tried to escape the disease by staying permanently in the open air. As a cure the open-air treatment was pioneered by Dr Leonard Hill in London, but it quickly took hold in New York at the Roosevelt Hospital and in Denmark and Milan, where glass was removed from many hospital windows. This fresh-air treatment seemed to do some good in reducing patient temperatures, but had little effect on the death rate, which continued to soar across the world.

Most bizarre of all perhaps was the hospital where the patients were placed on soaking wet beds and sprinkled regularly with cold water to keep them absolutely sodden. In one South African town bedding was in such short supply that mail bags were used to cover patients.

In hindsight, one of the most poignant moments during the pandemic of 1918 was the excitement and optimism generated by the discovery and identification of *bacillus influenza*, also known as Pfeiffer's Bacillus. For a while it was thought that this was the pathogen responsible for the worldwide pandemic, but this proved a dead end. Some patients, but by no means all, who died from influenza were indeed infected with Pfeiffer's Bacillus, but it was not the agent responsible for killing them. The truth was that a new flu virus to which few had any immunity was causing a massive overreaction in the immune systems of the young and healthy (see page 157 'Immune-system overload'). The resulting explosion of chemical activity in the body was allowing secondary infections that would normally be easily warded off to gain a foothold and kill the patient. Most commonly, of course, pneumonia was the culprit.

Towards the end of 1918 a number of scientists began to realize that the pathogen for which they were searching was probably too small to filter using available technology. Porcelain filters were trapping Pfeiffer's Bacillus as well as *pneumococci* and *streptococci*, but in tests filtered secretions were still infecting volunteers, which strongly suggested that the flu pathogen was slipping through the filter. An unknown and unfilterable pathogen was responsible.

We now know that the virus that caused such devastation in 1918–19 was closely related to a type of swine flu prevalent at the same time. No one would have guessed the connection, however, when, at the American National Swine Breeders Show in September, huge numbers of animals fell sick – they lay prostrate, breathing only with difficulty, coughing and sweating profusely. The show had to be cancelled, but of course animals had, by then, come together from across the country and been infected. They were now ready to take that infection back to their home farms across the United States.

The link with animals – one or two scientists were convinced that pig flu and this latest human flu were one and the same – no doubt reminded many doctors of the pioneering work of Edward Jenner who discovered the basic principle of inoculation back in the late 18th century (see Chapter 4). There were numerous attempts to inoculate members of the public, but trials were limited and of course it was impossible to inoculate successfully while the pathogen was still unknown and unidentified. Identification was not to come, as we have seen in chapter one, until 20 years later, with the invention of the electron microscope in 1938.

In their labs, the scientists of Europe and America eventually had some success in countering the effects of influenza, but only in terms of alleviating the symptoms. As we have seen, they were never going to create an effective vaccine because they could not isolate the pathogen responsible for the pandemic and without a national, coordinated health service they were bound to be overwhelmed by the scale of the pandemic. But they did develop a vaccine that helped where bacterial lung infections – secondary infections – were badly reducing chances of recovery. But those who developed cyanosis or severe respiratory problems were still beyond help. Opiates calmed the cough instinct; absolute rest enabled the body to fight the disease; staying in bed was still the best advice.

The people's response

Old ideas about the origins of illness re-emerged. In London it was blamed on mists rising from Flanders fields disturbed by millions of exploding shells; in Italy silkworms were seen as the carriers of the disease; elsewhere bedbugs were blamed, or chewing gum, or the position of the planets. Some British doctors blamed the wind; an American astrologer blamed the position of Jupiter.

In parts of Europe, America and Africa the levels of panic over the unseen killer reached such heights that people barricaded themselves in their houses, shutting up windows and doors and cramming paper and cloth into every nook and cranny. In some cases families died from suffocation (particularly where they used paraffin stoves for heating) or from malnutrition.

In America, understandably, soldiers began to be blamed for the spread of the disease and they were often shunned if seen in public places. Anyone of German origin was suspect and in at least one case a man was murdered after being accused of being a spy and spreading the disease. Sadly, in parts of Europe, particularly Poland, the Jews were blamed for the spread of the disease, and were attacked. In any country, foreigners were blamed for spreading the disease deliberately – a paranoid fear induced by the rising death toll.

But in many places acts of kindness greatly outweighed acts of intolerance. In the United States the wealthy citizens of San Francisco and other cities banded together to provide funds for hospitals. In Cape Town, South Africa, wealthy company directors, financiers and businessmen set up makeshift hospitals for the sick. In Lahore, then still part of India, free food and drinks were supplied to the poor in run-down areas of the city. In New York and Moscow health centres sprang up. In Chicago it became illegal for landlords to turn off the heating in flats where flu victims were living, even if the bills were not being paid. In Norway cars were provided free for doctors; in Venezuela free petrol was provided for bonfires to be lit in a vain attempt to ward off the disease. Cities across America and Europe used private cars and vans as ambulances and, where necessary, hearses to move the dead and dying around; volunteers with little or no medical experience were standing in for nurses and orderlies, themselves stricken by the disease.

Even prisoners were doing their bit – at the Deer Island Naval Prison in America, 50 prisoners volunteered to be deliberately infected with influenza to help scientists struggling to find some way to alleviate the worst effects of the illness. Ironically, at the top security Sing Sing Prison where some of America's worst criminals were housed, throughout the pandemic not one man died.

A small number of tiny, relatively isolated communities – most notably the town of Gunnison in Colorado – escaped the flu by enforcing at gun point a rigorous quarantine. No one was allowed to drive through the town nor alight from any train that passed through the town. As a result the town escaped without a single fatality.

Random success stories surrounded numerous supposed cures and prophylactics; people painted the inside of their noses with zinc, while newspapers and magazines were filled with advertisements for different mouthwashes. In reality, the reason that some people escaped infection during the second wave in the autumn, was most likely that they'd been infected with mild flu earlier in the year, and thus had some degree of immunity. Nevertheless, they were convinced that their escape was down to drinking camomile tea, or eating orange peel or garlic.

In Africa people drank whale oil or inhaled eucalyptus steam, and consumption of garlic and onions soared. Others drank and sprinkled vinegar in every room of the house or they burned bay leaves day and night. Elsewhere people tried even more bizarre cures – washing in cats' urine or bathing in ice water, for example. Even if it didn't work the view was that it was better to try something, anything, than to sit and do nothing.

Proving that odd-ball cures were not cures at all was even more difficult than discovering the cause of the disease. It is likely that bizarre cures such as these hastened the deaths of many victims. By the end of September and into October bodies were piling up in extraordinary numbers with few well enough in some regions to bury them.

Despite – or perhaps because of – the horror that had engulfed the world, jokes about Spanish flu became common place. Cartoonists and comedians had a field day. A famous children's skipping rhyme appeared, which was still being chanted by English schoolchildren in the 1950s, by which time its original meaning was long forgotten:

> I had a little bird
> Its name was Enza
> I opened up the window
> And in flu Enza

People made jokes about their friends being in bed or laid up with the 'Spanish lady'. In Copenhagen a cartoonist showed the Angel of Peace complaining that people were no longer interested in her but that the Spanish lady could go where she pleased.

The end of the world?

As the crisis worsened and reports from around the world confirmed that this was no ordinary disease, there were real fears that humankind might be annihilated. It is difficult to appreciate now just how real the fear was – some of those on what is now called the religious right believed that the flu was a Biblical plague sent by God to annihilate humankind before the second coming and the day of judgment. In

America's so-called Bible Belt the pandemic was blamed on immoral living. Christian Scientists joined Baptists and Evangelists of every hue to blame the godless age for the sickness that had come among them. They found it more difficult to explain why the righteous were carried off at the same rate as the ungodly.

The sense that civic society might break down completely was particularly acute in American cities, where hospitals ran out of doctors, nurses and medicines, and where the clamour for beds was so great that armed guards had to be posted to stop relatives of the sick forcing their way onto the wards. Coffins could not be made at a fast enough rate and mass burials were authorized. Relatives of the sick who had to be turned back at the hospital gates often tried to bribe the doctors, nurses and porters to find space for their sick relatives.

Public-health measures began to be instituted with strict penalties including prison for those who failed to comply. The wearing of gauze masks became compulsory in many cities, including New York. Spitting and coughing became criminal offences for which people were fined and imprisoned. The masks had no effect. Where city officials had at the beginning of the pandemic refused to act they now panicked and at last closed schools, theatres, churches and all public places of entertainment.

Mortuaries overflowed and bodies, often clearly visible from the streets, were stacked like firewood in yards while burial sites were hastily found for them. Undertakers were in extremely short supply as they, too, succumbed to the disease. By October the characteristic sudden and frightening collapse of individuals in the street had become commonplace across the world. It was indeed a time of apocalyptic scenes.

In many houses everyone was so sick that no one was well enough to go shopping. Where relatives left food they left the food at the gate rather than take it into the house or even as far as the front door. There is little doubt that many sufferers died from starvation – they were too ill to help themselves and their plight remained unknown to neighbours or officials. Those who, weakened by hunger, succumbed to the disease often lay undiscovered for weeks. In remote parts of America isolated farms were sometimes discovered with all the inhabitants dead; in dozens of Indian villages, as one commentator wrote: 'there were found one or two surviving children with each house filled with the rotting corpses of their dead adult relatives'.

Still the devastation continued with citizens wondering if it would ever end. Bus drivers collapsed at the wheel, occasionally causing accidents. Factories and offices were forced to close across Europe and America. At the Farrer Mine near

Bloemfontein in South Africa a mine lift operator collapsed and the lift cage he had been operating fell hundreds of feet killing more than 20 miners.

By the third week of September the death rate had reached more than 700 on one day in the third week of September 1918 in Bombay, India, alone. In Odessa, Russia more than 75,000 were reported to be suffering from influenza. In both Rio de Janeiro and Cape Town business life had to all intents and purposes ground to a halt. Down through Africa and across the Middle East reports continued of victims falling ill at an astonishing rate. The disease gained new nicknames as it infected new countries – the 'Spanish Lady' morphed into the 'Coquette' in Switzerland, the 'Bombay Fever' in Sri Lanka, the 'Bolshevik Disease' in Poland.

The speed with which people were dying astonished and terrified doctors. Those that managed to reach hospital deteriorated at an astonishing rate, showing new and deadly symptoms that baffled scientists and doctors alike – patients became catatonic, they suffered crippling headaches, soaring temperatures, profuse sweating, massive toothache, temporary blindness, unstoppable nose bleeds, amnesia, hallucinations and delirium. A number of patients became so deranged that they committed suicide. And of course there was pneumonia and the terrible cyanosis – invariably the sign that death was near. In many hospitals the rate at which patients was dying was so great that relatives could not find their deceased loved ones among the piles of bodies in mortuaries, corridors and even stacked in outhouses and sheds.

In Denmark the head of a special influenza unit at the Bidpebjetg hospital announced that it was pointless bringing flu patients to hospital, since they were just as likely to survive (or not) at home. Church halls, bus stations, garages, even city and town halls – all were used to house the sick and dying, but the dying went on. In Boston it reached an incredible 50 per cent of all those infected. On October 15 more than 1,700 died from influenza in Berlin. On October 17 more than 1,900 died in Paris.

In some parts of the world Christian missionaries helped the sick; in other parts of the world their obsession with carrying the word of God to remote peoples helped spread the disease and killed tens of thousands more people. On the island of Upolu, in Samoa, missionaries collected money from poor villagers and then refused to return any of it as the villagers fell sick and could no longer tend their fields. Other islands had extraordinary escapes – the Island of St Helena to which Napoleon had been banished was never infected.

Small isolated communities fared the worst in terms of their population being annihilated. The Australian-outback town of Byrock had 27 families, and in 23 of those every family member was ill with influenza. The local nurse, who also happened to be the level-crossing keeper, had to keep the whole town going – delivering food and medicines – single-handed.

The number of attacks and muggings fell dramatically in cities across the world, not just because criminals and good citizens alike were sick, but because assailants feared to approach anyone else for the purposes of their crime, lest they be infected. One girl told a reporter that going home alone late at night held no terrors for her any more – if anyone approached her, she said, she would just cough.

Spanish influenza was no respecter of rank or status. In the early months of the pandemic the rich thought that it would affect the poor but not them. They could escape to their country houses as rich Londoners had escaped during outbreaks of the Black Death centuries earlier. But this time there was no escape; influenza was just too infectious. The Chancellor of Germany, Crown Prince Max of Baden, caught the disease, as did the Spanish king. Both survived, but the same could not be said for Lu Kuyang whose attempt to become China's new emperor had only recently failed. He died along with the author Guillaume Apollinaire, British composer Sir Hubert Parry, South African Premier Louis Botha, Prince Erik of Sweden and the Maharajah of Jaiphur. Among celebrities and VIPs who survived were the queen of Denmark, Franklin D. Roosevelt, David Lloyd George and Mary Pickford, the richest woman in the world.

By late October industry and commerce across the world were severely damaged. Coffee crops in South America were left unharvested, gold and copper mines were shut down. Insurance claims ran into millions, and thousands of businesses of every sort were left bankrupt.

The biggest question at the end of October 1918 was whether the situation would worsen and, if it did, would civil society collapse? It had come perilously close already in cities across America, Europe, Asia and Africa. Most communities were still holding on – but only just.

CHAPTER 6

The Aftermath

As World War I entered its final weeks more than 16,000 American soldiers were completely incapacitated by flu in France and Belgium. In the United States where troops were still being mobilized, one soldier in five was dying in some camps. Given the scale of the disaster in the autumn of 1918, it is easy to forget that the majority of those who caught the disease *did*, in fact, recover. But whereas the mortality rate in a normal flu epidemic is probably 0.1 per cent, in 1918 it reached 20 per cent of those infected and occasionally 50 per cent.

End of the war … end of the pandemic?
There is little doubt that the flu pandemic hastened the end of the First World War. Unlike the British army, which had succumbed in large part to the first, milder wave of influenza back in the spring of that year, the German army seems to have suffered the full onslaught of the second and far more deadly wave in the autumn. The flu combined with a vastly weakened military position to force the German high command to capitulate.

It was the first week of November that saw the initial, tentative signs that the virus might be beginning to falter. In New York the number of new cases was dropping by some 2,000 a day. Across the world the tide was just beginning to turn although, in places, the number of cases of influenza increased for a little longer. In San Francisco and elsewhere it was hard to tell as the nightmare seemed to continue unabated.

World War I ended on 11 November 1918. Medical experts in London and elsewhere, such as Dr Leonard Hill and Sir Bertrand Lawson meeting at the Royal Society of Medicine, were still arguing about what they should do about the flu pandemic still raging. The only hope now – other than that the disease would naturally begin to abate – was vaccination. This had been tried with some measure of success already. Reports from Greenwich Hospital suggested that it gave immunity to 500 boys who, following injection, had remained clear of the disease. Evidence from anywhere else was hard to come by.

The victory celebrations following the declaration of the end of hostilities on 11 November actually made things worse for a while so far as flu was concerned. As people gathered together in squares and church halls, churches and market places across the United Kingdom and elsewhere, the death toll spiked again suddenly as the virus found a new opportunity to spread. In the week following Armistice Day deaths from influenza reached the extraordinary level of 19,000 in the United Kingdom.

By December 1918, a number of countries were reporting fewer new influenza cases. The world was still reeling from the death toll, however, and in Barcelona more than 1,000 were dying every day as November turned to December. In Tahiti 50 people were dying every day, and still the governor did nothing; he locked himself in his house and refused to meet anyone.

But, by the end of December, flu was definitely disappearing across the world, just as mysteriously and as quickly as it had first arrived.

Why did the disease begin to vanish so quickly? The answer has to do with the way viruses work (see Chapter 1). In the arms race between virus and host or victim there comes a point, particularly with a virulent virus like the 1918 'Spanish' flu, when it can no longer find enough victims to sustain its onward rush. At that point a pandemic is likely to implode.

Statistically, of course, something as virulent as the second wave was always likely to last a relatively short time and then diminish. The few places that had been untouched by the first and second waves of the disease were hit by what has been called the third wave – it was less virulent but still highly dangerous. It caused localized outbreaks around the world well into 1919, but since the bulk of the world's population had by then already been infected with a far worse version of the virus this last spasm of the killer could do little damage. By the end of January 1919 it was largely gone as a serious menace, although many of those who were already sick by this time would still die.

The disposal of the dead

The biggest problem in some parts of the world even as the worst of the pandemic seemed to be over was burying bodies quickly enough to prevent other diseases becoming rife as bodies decayed above ground. Mass graves were filled at night in scenes reminiscent of London during the plague of 1665; carts and trucks, horse-drawn vehicles and buses were used to ferry the dead to cemeteries. In Philadelphia mortuaries designed to hold 20 bodies were stacked with as many as 200 corpses waiting for burial.

In Norway and Finland bodies were simply left outside to freeze hygienically until the spring thaw allowed for burial; in America wood shortages led to coffins being made from old doors and packing cases; even cardboard boxes were used. Coffins were often re-used again and again – the body would be taken to the cemetery in the coffin, discreetly dropped into the grave out of the coffin's false bottom, and then the coffin would go back to the undertakers for its next incumbent. Relatives frequently had to dig the graves themselves when the gravediggers were incapacitated by the flu.

The troop ships that still left America for Europe as the war neared its end were now just floating coffins – instead of arriving with sick men as they had in the spring of 1918 they now dropped a seemingly endless line of men overboard. So fast did the men die that there was no time to organize proper burial services; they were simply slipped into the ocean one after another. Some 20 to 25 per cent of those who fell ill on these late ships died – thousands upon thousands whose watery graves have no marker.

The fear of death was great in 1918, but there was another, deeper fear – of being buried alive. A small but significant number of those who succumbed to the pandemic experienced a mix of symptoms that made them appear to be dead, when in fact they were still very much alive. In these individuals influenza frequently caused a death-like pallor and immobility, and with so many dying all around them and no time to issue death certificates it is almost certain than some victims were indeed buried alive. There are more than a dozen recorded instances where a body piled up with others ready for the mortuary was spotted breathing or moving slightly by a sharp-eyed attendant. In some cases these individuals went on to make a full recovery. Robert Coulter, aged three, is one of the best known examples. He was being taken to the cemetery in Wellington, New Zealand when, to the astonishment of the funeral director, he suddenly woke up and was heard mumbling and sighing.

The final death toll

Five per cent of the world's population probably died from flu and related illnesses in 1918–19. As many as 50 million people died worldwide, although in recent years that figure has been revised upward to a possible 100 million deaths. The figures for individual countries all around the world – carefully and accurately recorded at the time – are extraordinary.

In the United States 540,000 people were killed by the virus. New York City alone suffered a total of 33,000 dead. In Philadelphia nearly 800 died in one day in October, more than 4,500 in one week. Writing in the *American Journal of Epidemiology* in 1921, a doctor at the Harvard Medical School wrote:

> This fatality has been unparalleled in recent times. The influenza epidemic
> of 1918 ranks well up with the epidemics famous in history.
> Epidemiologists have regarded the dissemination of cholera from the Broad
> Street well in London as a catastrophe. The typhoid epidemic of Plymouth,
> Pa., of 1885, is another illustration of the damage that can be done by
> epidemic disease once let loose. Yet the fatality from influenza and
> pneumonia at Camp Sherman was greater than either of these. Compared
> with epidemics for which we have fairly accurate statistics the death rate at
> Camp Sherman in the fall of 1918 is surpassed only by that of plague in
> London in 1665 and that of yellow fever in Philadelphia in 1793.
> The plague killed 14 per cent of London's population in seven months'
> time. Yellow fever destroyed 10 per cent of the population of Philadelphia
> in four months. In seven weeks influenza and pneumonia killed 3.1 per
> cent of the population at Camp Sherman. If we consider the time factor,
> these three instances are not unlike in their lethality. The plague killed
> 2 per cent of the population in a month, yellow fever 2.5 per cent, and
> influenza and pneumonia 1.9 per cent.

It is odd that although one of the earliest disease centres for the 1918 pandemic was
America, Americans did not seem to benefit from the levels of immunity enjoyed in
Europe once the more virulent strain swept across the country in the autumn. The
early mild wave seems to have given Europeans far more resistance – it has been
estimated that as a result European deaths from flu were roughly half those in
America, a remarkable difference in mortality.

   In the United Kingdom 228,000 people died. That may not seem as significant
a figure as that for the USA, but hospitals across the UK were inundated with sick
patients who, where they did survive, struggled for weeks with severely debilitating
symptoms. A Manchester doctor wrote:

> Day after day the sick presented themselves at hospitals across the city.
> And we knew from colleagues elsewhere across the country that the
> situation was the same with them. In many cases they were brought by
> their relatives who could see that, as the days passed, their loved ones were
> growing dangerously and terrifyingly weak. There was little we could do
> other than reassure – and even that we did guiltily, knowing that our

reassurances were based on the triumph of hope over experience. Looking back it really did seem that the body's best chance of survival, once the initial and highly dangerous period of infection had passed, was simply to keep the patient in bed and well hydrated. For weeks and months we were putting patients in corridors and in the wards they were jammed together like sardines. As soon as a patient died his or her bed was filled by another. Wards remained unwashed, bed linen ran out or could not be changed nearly as often as it should and doctors regularly worked double shifts to try to cope with the seemingly endless stream of very ill patients. Even the window remained unwashed as people began to avoid hospitals – there was a real air of panic wherever you went. Catching flu wasn't seen as a death sentence at all – in fact despite its horrors most patients did recover – but there was a very real chance that you would die and that was something we had not seen in England for centuries – probably not since the last outbreak of Bubonic plague!

The Australian government had been among the most astute in the world. They had kept hundreds of ships out of their ports and isolated all suspected cases. As a result their death toll was significantly lower than it might otherwise have been. The Solomon Islands and New Hebrides were never infected.

The islands of the South Seas certainly suffered more than any other part of the world in terms of percentages – their isolated populations show us the worst that can happen when historic immunity to disease is almost entirely absent. In 1918 it was the passenger ship *Talune* arriving in Western Samoa from New Zealand on 7 November 1918, that signed the death warrants of 7,000 islanders. The ship was carrying infectious individuals who had yet to show symptoms themselves but were carrying the deadly virus. Within three months of their arrival more than 21 per cent of the population of the two islands Upola and Savii were dead. Roughly the same percentage died in the Fijian islands and Tahiti. The horror of that time was summed up by a local official soon after the disease had done its deadly work: 'It was impossible to bury the dead … Day and night trucks rumbled through the streets, filled with bodies for the constantly burning pyres.'

A staggering 10 per cent of the population, or 12.5 million people were lost in the pandemic in India, 250,000 of those deaths in the Punjab alone. This death toll was exacerbated by extreme poverty and overcrowding in the cities.

Between seven and 10 per cent of Russia's vast population was lost, approximately 450,000 people. This was no doubt exacerbated by the upheavals of revolution and civil war. The number of dead in China can only be guessed at, but it must have run into millions. Due to the lack of records it is also impossible to say how many people died in Africa, but as many as five per cent of the population of the whole continent may have died. In Italy 375,000 lives were claimed; in Japan, a staggering quarter of a million; 43,000 died in Guatemala. The list could go on.

Numbers alone do not tell the whole story. The deaths of 100 people in a small village could be far more devastating than the deaths of 10,000 in a large town, in terms of that settlement's future survival. In parts of Turkey, Persia (modern Iran) and Iraq whole villages were wiped out and no one was left alive to bury the dead. In Alaska and the Aleutian Islands Eskimo settlements hitherto isolated for centuries were annihilated. These deaths may not have been caused directly by the flu; with no one healthy enough to distribute food, the rest of the population died of starvation.

The demographics of the dead are also revealing. As many as five times the number of flu deaths occurred among young people compared to people over 50 – an astonishing statistic. Worst affected of all were pregnant women – as many as two thirds of pregnant women who contracted flu were killed by it. As we saw in the last chapter, one of the most alarming characteristics of the pandemic was that it claimed most of its victims from within the 15–40-year-old age group, those who would have had the best chance of surviving any previous flu epidemic.

The exposure of poverty

One of the good things to come out of the 1918 pandemic was an increased awareness of the terrible conditions in which most of the world's population lived. The incomprehensible scale of death reminded people – just as cholera outbreaks in London had reminded politicians in the 19th century – that ultimately the ill health of the masses would impact on everyone, rich and poor alike.

In 19th-century London cholera had led to the construction of the Thames embankment to house a new sewer to take the capital's sewage well down stream of the city. Similarly the disaster of the flu pandemic of 1918 made governments realize that they had to take more responsibility for the health of their citizens. In London Prime Minister Lloyd George spoke for many other world leaders when he said that if it had not been for the dreadful housing conditions ordinary people had to endure, far more men would have been able to contribute to the war effort. Across the world the way the poor lived became more conspicuous – children without shoes were common in the cities of the developed world, malnutrition was commonplace. In Cape Town whole families lived in stables; in

London two families might share a single room; in New Zealand the prime minister publicly stated that half the capital city, Wellington, should be rebuilt to eliminate the slums.

Far-reaching repercussions

Across the world the end of the war and the flu pandemic ushered in a new era in which the common people would no longer complacently accept the authority of the old order; the idea that certain sections of society had an automatic birthright to rule and an entitlement to respect and obedience was gradually jettisoned. Governments in future would be held to account, via a less malleable media, for the death of every soldier in war and every civilian in a pandemic.

In Great Britain, slums were cleared; public-health authorities were established with the two-pronged remit of treating the sick and communicating with each other to ensure that prompt and coordinated efforts would be made if and when pandemic or epidemic illness struck again. A Ministry of Health was set up to replace the local health boards that had failed the public so miserably. In Canada a public-health bureau was created for the same reason and new sanitary and hygiene codes were drawn up in cities as far apart as London, Athens, New York and Wellington.

The League of Nations Health Organization was established in 1920 to coordinate world health issues. It later became and remains the World Health Organization (WHO), which we shall learn more about in the next chapter.

One of the more bizarre after effects of the pandemic was that it was blamed for a number of otherwise inexplicable maladies. Chief among these was *Encaphalitis lethargica*, a kind of sleeping sickness that affected thousands of people. Its name simply describes what was happening – there was evidence of some kind of inflammation of the brain that caused acute tiredness. Women were more prone to the disease and in the worst cases it was completely incapacitating. Victims were struck down quickly and then remained almost permanently asleep, sometimes for years. No epidemic of the disease – which was previously unrecorded – has recurred since the 1920s, which led a number of scientists to argue that it was in some way related to the influenza pandemic of 1918, but there is no direct evidence to support this theory.

Survivors' stories

From amidst the carnage and death of both the war and the flu pandemic, it could be easy to overlook the fates of those who survived. The world was left with a vast number of orphans. For example, following the death of her mother, Edith Hill

Boyd had to care for her eight younger siblings; Benjamin Dorman's eight children and 20 grandchildren were left with no one to provide for them. Many survivors were left with psychological and neurological damage. In many cases the trauma remained with victims for the rest of their lives. Those who had been lucky enough to escape the virus had in many cases lost friends and family.

It is impossible to paint adequately the vast panorama of human suffering caused by the 1918 flu pandemic. Unlike the memorials to the dead found in almost every city, town and village that sent their menfolk to war, there are no monuments, plaques or remembrance services for the victims of the flu. Very few people who were alive at the time of the 1918 pandemic are still alive today, but there are a few who were children at that time. The letters, diaries, memoirs and reminiscences of these people are the only, and most poignant, memorial to the forgotten dead.

Thelma Trom, an American who lived beyond her 100th birthday, remembered accompanying the local doctor on his rounds in a small community in North Dakota. He had so many visits to make, she recalled, and so little time to rest during the worst months – October and November – that he often fell asleep while sitting in his pony and trap. Trom's uncle was the local undertaker and she recalled the dozens of coffins stacked up behind his shop and the fact that, though she accompanied the doctor, she was never allowed into the houses of the sick. She recalls that the doctor felt he could do little other than reassure and prescribe hot drinks – particularly lemon – and recommend that goose fat should be rubbed on the patients' chests. Several of Trom's relatives died, including her pregnant aunt. Eighty years later she still felt the loss keenly 'as if it were yesterday. The pregnant women had no chance.'

Cecelia McGrain recalled her mother talking about the 1918 influenza epidemic and the devastation it caused the family: 'Her oldest sister, Marie Burke Leonard, died, and so did Marie's only daughter, Betty, who was about nine years old. As I recall the story, there were two nurses who were hired to help, and they also died. Imagine four people in one household gone, though I'm certain many families suffered greater losses.'

William Walter Appel recalled that so many gravediggers had fallen ill or died that he and his brother Bernard had to dig their own aunt's grave when she succumbed to flu. Mary Alice Mauser remembered her great uncle Jules Bergeret who lived in New Orleans. He was 32, happily married with a second child on the way and running a successful business. Two weeks later Jules and his aunt were both dead and his widow had miscarried.

Aaron Thomas Bowden who grew up in Baltimore City recalled his parents' stories:

> We sat on our front porch or stoop and watched the world go by.
> But by 1918, the procession that passed the doors was made up of wooden
> wagons piled with caskets – some long and heavy and some pitifully small
> … Those same neighbours and friends now dragged wooden boxes (you
> could hardly call them caskets, really, because they could not make real
> caskets fast enough) into their homes for funerals and wakes.
>
> Neighbours avoided neighbours. Some stopped attending church. My
> father, a lithographic press operator … walked the 50 or so blocks to his
> job, because my mother was afraid he would get sick if he rode the
> streetcar. He was a healthy young man – one of the prime types who
> seemed to be succumbing to this sickness.

Frances McShea, who was 16 in 1918 and living in Manhattan, recalled:

> Everywhere around there were black crepes (or wreaths) on practically
> every door, indicating the death of someone in the home. The hospitals
> were filled to capacity, and any large, vacant building would be used to
> house the ill and the dying. Not too many people wanted to be part of
> picking up the dead.

An American nurse – whose name sadly has now been lost – left us her memories
of her work in the fateful year of 1918. She described how the corridors of every
hospital reeked with the smell of death. Patients could be heard gasping for breath
from every room, ward and corridor; everywhere there was a smell of urine, faeces
and disinfectant as the worst-affected patients were so weak they could not get to
the lavatory. So many medical staff were sick that there was no one – not even in the
biggest and best-run hospitals – to empty bedpans. There were not enough bedpans
to go around in any case, let alone bed linen, blankets or towels; bed linen was left
to become absolutely filthy. She had no doubt that many died needlessly because the
system broke down and routine infections – that might have been avoided under
normal circumstances when hospitals were kept clean and tidy – were able to run
riot in the filth and squalor.

Most vividly of all she recalled the never-to-be-forgotten sound of human grief
drifting continuously along corridors and through wards, as the relatives of the dead
and dying realized that nothing could be done.

Subsequent research into the pandemic

The pandemic of 1918 left many unanswered questions for the medical profession, some of which scientists are still wrestling with today. Among the most shocking manifestations of the disease at the time was cyanosis (see Chapter 5), the evidence of which was most graphically revealed on the autopsy table. There the lungs of the deceased were found to be drowned in fluid. This frothy liquid was a mix of blood and other body fluids, cell debris chemotoxins and macrophages – the result of what is now generally termed a cytokine storm (see below). It was the latter stages of this storm and the damage it caused that produced the terrifying blue pallour – cyanosis – with which flu victims were frequently afflicted.

Delicate alveoli that enable oxygen transfer to take place, along with delicate capillaries, were damaged by the counter attack made by the body's immune system. As the walls of cells broke down the result was a mass of blood, fluid, dead cells and chemical waste that effectively stopped the lungs functioning. Younger, stronger victims of the 1918 pandemic suffered what is now known as ARDS (Acute Respiratory Disease Syndrome) – a massive failure of the lungs caused by a viral invader sparking a massive overreaction in the body's immune system. It is therefore ironic that in 1918 a weaker immune system – typical of older and very young patients – sometimes gave a flu patient a greater chance of survival.

There is no doubt that the flu virus that hit the world in 1918 was a new strain and that it had almost certainly resulted from a genetic shift in an existing virus or through gene reassortment within an animal (see Chapter 1) – most likely a pig. Pigs are prone to infection both by avian and human flu viruses, and within their bodies the genetic melting pot occasionally produces something quite devastating for humanity.

The reason that the first, relatively benign wave of 'Spanish' flu turned inexorably into the second lethal wave has been endlessly debated. There is a remote possibility that the autumn flu was entirely different from the spring strain, and that it somehow went through a gene reassortment process, perhaps in pigs, and then re-emerged as a virus to which humanity had little or no immunity. That is certainly a possibility, but most scientists seem to agree that a more plausible explanation is that spring and autumn waves of infection were caused by the same virus, which had mutated and become increasingly virulent as the year wore on. It had adapted to man and as it adapted it increased dramatically in virulence. The science supports this idea, as tests have shown that 'passage' – the process by which a virus or bacteria increases in lethality as it is passed on – can be a key element in the way viruses work. If the 1918 virus really did jump from birds or pigs to man it would initially have struggled to survive in its new host but, as time passed, its strength would have increased until it was so potent that it destroyed rapidly and with horrible efficiency. This seems to have happened in 1918 and, ironically, it was the extreme virulence of the disease that made it disappear rapidly after December 1918.

Answers frozen in time

One of the most fascinating recent developments in studies of the 1918 pandemic is the discovery of deep-frozen and perfectly preserved traces of the virus. An Inuit woman who died from the disease in 1919 was exhumed from her permafrost grave in Alaska in the 1990s. Scientists were able to isolate the virus from her body and see for the first time its precise genetic profile and how that profile compared with the profile of flu-virus types in circulation today. Back in 1918, of course, the pathogen that caused the pandemic could not be isolated or even seen, let alone genetically profiled.

For the scientists studying the structure of the extracted genetic material the work was difficult and highly dangerous – bio-security measures put in place were the toughest ever imposed on researchers engaged in medical work, but they were vital to prevent the virus escaping once again into the general population. The consequences of such an escape might easily have been once again millions of deaths, since our historic immunity to the 1918 flu pandemic would have diminished greatly since the virus disappeared almost 90 years ago.

The ultimate aim of the genetic work was to discover the precise structure of the H1N1 virus, as Spanish flu is now known. In this respect the research was spectacularly successful – we now know that the 1918 virus does bear some strong resemblances to the avian flu viruses with which we are currently threatened.

Using highly sophisticated methods that have been available only in the past 20 years or so, researchers were able to recreate a fully functioning live version of the 1918 virus and infect first mice and then monkeys with it. The results were astonishing – and terrifying.

The lungs of infected monkeys were almost completely destroyed by the virus in a matter of days as their immune systems went into overdrive. First symptoms appeared within 24 hours of exposure, and the subsequent destruction of lung tissue was so widespread that, had the monkeys not been killed a few days later, they would have drowned in their own blood. That is precisely what happened – according to contemporary reports – to so many human patients back in 1918–19.

The general effects on the monkeys also matched those observed when mice were infected in an earlier study, and they were remarkably similar to the whole range of symptoms described in human patients at the time the pandemic was at its height.

Immune-system overload

Scientists were astounded by the speed at which the virus worked, but amid all the gloom there were some grounds for optimism. The researchers discovered a human gene that may help explain why the 1918 virus (and its re-created clone, H1N1) was able to create the massive immune system overreaction that seems to have done far more damage and caused far more fatalities than the virus alone would account for.

Immune-system proteins that can seriously damage infected tissue were found at much higher levels following H1N1 infection, compared to other viral infections. A key component of the immune system, a gene called RIG-1 seems to be involved. Levels of the protein produced by the gene were higher in tissue infected with the 1918 virus, suggesting the gene had somehow switched off, causing immune defences to run completely wild. This ability to alter the body's immune response is shared with the most recent candidate for mutation into a pandemic strain, the H5N1 avian flu virus. We know that compared to 'normal' flu, avian flu can kill rapidly, just like the Spanish flu of 1918, largely because it causes this massive immune system overreaction.

There are even today no certainties in this area of diagnosis but the most recent and now generally accepted explanation for the high number of deaths among the young and healthy in 1918 – and it is an explanation supported by a considerable amount of evidence – is that a strong immune system can, under certain circumstances, cause what has been termed a cytokine storm. This storm causes the release of a vast quantity of immune system protein which in its turn causes inflammation and serious tissue damage. Researchers are puzzling still over the results and, as in so many areas of scientific enquiry, there are no easy answers here.

While scientists continue to pursue ever more effective vaccines, they are also searching for a means to control that fatal overreaction of the body's immune system – an overreaction that is likely to be a key element in the threat posed by any future avian flu pandemic. Our ability to modify certain genes is likely to be central to this. If the RIG-1 gene can be modified in some way so that the immune system will continue to work normally (rather than overreact), far fewer people will die in the event of an avian bird flu pandemic. That at least is the theory.

As part of this research work other sources of 1918 virus are being sought – in the United Kingdom permission was obtained to exhume the Boer War veteran and Tory MP Sir Mark Sykes who died in 1918 after contracting the Spanish flu. There was so much fear at the time he died that the very process of burial was seen as potentially hazardous for the mourners; as a result his family decided to bury him in a sealed lead coffin. His remains are therefore likely to be so well preserved that yet more 1918 virus may be made available to scientists. With every new piece of information we are certain to move closer to controlling a disease that – should it return – might otherwise cause millions of human deaths across the world.

CHAPTER 7

The Mutant Enemy – Asian Flu (1957) and Hong Kong Flu (1968)

In the decades after the worldwide disaster of the 1918 flu pandemic, various flu viruses continued to circulate in human populations across the globe. Some years the dominant virus was more dangerous than in others, but the threat of another terrifying influenza pandemic seemed to recede.

The flu pathogen identified

A number of scientists back in 1918 had, it is true, some inkling that they were dealing with an agent smaller than any then known; despite the fact that their microscopes, which relied on ordinary light, could not see the pathogen a number suspected it existed. It was more than two decades before their suspicions were confirmed.

The flu virus was first discovered in pigs in 1931, but its presence and nature could only be inferred since no microscope then available was powerful enough to see something so small. Richard Schape carried out this pioneering research, which was followed up by work carried out by a London-based team headed by Patrick Laidlaw to isolate the virus. Then, in 1935, Wendell Stanley managed to crystallize tobacco mosaic virus (a virus that damages the leaves of the tobacco was a commercial disaster at a time when smoking was very popular), which was the first virus to be discovered.

The process of discovering the flu virus was a slow one and one to which many people contributed their skills and time, but by the late 1930s the pathogen that caused influenza had been isolated and seen for the first time using powerful new electron microscopes that gave a glimpse into the extraordinary world of sub-microscopic life. The development of the electronic microscope made viruses visible for the first time, confirming earlier work.

One problem with the new electron microscope (which could magnify up to 1,000,000 times compared to about 2,000 for a light microscope) was that unlike the older light microscopes it did not show the virus (or anything else) alive – the electron bombardment that enabled the virus to be seen also killed it. Nevertheless, it could be studied and its particular properties understood in such a way that scientists began to hope that an effective vaccine might one day be possible.

The discovery of antibiotics

The viruses that swirled about the world in the years following the devastation of 1918 claimed the lives of the young, old and those already weakened by other illnesses, but this was not unusual. Though infection rates were high each year, mortality rates remained relatively low, and well below levels that suggested influenza was powering up for another devastating attack.

Deaths from influenza complications and secondary infections decreased during this period because the biggest killer of those suffering from influenza was still bacterial pneumonia, and bacterial pneumonia was now fought with the most powerful weapon ever to be discovered by the medical profession: antibiotics.

When, in 1929, Alexander Fleming accidentally discovered in his cluttered and untidy room in St Mary's Hospital, London, a mould that killed bacteria without killing surrounding healthy cells, he did not at first realize how revolutionary his discovery truly was. It took almost a decade before the first widespread use of commercially produced penicillin began. It revolutionized the treatment of bacterial infection and saved countless millions of lives.

Within a few years of the widespread use of penicillin there were problems. Bacteria became resistant to penicillin, for example, but other antibiotics were sought and developed in an attempt to stay ahead of resistant strains as and when they appeared. This battle continues today with methicillin-resistant staphylococcus aureus (MRSA) the so-called super-bug at the centre of frightening reports in the media.

Back in the 1940s and early 1950s antibiotics were hailed as having the potential to cure pretty much everything. While hugely effective against *bacterial* infections, they were useless against one of the biggest of all killers – the virus. They could do nothing to protect against yellow fever, dengue fever, Ebola – or influenza. Nevertheless, the scientific world remained optimistic, and it was regarded as just a matter of time before viruses too would meet their nemesis.

As the years passed, various strains of influenza steadily mutated. This process of antigenic drift (see Chapter 1) was never likely to be a huge problem because these new varieties of influenza were sufficiently similar to older varieties already circulating, to which human populations had at least some immunity. This meant, as we have seen, that though morbidity might be high with each year's new flu outbreak mortality remained relatively low.

The World Health Organization

All these scientific developments were most promising. Another weapon in the arsenal against any future pandemic was, and is, the World Health Organization (WHO). The WHO is part of the United Nations – a product of new optimism following the end of World War II and an organization with 191 member states. Where various world governments bicker and argue in other international arenas they are largely – though by no means entirely – able to cooperate through the WHO to coordinate a worldwide response to disease of all kinds. By 1949 a World Influenza Centre had also been set up to link 84 laboratories in 45 countries. Their responsibility was to know in advance which influenza viruses were circulating in the human population and to coordinate future efforts to alleviate their worst effects.

The WHO promotes scientific and medical cooperation for health between different nations, and undertakes programmes to control and eradicate disease. It also spends huge sums of money and much time and effort trying to improve the quality of human life across the globe. The WHO's four main functions are: 'to give worldwide guidance in the field of health; to set global standards for health; to cooperate with governments in strengthening national health programmes; and to develop and transfer appropriate health technology, information and standards'.

The WHO's greatest success so far has been with the eradication of smallpox. It has also been singularly successful at reducing the incidence of polio – a disease now on the verge of extinction – and leprosy. The latter disease, though still common in some parts of the world, is relatively easy to treat and prevent, and ultimate eradication is therefore a real possibility.

The success of the WHO can be judged both in terms of human happiness but also in purely financial terms. According to one source, for example, 'The United States alone saves its entire investment in the disease-eradication programme every month because costly protection measures are no longer needed.'

The WHO works to improve the general health of world populations, delivering essential drugs, improving medical services within cities and promoting healthy lifestyles. As well as targeting serious diseases such as influenza, the WHO targets vulnerable populations such as the elderly and pregnant women, promotes access to safe drinking water and better sanitation facilities.

The WHO believes passionately that ultimately even the world's worst health problems can be alleviated or even eliminated (as smallpox). As one WHO spokesman put it:

Fifty years may seem a long time to individuals, but it is a short spell in human history. For two centuries it was known that smallpox could be prevented, but only in the twentieth century was a coalition organized by WHO able to do something definitive about it. With political will, commitment and a willingness to work together, there is no reason why this success cannot be continued.

A deadly new strain

For nearly forty years after the terrible 'Spanish' flu pandemic, the world suffered no other frightening outbreaks. That situation changed dramatically in 1957. In February of that year a new strain of influenza was identified in the Far East as small numbers of individuals came down with severe, flu-like symptoms, and a number of people died. The new strain differed sufficiently from known strains of the disease to ensure that anyone under the age of 65 was unlikely to have any immunity; the alarm bells immediately rang through the World Health Organization influenza monitoring system. A pandemic was expected.

With the precise nature of the flu strain identified, a huge effort immediately got underway and mass vaccine production started in May of that year. In Britain the vaccine was produced at the Wright-Fleming Institute of Microbiology in West London. It was administered free of charge but was effective only if administered in two stages – two injections were needed at an interval of roughly three weeks. The elderly and other at-risk groups were given the vaccine first along with doctors, nurses and other medical staff.

Monitoring services across the world were put on red alert for the first signs that the new strain was causing illness and spreading. By August the new vaccine was available in many Western countries, but like all flu vaccines it was only ever of limited use. The new strain of what was now being called Asian flu reached the USA where outbreaks were reported through the summer of 1957. In Britain, America and many parts of Europe it was the return of children to school in the autumn combined with colder weather that caused a sudden rise in reported cases. Classrooms were a perfect dispersal centre where the flu could transmit rapidly and then be taken home and spread further afield by newly infected children.

By October doctors across the world – but particularly in America – were reporting serious cases of flu in the very young, the elderly and among pregnant women – all traditionally high-risk influenza groups. There was no sign that this outbreak would kill the young, vigorous and healthy (as in 1918), and doctors and governments across the world breathed a sigh of relief as the true measure of the pandemic became clear. If it was far less severe than 1918 it was nonetheless serious and occasionally devastating. The elderly suffered the highest mortality rates and as the winter wore on death rates reached their peak, levelling out in the spring of 1958.

Old lessons relearned

The spread of the new strain through schools was highlighted by the World Health Organization and this was paralleled by its spread through army camps and other large gatherings of people – marches, conferences, camps, theatres and cinemas were all linked with the spread of the new strain. As in 1918, it was difficult to persuade individual governments across the world to implement strict procedures as a way of lessening the spread of the disease.

The consequences of not acting quickly enough to prevent people gathering together in large numbers in the early stages of an epidemic or pandemic was a lesson learned the hard way in 1918. Despite this experience governments were slow to close schools and other places where the public gathered. The social and economic cost of a major shut-down was almost certainly deemed to be too high since it could be months before it was safe for normal life to continue.

But the WHO recommendation for this and future epidemics and pandemics was unequivocally that social gatherings aided the spread of the virus and should therefore be avoided once a particularly dangerous flu strain had been identified. Sadly, the WHO – then as now – had no power to force governments to act.

Where schools were closed in 1957 the number of flu cases dropped, particularly in children aged six to 12. Most stayed closed for little more than a month before it was safe for them to re-open – the one-month break in the infection cycle was clearly enough to disrupt the rapid spread of the disease. Despite this, however, in the United Kingdom and the United States up to 50 per cent of all school children were hit by the new strain – this steep rise in childhood cases occurred as part of the first wave of infection.

The lightning strike

The speed of that first wave astonished scientists and doctors – a number of American schools found that in a two-week period that autumn they went from no cases at all to 90 or even 100 per cent infection rates. In London polluted air caused by the millions of domestic coal fires exacerbated the effects of the flu. Large numbers of elderly people developed pneumonias that were resistant to penicillin and other antibiotics, and as a result there was a frightening rise in the death toll.

In Liverpool and other British and American cities health professionals were particularly hard hit – in some areas more than one in five nurses were struck by the disease during that first wave of attack; in pockets of infection that figure rose to one in three with a similar rate of infection for city-based hospital doctors. Hospitals were inundated with far higher numbers of sick patients than in a normal winter; many had to set up beds in corridors to cope with the extra demand. The long shadow of 1918 seemed to be marching across the land once more. As one Manchester doctor put it, 'Among my colleagues there was a real feeling that the increase in flu cases that had to be admitted to hospital was so sudden and individual symptoms so severe that we really thought that there was a danger of the kind of system collapse that occurred in 1918–19.'

With many nurses and doctors themselves sick the situation quickly reached crisis point. A more virulent strain of flu could have led to a situation comparable with 1918, but thankfully the 1957 strain was milder and contained enough genetic material to which the human population worldwide had a large degree of immunity. As a health-service breakdown loomed in some parts of the world – notably America and the United Kingdom – the peak of infection passed and crisis was averted, but this was more a matter of luck than anything else.

The two key months were September and October 1957 and during that period in the United Kingdom alone an extra 25,000–30,000 cases of serious respiratory infection were admitted to National Health Service (NHS) hospitals in England and Wales than would have been predicted in an autumn/winter period when a 'normal' influenza strain was circulating. Statistics reveal that in those first months of the pandemic in London hospitals 20 per cent of patients admitted with pneumonia were dying. The problem in many cases was antibiotic-resistant or viral pneumonia. By late autumn some 30 million doses of the new vaccine were available in America alone, but this fell far short of the 60 million doses that were thought to be needed. Nevertheless it showed how far medicine had come in terms of organization and distribution since the chaos of 1918.

There were similarities with 1918, however. Then as now the disease seemed to come in waves. By December it looked as if the worst of the first wave was over, but the New Year brought little relief. In fact there was a sudden increase in the number of reported cases and an increase in the number of victims reporting serious complications, particularly among the elderly. This second-wave phenomenon is probably characteristic of all pandemic outbreaks of influenza and is caused by the virus mutating and becoming more powerful. As it becomes better at infecting people it will often become far more efficient at killing them too.

Flu in Communist China

Most of what we know about the 1957 flu pandemic comes from Europe and America. Having swept across those two continents, however, we know that it was equally devastating in Asia, and particularly China, where it originated.

Chairman Mao's 'Great Leap Forward', instituted in the late 1950s and reaching a peak of intensity in 1957, caused somewhere between 14 and 30 million deaths from starvation. As collectivization was forced on the rural population, harvests collapsed, while the propaganda machine claimed harvests were at record levels. With a seriously undernourished population influenza would have been a lethal killer. But, as China was effectively a closed society at that time, we simply do not know how badly the general population was affected. By the same token, it is difficult to know to what extent the influenza pandemic of 1957 contributed to the overall death toll caused by the Great Leap Forward. We do know that the 1957 pandemic began in China, and it is unlikely therefore that their death toll was significantly lower proportionately than elsewhere in the world. One or two researchers have argued that the huge death toll that has generally been attributed to the famine caused by the Great Leap Forward actually had far more to do with flu than starvation.

Counting the dead

The global death toll from flu in 1957 has been estimated at two million, but given that there is so little evidence from more remote parts of the world the true figure is almost certainly much higher. We know that though the disease was far less dangerous than the 1918 strain, it still caused at least 70,000 deaths in the United States and as many as 30,000 deaths in the United Kingdom. Without the vaccine that was distributed towards the end of 1957 that death toll would certainly have been far higher.

Typically – and despite attempts to distribute the vaccine as widely as possible – the death rate did continue to rise through the autumn and winter, but not as fast as it might otherwise have done. With future pandemics in mind it is worth remembering – amid media stories of doom and gloom – that the speed with which vaccines can be manufactured, and their effectiveness, has improved greatly since 1957.

Just like in 1918, the 1957 pandemic hit hardest in India and Asia where most of the two million worldwide deaths occurred. The reason fatalities were greater here was due to poorer nutrition and health care, population density and the proximity of humans to pigs and birds.

Hong Kong flu in 1968

Like all pandemic strains, the 1968 outbreak of flu began in bird populations and mixed with human strains to create a strain to which there was little existing immunity in humans. It was first recognized in the Chinese province of Guizhou, from where it spread rapidly to Singapore and Hong Kong. Just as in 1918 it was not named after the area in which it started but in which it was first widely publicized – Hong Kong.

In 1968 China was still a closed country ruled by a totalitarian regime. All talk of problems and epidemics, famine or poor harvests was condemned as 'bourgeois' and 'counter-revolutionary'. News of the disease only emerged when cases were reported across the border in the then-British colony of Hong Kong. Once again the alarm bells began ringing around the world; here was a new and potentially deadly strain of influenza.

It seems to have taken roughly two years for the Hong Kong flu to work its way around. As usual it came in at least two waves: the first caused more deaths in some countries, the second in others, which may be explained by the fact that a mild version may have given partial immunity to some groups in some countries. The worst months for flu are almost always in the winter and 1968 was no exception, with deaths reaching a peak in December of that year and then declining in the spring of 1969.

As many as four million people worldwide were probably infected, which makes the outbreak seem almost insignificant compared to 1918. In the United States it caused roughly 34,000 deaths. That figure, though far lower than the death count in 1918 or 1957, does not reflect the disruption and suffering caused by the disease, which infected at least ten times that number in the Americas alone. Business and commerce took months if not years to recover. Worldwide, it resulted in more than one million deaths, a huge figure given that 1968 is well within the era of modern high-tech medicine. That total might have been far worse had it not been for the massive improvements in disease tracking and vaccine production.

In the UK, the pandemic caused a sudden surge in hospital admissions and a rise in the rate of deaths as compared to 'normal' flu outbreaks. Hospitals were put under enormous pressure but coped far better than in 1957. In comparison to 1918 of course there was little to cope with and the National Health Service, which came into being in 1948, showed how much a co-ordinated health system could do. Vastly increased sums were spent on health compared to 1918 and there is no doubt this contributed to the sense in the UK at least, that the authorities could and would cope. This sense of being in control – a sense entirely lacking in 1918 – was reinforced by the vast increases in medical and scientific knowledge.

Pandemics on a smaller scale

The world had changed dramatically by 1969. Even in 1957 air travel was not that common, but by 1968 we had entered the era of the charter flight – millions of people were travelling regularly and rapidly between countries every year; with them went the influenza virus.

Unlike the Spanish flu of 1918 but resembling the 1957 pandemic, Hong Kong flu tended to kill the elderly and the very young rather than those in the prime of life. When the second wave came, the disease hit the United Kingdom particularly badly in terms of the number of reported cases, reaching a peak in early 1970. The development of effective vaccines had begun as soon as the earliest cases developed, and that simple fact massively reduced the number of fatalities. The 1968–69 pandemic was in fact the least damaging of all 20th-century influenza pandemics.

Improved health and nutrition, and the ability to control secondary bacterial infections all played their part too, but the main reason the pandemic was essentially mild was that it was caused by a strain whose chemical profile was similar to that of the strain that swept around the world in 1957. That meant a major part of the world's population probably had some immunity.

Another chance event reduced the spread of the disease. As it worsened in the USA and United Kingdom, schools closed for the Christmas holidays, effectively breaking the chain of contacts that might otherwise have ensured an even greater disease spread.

The pandemics of 1957 and 1968 did present problems for scientists, doctors and governments but the international monitoring service, an element of luck, and advances in medicine ensured that they never reached the scale of the 1918 outbreak.

Identifying the strains

The 1957 Asian flu pandemic was caused by a flu strain known as H2N2 – the 1918 pandemic, by contrast, was caused by an H1N1 subtype and the 1968 pandemic by the H3N2 virus.

In 1957, human H1 influenza almost certainly mixed with bird flu viruses carrying the surface protein H2. The strain of flu created by the mix – which probably occurred in rural China – was far more dangerous than the existing H1 strains of influenza. Human populations would have had some immunity to H1, but had never before encountered the H2 protein.

By the time the 1957 pandemic was officially over doctors and scientists noticed that the H1-virus flu in humans had completely vanished. It had been replaced by the H2 strain. This process of substitution was to happen again a little over a decade later when, in 1968, another deadly virus emerged once more in rural China. The 1968 virus was characterized by haemagglutinin H3 which superceded the H2 strain. As each strain superseded the last, levels of human immunity plummeted – no sooner has the body armed itself against the new invader than another entirely different invader appears on the scene.

As time passes human populations lose their immunity to earlier forms of influenza – anyone born after the H2 virus disappeared would have no immunity to that strain should it return. The same is true of the strain that caused the 1918 pandemic. Its return could again trigger deaths on a truly colossal scale because no one alive now – no one that is except perhaps the extremely elderly – has any immunity.

By 1968, influenza of every known type was carefully monitored and categorized across the world according to strict scientific principles – the Asian flu of 1957 was officially a category-two pandemic, not catastrophic, but highly dangerous nonetheless.

When the Hong Kong flu of 1968 was first identified as a completely new strain there were fears that it might be very serious indeed. The reason for this fear was that in terms of its chemical and genetic structure it showed the effects not of antigenic drift but of far more serious genetic shift – a sudden genetic leap that left immunity too far behind to give human victims much chance of fighting the disease without medical intervention. Hong Kong flu was officially identified as the strain H3N2. In the event it caused a milder pandemic than that which occurred in 1957, but it was another serious outbreak nonetheless.

One scientist has neatly summarized the difference between the 1957 and 1968 flu strains and that of 1918: 'While the pandemic human influenza viruses of 1957 (H2N2) and 1968 (H3N2) clearly arose through reassortment between human and avian viruses, the influenza virus causing the Spanish flu in 1918 appears to be entirely derived from an avian source.' That distinction – between flu viruses that are a mix of avian and human strains, and viruses that are of purely avian origin – has now been at the heart of flu monitoring and research for decades. The risk to humans will always be greatest where a new flu strain does not resemble or at least include some elements of human influenza. A pure avian strain that mutates in humans to the extent that it can be spread from human to human rather than from bird to human is the ultimate fear.

It should be pointed out, however, that not all scientists accept the Domesday arguments of the pessimists. Among the optimists are those who believe that avian flu is unlikely to mutate to the point at which human to human infection becomes a serious threat. They point out that many factors were at work in 1918 that do not apply now: a world population weakened and relatively undernourished after more than four years of war; a system of collecting troops together (particularly in the United States) that took little or no account of medical and hygiene good practice; and a profound ignorance of the nature of the virus they were up against. We are, in short, much better equipped to deal with a major assault by the virus, even by a dangerously mutated avian flu.

But that is the optimistic view – the pessimists (or realists as they might style themselves) argue that we cannot ultimately be properly prepared for a virus that will have a genetic make-up we cannot predict. They also point to one or two places in the world that provide the ideal breeding ground for an emerging pandemic virus.

As the world's population has continued to expand and the speed of communication increased, the vast pool of potential infection in China has come to loom large in the imagination of Western democracies. The WHO has stepped up its monitoring activities and scientists continue to work on vaccines. Despite all their best efforts, however, we are still faced with a genuine risk that when a pure type of avian flu hits us again, as it did in 1918, the death toll will be catastrophic. As we will see in the next chapter there is currently not much we can do to stop it.

CHAPTER 8

Jumping the Species Barrier – Avian Flu

As the world becomes ever more crowded and once-remote regions are gradually encroached upon by man – a process that has accelerated alarmingly in the past century – man has come to live in ever closer proximity with animal species with which he previously only had rare contact. This has all sorts of implications for animal conservation. As we deprive these species of their habitats at such a phenomenal rate, many face extinction; other animal species are trying to find ways to adapt and survive by encroaching on our turf in turn; whether it be the grizzly bears of North America raiding suburban dustbins, tigers creeping out of the jungles of India to prey on neighbouring cattle, or bold-faced foxes prowling the streets of London for food, these are all becoming increasingly common sights.

A question we probably think about far less frequently is the impact this process could have on the survival of the most successful species of all – humankind. Zoonosis – the process by which animals pass their diseases to humans and vice versa – has become a potential nightmare for disease monitors across the world. It results from animals and man sharing habitats too closely, and is only likely to get worse as the world becomes ever more densely populated.

Population growth – a moral question?

With the sole exception of China no country in the world enforces a limit to the number of children a couple may have. But even China's one-child policy is widely flouted by the wealthy and criticized by democratic countries in the west that regard it as an infringement of fundamental human rights.

Population growth is currently seen almost universally in purely economic terms. Despite the terrible poverty in which the vast majority of the world's population lives, there is enough global wealth – today – for everyone to live comfortably, with access to basic sanitation, education and healthcare. But – in the very simplest of terms – until the wealthiest countries do more to redress this balance, the poorest countries are left to pursue policies that support their immediate economic needs, such as the 'slash and burn' of the Amazonian rainforests in order to create both arable land and pasture for cattle to supply the demand for beef consumption in the West.

In poor countries where there is very high infant mortality due to malnutrition, disease, or, in some cases, civil war, the impetus is thus to continue to have large families in order to overcome this statistic. And they are succeeding; populations in the developing world continue to increase dramatically. In the West a high birth rate is seen as good because countries with growing populations, such as the United Kingdom, tend to have stronger economies than countries with falling populations, such as Russia.

From the comfort of our sitting rooms in the wealthy and democratic West, it is easy for us to sit in moral judgement upon those – whether individuals or governments – who, out of ignorance or necessity, cause terrible damage to their immediate environment or endangered animal neighbours. It is easier for the privileged few to see uncontrolled population growth as a moral problem that leaves other animals on the planet in a disastrous, often irreversible spiral of decline as their habitat is destroyed to make way for yet more humans or to grow food for yet more humans. *Do* animals have a right to retain their habitat if human populations need that same habitat? And what of the catastrophic impact on the global environment? These are vast and complex questions that fall beyond the scope of this book, the consequences of which we will undoubtedly face in coming decades.

The fact is that for the many millions of people in the world today living hand-to-mouth, these questions are an irrelevance. Despite the dubious moral basis for allowing the wholesale destruction of the world's few remaining pockets of pristine jungle, forest and savannah, the farmer trying to feed his family does not have the luxury to worry that there is one less acre of forest, or one less tiger living in the wild.

Perhaps, then, in this present global state of affairs, we are approaching this question from the wrong angle. The moral question is obviously premature for most of the world's population. Perhaps it is not a question of wealth, but *health*? Perhaps the threat of new, deadly diseases could serve as a more effective counterbalance to the destruction of natural habitats? The terror of AIDS should serve as a cautionary tale. The irony is, of course, that as we continue to destroy those habitats, we are also destroying natural sources of medicinal cures that could very well save us from some of those diseases.

A case study – the Hendra virus

This is all very interesting, but what has this got to do with a social history of influenza, I hear you ask? Well, since our latest fear is of a pandemic of the newly emerged bird flu, it is imperative that we try to understand the context in and mechanisms through which such a pandemic might occur. And, more importantly, is there anything we can do to prevent it?

A good example of what can happen when a particular species loses its habitat as a result of human encroachment can be seen in Australia where a deadly virus – one never before seen in humans – erupted in 1994. The new virus was called Hendra, and we can learn a great deal about how future flu pandemics may progress by studying the emergence of this new and deadly virus.

It all began in 1994 on an equine farm at a place called Hendra (later to give its name to the disease) just outside Brisbane in Australia. A pregnant mare called Drama Series was happily feeding in a meadow one day only to be discovered fever-ish and frothing at the mouth the next. Stable foreman Ray Unwin, and the horse's trainer, Vic Rail, immediately called in veterinary help. They tried everything they could think of to save the horse and her foal but it was hopeless – a bloody froth poured from the mare's nose and mouth, her fever became worse and within 48 hours she was dead.

Drama Series had been killed by a new and previously unknown virus. The power of that virus can be judged by the fact that within three days 12 more horses on the farm had succumbed to the same disease and Unwin and the trainer were fighting for their lives. Unwin survived; Rail died. Unwin has never fully recovered. For doctors and researchers called in to discover the identity of the killer the big questions were: what was it and where did it come from?

It was first thought that the horses might have been poisoned or bitten by snakes, but nothing quite matched what they were seeing. It was soon discovered that the virus lives in fruit bats, and the outbreak near Brisbane was almost certainly the result of the loss of fruit-bat habitat. As humans took their habitat the bats found themselves living cheek by jowl with the farmers. Trees on Ray Unwin's farm certainly had bats living in them and the close proximity over a lengthy period of time of horses and bats eventually allowed the Hendra virus – to which the bats were largely immune – to jump species with the devastating effects described above.

Getting too close to the neighbours

In most cases viral diseases suddenly appear from nowhere and then seem to disap-pear as quickly as they have come. In fact, they don't disappear at all. They merely retreat to the host species in which they have usually lived for tens of thousands of years – long enough, in fact, for host and virus to have learned to live in relative peace with each other. If we compare this with avian flu we see the immediate parallels – avian flu as the name implies lives in wildfowl and only rarely kills its host animals.

It is estimated that something like 60 per cent of all the infectious diseases that affect humans are shared with animals. As we encroach further into animal territories we are more likely to experience the sort of devastating outbreaks of disease seen at Hendra. Once that virus had jumped from the bats to the horses it had entered a species that had no historic immunity, which explains why horses – and humans – were so quickly overwhelmed and killed.

Proximity of host and victim is key and parallels precisely the situation with wild and domestic birds and humans in southern China, where the vast majority of cases of avian flu jumping the species barrier have occurred.

In some cases it has taken years to discover the host species of particular viruses. Ebola, which first broke out in the 1970s in Africa killing 98 per cent of its human victims before burning itself out, remained a complete mystery for more than two decades. Scientists were convinced that an animal host must exist, but they could not find it. Then, in 2005, researchers in Franceville, Gabon, isolated the virus in several species of fruit bat. But their evidence was tentative. Researchers had no idea whether the bats infected humans directly or through some intermediate animal. They are convinced, however, that outbreaks have occurred where humans have had contact with dead apes and monkeys; catching, killing and butchering bush meat – usually chimpanzees – looks like the most high-risk behaviour for becoming infected with Ebola. But making definitive pronouncements about Ebola, as about every virus, is difficult, doubly so with Ebola as the virus tends to strike in remote regions of Africa; by the time researchers are in place the disease has usually run its course.

Whether we talk about Ebola, Hendra or any other virus that jumps species, what we should worry about most is not whether the virus simply jumps species, but whether it jumps species regularly, and mutates at a very quick rate. Some species-jumping viruses, such as Ebola and Hendra, while lethal, are so deadly that they burn themselves out before any infected humans have had a chance to spread the virus very far. On the other hand, influenza already has a track record of mutating at incredible speed into forms to which humankind has no immunity. The nightmare virus is thus flu, and more specifically, avian flu.

In the first few years of the new millennium, a growing number of human H5N1 cases – in other words, pure avian flu cases – were reported across Asia and Africa: in Azerbaijan, Cambodia, China, Djibouti, Egypt, Indonesia, Iraq, Nigeria, Thailand,

Turkey and Vietnam. More than half those infected died – a far higher death rate than that for the 1918 'Spanish' flu pandemic.

All these cases were almost certainly caused by exposure to infected poultry and it is sheer good fortune that, so far, H5N1 has not mutated to the extent that having infected humans it can then be passed from human to human. The results of that would be catastrophic. It is worth taking a moment to absorb that key difference. Bird-to-human transmission is certainly frightening, but while transmission is only ever directly from bird to human, that simple fact tells us that the virus has not mutated (or been genetically reassorted) sufficiently to cause widespread human infection. Only those in regular and close contact with the bird hosts of the disease have so far been infected with avian flu. While that situation continues we are relatively safe and avian flu will not be able to lay waste to huge urban populations, the ultimate fear.

So, the concern – and it is something being closely monitored by the WHO at a cost of millions of pounds each year – is that H5N1 will evolve into a virus capable of rapid human-to-human transmission.

How bird flu functions … at present

Avian flu is caused by influenza-A viruses that occur naturally among birds. Different subtypes of these viruses exist because of changes in certain proteins – haemagglutinin (HA) and neuraminidase (NA) on the surface of the influenza-A virus – and the way the proteins combine. Each combination represents a different subtype. All known subtypes of influenza-A viruses can be found in birds. The avian flu currently of concern is known as the H5N1 subtype.

Wild birds across the world carry avian influenza viruses in their intestines, but over countless generations virus and host have learned to tolerate each other and the birds do not usually suffer any ill effects. For domesticated birds, including chickens, ducks and turkeys, however, the avian flu virus is highly contagious and frequently lethal. Once a bird has been infected it will spread 'live' virus in vast quantities in its saliva, nasal secretions and faeces. Domesticated birds may become infected with avian influenza in many ways: through direct contact with infected wildfowl (ducks and geese) or other infected poultry, or through contact with infected dust and dirt, or even materials (such as water, feed or the utensils in which they are contained) that have come in contact with the virus. The virus can survive for a considerable time outside the body of its host.

Avian-influenza infection in domestic poultry causes two main forms of the disease – a low-virulence type and an extremely high-virulence type. The low-virulence form is often virtually undetectable because it causes mild symptoms and victims quickly recover, but the high-virulence form is terrifying both in the speed with which it will infect a flock of birds and in the high mortality it will cause: in some instances mortality rates can reach 95 or even 100 per cent. The H5N1 virus – the strain with which humans are concerned – is, unfortunately, of the high-virulence type.

It is likely that some genetic parts of current human influenza-A viruses originally came from birds; that is by no means certain, but it is an idea that has the support of many in the scientific and medical community. There are three known A subtypes of influenza viruses (H1N1, H1N2, and H3N2) currently circulating among humans. The A-virus subtype to which avian flu belongs – H5N1 – is split into two groups or clades, and there are further sub-clades also. Influenza-A viruses are constantly changing – through antigenic drift and genetic shift (see Chapter 1) – and other strains might adapt over time to infect and spread among humans. This is why it is so difficult for humans to protect themselves against the disease in advance. It is when a human-influenza virus's genes are reassorted inside another animal (usually a pig) with avian-virus genes that the problems can really start.

Although influenza viruses and their subtypes have jumped occasionally between species, the traffic has not always been one way – i.e. from birds or pigs to man. Flu subtypes H1N1 and H3N2, which are currently circulating in human populations, have crossed the species barrier to infect pigs, for example. In 1998, H1N1 viruses circulated widely in the American pig population, and in the same year H3N2 viruses from humans were introduced into the pig population causing huge animal-welfare problems. More recently, H3N8 viruses from horses have crossed over and caused outbreaks in dogs.

For most people the risk from avian influenza is low, because it is still extremely rare for the virus to infect humans. H5N1 is one of the few avian-influenza viruses to have crossed the species barrier to infect humans. Despite the fact that it is the most deadly of those that have crossed the barrier it has not yet become widely trans-missible from human to human.

The absence of immunity

Since avian viruses do not usually infect humans, there is virtually no historic or existing immunity to them in the human population. If the H5N1 virus were to gain the capacity to spread easily from person to person, a pandemic would almost certainly begin for this very reason. No one can predict when a pandemic might occur, but experts from around the world are watching the H5N1 situation very closely. They are preparing for the possibility that the virus may at any time evolve and begin to spread more easily and more widely from person to person.

Identifying bird flu in humans

Most cases of H5N1 influenza infection in humans have resulted from contact with infected poultry – domesticated chicken, ducks and turkeys – or surfaces contaminated with secretions or excretions from infected birds. Infection occurs from bird to human and usually stops there.

The spread of H5N1 virus from person to person has been limited, and has not continued beyond one additional person or, in very rare cases, a small cluster. Most cases have occurred in previously healthy children and young adults. However, it is possible that the only the most severe cases are currently being reported, and that the full range of lower-level illness caused by the H5N1 virus has not yet been identified. In other words there may be large numbers of humans infected with the H5N1 virus but suffering only relatively mild symptoms or symptoms that appear to be caused by something else.

The difficulty is the wide range of symptoms caused by all types of flu. The typical symptoms of fever, cough, sore throat, aches and pains and lassitude are usually present, but many others are not typical human-influenza-like symptoms; eye infections, pneumonia, severe respiratory diseases such as ARDS, and other severe and life-threatening complications have also been recorded. The symptoms caused by avian influenza may depend on which precise virus caused the infection.

Avain flu attacks birds and humans in very different ways. In birds without immunity it spreads quickly affecting muscle, brain, lungs and every major organ. In humans the damage to lungs usually comes first and is often so massive that the patient dies before the disease can spread much beyond the lungs. 'It's like inviting in trucks filled with dynamite' said one doctor in Hong Kong. This is very similar to the situation in 1918 where the cytokine storm led to a massive overreaction in the flu victim's immune system. That overreaction then became a major problem in itself, massively increasing the destruction of the lungs caused by the virus.

Researchers at the University of Hong Kong have noticed other worrying and fatal reactions to the disease. One young Vietnamese boy arrived at hospital in Ho Chi Min City in a delirious state. His lungs were perfectly healthy and remained unaffected until he died. An autopsy revealed that the cause of the boy's death was a catastrophic brain inflammation caused by the H5N1 virus. This finding suggests that, should the H5N1 virus gain a foothold in human populations, the range of killer symptoms might move far beyond the lung damage that was so central to the Spanish flu pandemic of 1918.

Our ignorance about avian flu is astonishing – the world's top influenza experts in Atlanta, United States and in London still don't have the answers to the most basic questions. They do not know, for example, how many people are infected at any one time; many of those who catch the disease are presumed to show few or no symptoms. Nor do they know all the countries that have suffered outbreaks; eight countries are listed by the World Health Organization, but scientists are almost certain cases have gone unreported elsewhere. Nor do they know much about how people become infected. As one researcher put it: 'We assume that people catch avian flu by close contact with infected poultry but what does this mean? Does it mean they are exposed to sick or dying poultry – did they touch those birds or eat them? Did eating them cause infection or was it enough just to handle the birds? The truth is we don't yet know.'

Other possible infection routes favoured by a number of specialists include the inhalation of dust containing particles of infected poultry faeces. But how intense and prolonged does contact with dead or dying birds and their faeces have to be before infection becomes likely? Despite years of work and the most sophisticated monitoring and research equipment we still don't know the answers to these basic questions. 'And without answers, fighting back is like fighting with one arm tied behind our backs,' laments one researcher.

A drug-resistant virus

There is no vaccine available to counter the bird flu virus currently affecting very small numbers of humans in Asia, Europe and Africa. No one is going to manufacture large stocks of vaccine while the strain of avian flu behind these cases is a bird-to-human strain only. A pandemic vaccine can only be produced when a new human-to-human influenza virus emerges and is identified – once that happens it will be a race against time to produce an effective vaccine in time to save millions of lives.

Unfortunately, the H5N1 virus that has caused human illness and death in Asia is resistant to two of the best antiviral flu drugs currently available – the M2 inhibitors amantadine and rimantadine. M2 inhibitors work by stopping the viral genome being released so that replication stops. Two further antiviral medications, oseltamivir (brand name Tamiflu) and zanamavir, would probably work to treat influenza caused by H5N1 virus, but the outlook is still bleak because we do not know precisely how humans will react to infection. All antiviral medications have a limited life as the virus (or viruses) constantly mutate to outwit them.

Oseltamavir and zanamavir are neuraminidase inhibitors (that is, they prevent the virus budding from the host cell), but their effectiveness depends on their being administered within 48 hours of the first signs of illness. Clinical data and hard evidence that they are genuinely effective is hard to come by, and at best they probably only reduce the severity of the symptoms and improve prospects of survival.

Another problem is that we do not have the capacity to produce sufficiently large quantities of these drugs in the event of an emergency. And they are expensive to produce, certainly too expensive for poorer countries. According to an industry insider: 'At the present rate of manufacturing capacity, which has recently quadrupled, it will take a decade to produce enough oseltamivir to treat 20 per cent of the world's population.'

Using antiviral medicines on large numbers of people over a long period would accelerate the development of resistance. This is why the vaccine route is most favoured by doctors and scientists for long-term strategic anti-flu measures. Antivirals are preferred for early use in viral hotspots – to try to limit the spread from these hotspots while large quantities of vaccine are prepared – and for health workers. That at least is the option recommended by the WHO, though whether even the WHO could persuade governments across the world to agree to their plan is another matter.

Already the west is stockpiling Tamiflu, which is known to offer some protection against the worst effects of avian flu. The United Kingdom alone has enough stockpiled antivirals to treat some 15 million people, just a quarter of the total population. Other countries in the West have similar stockpiles but the real effort is being concentrated on trying to find an effective vaccine, prevention inevitably being better, cheaper and less disruptive than cure.

The cases so far

Most cases of bird flu so far have been recorded in the Far East – particularly Thailand, Vietnam and China – with a few cases also occurring in Turkey and other Near Eastern countries. Interestingly, no two cases have presented precisely the same symptoms, and those cases carefully studied by doctors have revealed a surprising range of means of infection. In Vietnam in 2005, for example, two people were infected after drinking raw duck blood. In other cases children have been infected after playing with feathers taken from birds; there have also been cases where workers on poultry farms have become infected as a result of breathing infected dust.

The world's first instance of avian flu in a human population was recorded in 1997 in Hong Kong, when vast numbers of chickens died from the disease in Hong Kong's predominantly rural New Territories. Eighteen people were hospitalized and six died.

It all started when a three-year-old boy was admitted to hospital suffering from what looked like classic flu symptoms – he had a high fever, difficulty breathing and a terrible cough. He was immediately placed on a ventilator and given massive doses of powerful antibiotics. Within days he was dead and an autopsy revealed the grim truth – he was the first recorded human to be infected with H5N1. To the astonishment of doctors at the hospital the strain of H5N1 precisely matched the strain that had killed millions of chickens earlier that year. Within a few days 17 more infected people materialized, five of whom died. Translate that ratio into a worldwide pandemic and the death toll would be catastrophic.

The victims all had at least one thing in common – they had either regularly visited or worked in and around one or other of the huge local poultry markets. In southeast Asia most poultry markets sell live poultry. Experts from across the world travelled to Hong Kong in the weeks that followed. More than a million chickens and other domestic fowl were slaughtered as a precautionary measure and, to the surprise of many, the virus disappeared.

A different strain of bird flu known as H7N7 unexpectedly hit the Netherlands in 2003. Ninety poultry-farm workers were infected, but the outbreak showed clear signs of low mortality, and only one of the 90 infected workers died. The origins of this outbreak are not clear, but there have been no new cases of H7N7 in humans since.

There are one or two cases where there has almost certainly been human-to-human infection of avian flu. In Indonesia in 2006 seven people from one family died, and the evidence strongly suggests that, after one member of the family was infected by direct bird contact, he or she then infected the other members of the family – but the spread of infection ended there. This could so easily have been the flashpoint for a pandemic the like of which the world has never seen, but on these occasions we have been lucky – and we have no idea why.

So far it seems as if the virus can infect humans, and then, in very rare cases, those infected humans have been able to infect one other human. There is nothing yet to suggest that infection via human-to-human contact has ever gone further than that – i.e. one level of transmission. At the moment, the virus appears to weaken or deteriorate as it passes from human to human.

In Vietnam, where avian-flu-infected humans died, it was found that – as in 1918 – they sometimes suffered a cytokine storm in which the immune system overreacted so massively that it contributed to the death of the patient. At the Hospital for Tropical Diseases in Ho Chi Minh City, a Vietnamese doctor holds a set of x-rays up to the light. They show the lungs of an otherwise healthy 18-year-old girl brought to the hospital two days earlier by worried relatives. The x-rays show the lower area of the girl's lungs are so filled with fluid that they can no longer function. A set of x-rays taken just two days later show the same lungs completed obscured from top to bottom by the same haze – the girl died just like so many in 1918 because her lungs were so damaged by the virus that she was starved of oxygen until she either suffocated or her other organs began to fail. Nothing the hospital could do had any effect on the progress of the disease.

Because doctors at this hospital were regularly in contact with flu-monitoring services around the world they knew what to do. An isolation ward was established with strict protocols. For the dozen and more patients admitted in the ensuing days with the tell-tale signs of avian flu everything possible was done – they were given the most powerful antivirals available, including Tamiflu, and were given oxygen masks. Despite these efforts all those who contracted the disease died.

Most cases of avian flu have been found in children and adults under the age of 40 rather than, as might have been expected, in older people. Ten to 19 year olds were the most likely to die as their respiratory systems were particularly hard hit.

The total number of confirmed cases of avian influenza in humans worldwide up to 2007 is 318. In global terms that figure is tiny, but it remains small only because the virus, though able to infect these individuals, did not then mutate to such an extent that it was able to pass quickly onward from human to human. There is some evidence, too, that the bird flu virus may hit particular families or create clusters of infection because particular families have a genetic susceptibility to avian flu infection.

Other cases of different viral strains – including H9N2, H7N3 and H7N2 – have all occurred in very small numbers across Asia. It may be that this has been happening in a small way for centuries and that we have only become aware of it since our technology and medical knowledge has become sophisticated enough to register and study events. There still remains a real sense that each additional case in humans of any type of avian flu is a serious cause for concern.

There is no question that avian flu is a killer and that its killing technique is not unlike that associated with the 1918 Spanish flu pandemic. Victims appear initially to develop symptoms associated with 'normal' flu – high temperature, aching limbs, headache, listlessness and loss of appetite. As the disease develops, the lack of an adequate immune response (or the fact of a massive overreaction in the immune system) can then trigger a range of symptoms that are not usually associated with 'normal' flu – internal bleeding, massive damage to lung tissue and, ultimately, organ failure. It is a pretty safe bet that, with modern medical care, the victim of avian flu today or at any time in the future would have a far better chance of recovery than his counterpart in 1918, but only in the technologically advanced parts of the world. In Asia and Africa avian flu might well spread rapidly, unchecked by the sort of medical and scientific interventions we take for granted in the West.

Southern China – the pool of infection

Just four years after the first recorded outbreak in 1997, a similar crisis occurred in Hong Kong. Birds in Hong Kong's live markets were found to be infected with a slightly different H5N1 virus and a mass slaughter began. By this time, however, a few Hong Kong doctors were aware that the real source of the H5N1 virus was in mainland southern China. Whatever they might do to stop this or any other outbreak in its tracks, it would only be a matter of time before another arose from the pool of infection almost certainly in existence – and out of their control – in the province of Guangdong.

In Guangdong a vast and largely poor rural population lives among hundreds of millions of ducks, geese and chickens. The bulk of these birds are free to roam over a wide area, crisscrossing each other's territory endlessly. These birds inevitably mingle with wild populations of ducks and geese (or come into contact with wild bird faeces) in whom avian flu is endemic. In 2003 two cases of H5N1 were found in a family that had recently travelled to China from Hong Kong. One recovered, the other died.

Avian flu is highly contagious. As wild birds have access to the farmland and ponds that domestic Chinese ducks and geese use, it is very difficult to control the potential pool of infection. One Chinese government official is quoted as saying 'We cannot put a lock on the skies.' This leaves world scientists with the problem that different strains of H5N1 will continue to appear at an alarming rate infecting Guangdong in the first instance and then quickly transferring to Hong Kong and, if we are very unlucky, the rest of the world. With infections and mutations running rife between wild and domestic flocks even the wild birds succumbed – millions of wild geese and sea birds died at one nature reserve in western China, for example.

Curiously, despite the certainty that wild birds are the host animal for avian flu, they appear not as yet to have carried the disease beyond southern China and Hong Kong. Some experts believe this is simply because birds carrying the mutated version of H5N1 die before they can travel any real distance. After 2001, H5N1 strains were found in Japan and in South Korea before being tracked to Indonesia. However this spread probably has more to do with the southeast Asian habit of shipping live poultry around the region.

The real problem is a cultural one. In most of southeast Asia there is neither the money nor the inclination to organize poultry farming in such a way that chickens are kept within boundaries while they are growing and then slaughtered before being taken to market. The demand for freshness (and the lack of money and infrastructure for refrigerated transport) means that millions of live chickens from many different parts of the countryside are brought together at markets where there is no chance of maintaining biosecurity. Add to this the fact that on farms across southeast Asia growing chickens mingle freely with each other, with chickens from other farms, and with wild birds, and it is easy to see why conditions are ideal for the H5N1 virus.

After coming together in their millions at live poultry markets, unsold birds return home taking with them any virus they may have picked up. They then continue to peck around their home farms mingling once again with other domestic and wild birds. Any farmer who suspects his flock may be infected is likely to say and do nothing – he knows that if he reports his suspicions his flock will be destroyed and he will receive no compensation. So he keeps quiet and sells or eats his infected birds if and when he can.

In China and Vietnam the usual method of duck rearing involves driving the ducks from farm to farm and field to field where, following the harvest, they feed on spilled grains. In the process they spread their faeces over an incredibly wide area leaving infected droppings as they go.

The disaster of a worldwide pandemic – if that ever happens – will be of our own making. We can hardly blame the wild bird populations; it is up to us to abandon these hazardous poultry-rearing and selling practices.

Culls and controls

Such is the level of that concern that in recent years in Hong Kong and other parts of Asia governments have been forced on a number of occasions to slaughter millions of chickens following the discovery of H5N1 in flocks. This measure may seem drastic – 1.5 million chickens were slaughtered in Hong Kong during one weekend in 1997 – but this is seen as the only way to minimize the chances of avian flu mutating and becoming deadly to human populations. Strict measures also immediately came into play to halt the transportation of all birds to and from affected areas. These measures will be implemented again in the future whenever there is an outbreak of avian flu. This will undoubtedly help, but it will only ever remove the source of any infection; it will not halt the spread of disease once it gets going.

By 2004 the death toll from avian flu in Vietnam alone was 40. In many parts of southeast Asia bird flu has become almost as terrifying as AIDS, with the result that people who once relied heavily on eating chicken and duck now refuse to touch it. Combine that with the financial consequences of the loss of millions of birds – either to the virus itself or to culls – to some of the world's poorest people, and avian flu is a serious menace in more ways than one. When people in Vietnam stopped eating chicken and duck, the huge chicken export industry in Thailand was suddenly badly hit. No one wanted to buy Thai chicken, businesses collapsed and jobs disappeared – 20 per cent of all poultry-related jobs vanished in Indonesia alone.

The tragedy is that chickens and ducks are an ideal protein resource for poor people in the Far East. Agricultural costs are zero because the birds forage and scavenge for themselves. Wiped out by flu or controlled culling, their absence from local diets could, in the worst-case scenario, lead to malnutrition. In Vietnam in 2004 more than 40 million ducks and geese were either slaughtered as a precautionary measure or died from avian flu – a huge loss of protein for human populations.

When bovine spongiform encephalopathy (BSE) and its human form Creutzfeldt-Jakob Disease (CJD) hit the United Kingdom, officials went out of their way to try to bolster support for the beef industry – most famously one minister organized a press conference where the BBC filmed his daughter eating a beefburger. But in Vietnam and other areas of southeast Asia the fear of avian flu remains so great that officials have made it known that even they will no longer eat chicken.

A massive programme of poultry vaccination in Hong Kong in 2003 and 2004 kept the former British colony free of the disease for that year, but outbreaks of H5N1 in poultry have continued to occur in mainland China, Vietnam and else-where. Live poultry markets were shut down completely twice a month throughout 2004 in order to disinfect them, and a team of inspectors kept an unremitting eye on markets and farms. But, while live birds are moved and brought together in huge numbers it will only take one bird to slip through the net to infect perhaps millions of others. The task seems hopeless; keeping avian flu out of Hong Kong will have no effect on Vietnam, Korea, Thailand or anywhere else. International agreements on these matters are proving notoriously difficult to organize and maintain.

At the end of 2004 avian flu was back with a vengeance – almost every one of Vietnam's 64 provinces reported outbreaks of the disease. Tens of millions of chickens were slaughtered in an attempt to halt the progress of the disease. The epidemic gradually abated and the Vietnamese government declared that it had been eradicated.

Scientists were not so sure, suspecting that it might well have simply faded away anyway as it had done elsewhere.

Officials within Vietnam and other countries admit that there is little they can do to stop the next outbreak of avian influenza. As one official put it: 'Avian influenza is a product of agricultural practices that the people cannot afford to abandon although the government would like them to change their ways. As a result it is always only a matter of time before the next outbreak of avian flu kills millions of birds.'

Compared to Vietnam, Thailand shows some progress in tackling these problems. Farmers are encouraged to report the fact that their birds are showing signs of infection by the promise of financial compensation, for example, and ducks are tested for H5N1 before herders are allowed to move them around the country. Almost one million villagers have been recruited to watch for signs of flu in chickens and other bird flocks. As a result avian flu has retreated to only a few provinces.

But any respite is likely to be temporary. Thailand has long, uncontrollable borders with Cambodia and Laos, where control measures are non-existent and outbreaks frequent – even if chickens kept in remote farms on either side of the border do not infect each other, animals are moved across the borders to be sold. Only one bird needs to be infected to spread the disease far and wide.

It is in some remote rural area like this – on a farm miles from any monitoring station – that avian and human flu is most likely to mix in a way that produces the ultimate explosion of contagion. If the mix is right the first person to be infected will quickly spread the disease to his family and then his village. It would then spread to other villagers before reaching the towns and the cities. Before too long dozens, perhaps hundreds, of people would travel out of Asia by airplane, unaware that they were harbouring a disease capable of killing millions. If this all sounds rather far fetched, it is worth remembering that this is precisely what happened with AIDS back in the 1970s. An infection from Africa was quickly spread to the United States and Europe, probably by just a few individuals. The rest, as they say, is history.

Current lines of research

Of course it remains a fact – though one that cannot yet be explained – that some of those who have contracted avian flu have made a full recovery. It is even thought that some individuals contract the disease and barely exhibit any symptoms. In 1918 the case was similar. Inexplicably some individuals seem particularly susceptible to the worst effects of avian flu infection while others (who are no more likely to enjoy any historic immunity to the disease) recover relatively quickly. Clearly genetic differences are at work here and the genetic route is in fact one that scientists are pursuing with enthusiasm, though research in this notoriously complex area is inevitably slow moving.

Take the case of Nguyen Thanh Hung from Hanoi, Vietnam. Nguyen contracted avian flu and survived. Doctors believe that he caught the disease after eating a local delicacy – raw duck blood. Nguyen may also have had contact with infected poultry in some other way, but the duck blood seems the most likely culprit because Nguyen's brother shared the dish, and he too fell ill. Nguyen at first showed no symptoms while his brother became dangerously ill. A fortnight later – ironically, on the day his brother died – Nguyen was rushed to hospital suffering from suspected avian flu. Tests confirmed the diagnosis and after treatment with antivirals he recovered. The question here, as yet still unanswered, is that if Nguyen and his brother were both infected by the duck blood why did it take two weeks for symptoms to develop in Nguyen? The most likely explanation is that Nguyen caught the disease from his brother while nursing him. But all this is highly speculative.

As we know, one great fear is that the avian flu virus mutates to become rapidly transmittable from human to human. But another possible nightmare scenario is that the virus could mingle – or reassort – its genes with those of a human flu virus, either in a particularly susceptible human or in a pig or other animal we know to be prone to such gene mixing.

Rather than wait until this happens scientists have decided to steal a march on the virus by trying to make it happen under controlled – and ultra-safe conditions. In the United States, United Kingdom and the Netherlands the race is on deliberately to mix human-flu and avian-flu genes. The plan is to test the resultant mix to see if it produces a virus that combines human flu's incredible ability to spread with avian flu's incredible ability to kill. The scientists will then try to find an antiviral that will kill or disable the hybrid before it occurs naturally in the wild and starts to kill us in our millions.

Creating a pandemic strain of avian flu crossed with human flu may give us a head start on any future outbreak, but as every scientist worth his salt agrees, flu is a tricky customer; no sooner has a strain been isolated or named than it has turned into a different strain or vanished, only to reappear when least expected and in some utterly unpredicted location.

For now, creating this Frankenstein monster in the lab is the best hope we have of learning something about what we might – or as many believe what we will –

face in the future. It is possible that the theoretical deadly hybrid will never be created in the wild because it a genetic mix that is simply impossible. But that optimism is not justified from what we know of flu viruses in general. Indeed, the more plausible forecast is that unless we do something now avian and human flu *will* eventually get together to create a virus of unparalleled ferocity.

Perhaps our greatest ally at present is time – time we can spend working on practical plans to counter widespread sickness should it occur, and watching for early-warning signs in avian and human flu strains that suggest the big one is on its way. One of the most obvious practical measures would be to completely eradicate H5N1 in poultry, but for reasons outlined above it is likely to prove extremely difficult indeed.

The difficulties involved in creating an effective vaccine are legion – as we will see in the next chapter. Central to the difficulty is that the only effective medium currently used for vaccine cultivation, fertilized chicken eggs, is difficult to use with avian flu virus, as the virus tends to kill the eggs. Safety measures required to carry out the work are also extremely difficult to implement as influenza is among the most contagious of all viral illnesses.

Instead of using eggs scientists are now focusing on the new science of genetic engineering. The idea is to isolate the H5N1 virus and then alter part of its genetic make-up effectively to disable it. Once disabled it could not harm those to whom it was given but it would, according to the theory, kick start the individual's immune system so that it was fully primed in the event of infection by the real H5N1 virus.

The other great advantage of a genetically engineered vaccine is that it can be produced very quickly compared to a conventional vaccine because it does not rely on the laborious business of egg culture. Tens of millions of doses could in theory be produced within weeks. This would reduce the need for expensive stockpiling of a vaccine that would not necessarily match an emerging virus if that virus occurred a year or two after the stockpiling began. Genetically engineered vaccines would be made in response to the specific profile of a particular strain of H5N1 (or any other flu virus) as and when the strain was identified as the culprit in a predicted pandemic.

There is still the problem that the flu virus will mutate over time and even during the course of a pandemic, and any vaccine might fail in the face of these changes, but at the moment the genetically engineered vaccine offers the best hope we have.

The situation is complicated further by the fact that researchers believe that H5N1 may not be the only bird flu virus that we have to fear; scientists have isolated a number of other bird flu viruses that look as if they may be able to infect humans. So far the suggestion is that, even if they could infect us, these less well-known bird flu viruses are not as deadly as H5N1. As with everything to do with flu, however, what is true one day or one year tends to be completely outdated the next. The only certainty we have when dealing with flu of all kinds is that very little is actually certain – all predictions and apparent facts about H5N1 and other flu viruses can only be, at best, approximate.

A plan of action

In the event of an avian flu pandemic the first priority would be to isolate and identify the particular strain of influenza involved and then begin the rapid manufacture of a suitable vaccine, but there are other measures that would certainly be taken in the West and possibly (funding permitting) in Asia and elsewhere too.

Community strategies would gain time for scientists and researchers hunting for antivirals and manufacturing vaccines. These would include obvious measures such as closing schools, bars and clubs, theatres, cinemas, churches and other places where the public gather. Strict quarantine would be enforced for all those infected.

The exponential rate at which even a well-managed avian flu pandemic would probably spread was calculated in a computer simulation for the city of Seattle in the United States. The computer calculated that infection would go from day one – no cases – through day 28 – 31 people sick – to a maximum of 90,000 cases at the peak of an outbreak, on day 86. The pandemic would then decline rapidly until the disease burned itself out on day 182.

Any outbreak following that particular trajectory would, if it were caused by a high-mortality strain of avian influenza, leave tens of thousands dead. Globally a runaway avian flu virus might well leave tens of millions dead. It would be of little comfort to them, but in the wider picture of human history and evolution, the arrival of a deadly flu bug would merely parallel great natural disasters of the past that all species have suffered. It would not be as bad as the extinction of the dinosaurs, and probably not as bad as the Black Death of the Middle Ages, which, at a conservative estimate, killed something between one third and two thirds of Europe's population.

The truth is that all speculation about the likely effects of an avian flu pandemic is just that – speculation. It may be that a new and deadly avian flu virus that is able to move quickly from human to human would be so incapacitating that it would burn itself out quickly for reasons we simply cannot at present even guess at. Ebola virus kills something like 90 per cent of those it infects and few have suggested that an avian flu pandemic would be that bad; where avian flu infection has so far occurred in humans, most notably in China, other parts of Asia and Turkey there is little evidence that it wipes out whole families or communities. If avian flu does hit us and hit us hard many will still survive – our own vast pool of genetic variation will ensure that some are less susceptible than others. But if the human species survives it may be in a world that it is difficult now to envisage – a world where communications, the economy, and economic and business life are severely disrupted.

Those who survived any bird-flu pandemic would pass on immunity to future generations. From a worldwide population crash of whatever magnitude, the human species would return slowly to pre-disease levels. Those who believe in the idea of planet earth as a self-regulating entity – the Gaia theory – might well argue that any pandemic that reduced the human population by 50 or 70 per cent would be a good thing from the planet's point of view – nature simply taking its course. The fruit bats that killed those horses and their trainer in Australia were simply acting out their part in a kind of evolutionary drama that strains to correct the massive over population of the world by *homo sapiens*. As we encroach on every acre of the world we risk our future by allowing no room for other animals and the diseases they usually keep to themselves. It is a risk we ignore at our peril.

CHAPTER 9

Finding a Cure

In our present age of technical wizardry and scientific innovation, the humble flu virus still escapes our domination, despite our best efforts. The nature of the virus is such that, just when we seem to have made a breakthrough, it mutates once more and once again jumps ahead of us in the game. Most worrying of all in the 21st century is the possibility that bird flu will truly jump the species barrier, and possibly cause another pandemic like that of 1918. While the holy grail of an outright cure still eludes us, however, there is much else that we can do to try to prevent, or at least prepare for any future major outbreak.

A man-made problem?

The rise of infectious diseases of catastrophic potential is largely attributable to aspects of modern human civilization. This is true of AIDS, the Ebola virus, avian flu and of the great influenza pandemic of 1918. Before we can begin to understand the possible route to a cure for influenza (or at least a reliable way of preventing infection) we need to understand the way in which these diseases arise. Anthony S. Fauci of the National Institute of Allergy and Infectious Diseases in Maryland, United States, neatly summarizes the problem:

> Infectious diseases are the second leading cause of death throughout the world. In 2002, according to the World Health Organization more than a quarter of approximately 57 million deaths worldwide were caused by infectious diseases. Millions of additional deaths are due to the secondary effects of infections. Among people under the age of 50 years, infectious diseases are the leading cause of death and account for nearly one-third of all healthy years lost to illness.
>
> An estimated 75 per cent of emerging infectious diseases in humans are zoonotic in origin, that is, they arise from microbes that infect other animals. Most microbes have evolved to reach equilibrium with their natural hosts without causing disease. However, factors such as economic

development and land use leading to perturbations in the natural microbial environment, human demographics and behaviour, and international travel and commerce can create an imbalance in the established microbe-host equilibrium and trigger the emergence of new infectious diseases.

As the world shrinks and the human population expands at an almost exponential rate, humans move into rainforests and other previously remote areas where they are exposed to new viruses. We know that AIDS almost certainly arose from peoples of some African countries killing chimpanzees and other primates for food. The AIDS virus almost certainly jumped from a primate to man when an injured primate bit or scratched a hunter. The same is almost certainly true of the Ebola virus. As Dr Fauci puts it: 'Human intrusion into settings such as rainforests has led to exposure of humans to viruses and other microbes that otherwise would not have occurred.'

The mass movements of people during World War I contributed hugely to the spread of the deadly 'Spanish' flu virus, and similar vast movements of people are taking place today. This adds greatly to the risk of infection by some new deadly virus or a mutated and deadly influenza virus. Over the past decades millions of rural dwellers worldwide have migrated to live and work in cities at home and abroad. People are more than ever on the move, whether for work or leisure travel. Urban poverty in the world's great cities is also a huge problem, along with increasing sexual promiscuity.

The effects of our gradual encroachment on the few remaining areas of the world where humans have not traditionally lived has put wildlife under pressure too, which can mean that species with which we have not often come into contact are now our neighbours. If we do not kill them – which is what humans usually do – we find that we are living cheek by jowl with them. In one such instance there was a severe outbreak of Nipah virus in Malaysia. This probably happened when domestic pigs contracted the virus from bat droppings. The bats had lost their traditional home well away from human areas of population when their forest habitat was cut down. They moved into a fruit orchard near to which the pigs were penned. Once the pigs were infected with the virus it was passed to their owners. In another instance, the United Kingdom largely created the disease bovine spongiform encephalopathy (BSE) or 'mad cow disease' (and its human form Creutzfeldt-Jakob disease) by feeding cattle the remains of other cattle, effectively turning herbivores into carnivores.

Diseases – including new forms of influenza virus – develop because of the way humans live. They do not develop in a vacuum. But unfortunately what sometimes starts as a rare disease can become endemic – AIDS is the best and perhaps most terrifying example, but this may also turn out to be true of Lassa fever and, of course, avian influenza.

The way forward

Many people assume that avian flu and pandemic flu are one and the same thing, which they are not. The 1918 pandemic of Spanish flu which, as we have seen, caused tens of millions of human deaths was not avian flu. It almost certainly shared one or more characteristics with avian flu, but was in other respects very different. The 1918 pandemic was such a spectacular example of a runaway, virulent strain of flu that scientists and other researchers are inevitably drawn to its study. Whether the results of their research will help us plan for a future outbreak of some other type of flu – most notably of course avian flu – remains to be seen, and the idea is contentious. Some scientists argue that drawing conclusions about the likely progress of a future avian flu outbreak from the experience of 1918 may even be counter-productive. Writing in the *Journal of Infectious Diseases* review, Doctors David M. Morens and Anthony S. Fauci are cautious, taking the view that we can learn some lessons from 1918, but that more research is also needed:

> Today, nearly a century after the 1918 influenza pandemic, its mysteries remain largely unexplained. Much work remains to be done, by scientists as well as by historians and other scholars, with regard to the many unanswered questions surrounding this historic pandemic. These studies must be part of our preparedness efforts as we face the prospect of a future influenza pandemic.
>
> In addition to ongoing laboratory studies, we feel that much can be learned from examining the vast scientific literature related to the 1918 influenza pandemic and previous influenza pandemics. A treasure trove of journal articles and other materials exists in many languages that can be mined for novel information with practical applications relevant to the threat of pandemic influenza we face.

Mostly, of course, it is a question of learning from our mistakes. In 1918 local and national authorities failed to act for a number of reasons – until it was too late. They felt they were justified in delaying drastic quarantine measures by the need to mobilize for war and by a belief that influenza was not a killer disease. This failure was of course partly due to ignorance – the pathogen that caused the disease was as yet undiscovered – and it followed that no amount of work was going to produce a cure or an effective vaccine.

We are in a stronger position today and would be likely to move far more quickly to prevent the spread of avian or any pandemic influenza. We know that it would be impossible to maintain 'business as usual', unless we were sure that we had created an effective vaccine in time. Our governments are held far more accountable today via the media and the ballot box.

Our increased knowledge of the whole range of influenza viruses has led some experts to argue that a new influenza pandemic would not affect the world's population as badly as the Spanish flu in 1918. We are generally healthier now and in a better position to control secondary bacterial and viral infections. But we are not in any position to be complacent.

Prevention rather than cure

The World Health Organization, fully aware that vaccines are likely only to be partially effective, has issued a six-point plan covering its own strategy should pandemic flu occur. The WHO would:

1   Support Member States for the implementation of national capacities for epidemic preparedness and response including laboratory capacities and early warning alert and response systems.
2   Support national and international training programmes for epidemic preparedness and response.
3   Coordinate and support Member States for pandemic and seasonal influenza preparedness and response.
4   Develop standardized approaches for readiness and response to major epidemic-prone diseases (e.g. meningitis, yellow fever, plague).
5   Strengthen bio safety, bio security and readiness for outbreaks of dangerous and emerging pathogens outbreaks (eg SARS, viral haemorrhagic fevers).
6   Maintain and further develop a global operational platform to support outbreak response and support regional offices in implementation at
  · regional level.

In the report by Doctors Morens and Fauci mentioned above, the authors write:

> In 2007 public health is much more advanced, with better prevention
> knowledge, good influenza surveillance, more trained personnel at all

levels, well-established prevention programs featuring annual vaccination with up-to-date influenza and pneumococcal vaccines, and a national and international prevention infrastructure.

They also point out, however, that little of this will apply in poorer parts of the world where containing the disease will turn out to be a question of access to medical care and resources. The authors suggest that prevention is key; efforts, they say, should be made to improve planning and surveillance, and above all to be ready to produce vaccine in sufficiently large quantities.

Prevention rather than cure is generally agreed to be the best world strategy – and that explains the WHO's monitoring policy with regard to human influenza. For the purposes of worldwide surveillance the WHO splits the year into date segments, which are then studied and analyzed as data comes in from across the world. The following extract comes from the WHO report on seasonal influenza during weeks eight to 11 in 2007:

> Overall influenza activity in the northern hemisphere remained moderate in weeks 8–11. In North America, influenza activity declined in general, while in Europe and some Asian countries and areas, widespread activity continued, with influenza A (H3N2) viruses predominating. Influenza A (H1N1) viruses circulated in the United States and in a few eastern European countries. Influenza B viruses circulated at low levels.
>
> **Austria.** Widespread influenza A activity continued in weeks 8–11.
>
> **Canada.** A decline in influenza activity was observed in weeks 10–11, with the overall influenza-like illness (ILI) consultation rate remaining within the expected range for this time of year. Widespread influenza A activity continued to be reported in some parts of the country.
>
> **Croatia.** Influenza A (H3N2) activity declined from week 8 and was reported as sporadic in week 11.
>
> **Denmark.** Widespread influenza activity continued in weeks 8–11, with A(H3N2) viruses predominating.
>
> **Japan.** Widespread influenza activity was reported in weeks 8–11, with A(H3N2) viruses predominating.
>
> **Russian Federation.** Regional influenza activity continued in weeks 8–11. Influenza A(H1N1), A(H3N2) and B viruses co-circulated.
>
> **United Kingdom.** Regional influenza A activity stared to decline in week 8, with sporadic detections reported in week 11.

United States. The number of states reporting widespread influenza activity started to decline in week 9; activity was reported as regional for America as a whole in week 11. The overall ILI consultation rate was still above the national baseline, but the percentage of deaths due to pneumonia and influenza remained below baseline level. During week 11, 69% of the influenza viruses detected were influenza A and 31% influenza B. Of the A viruses sub typed, 61% were influenza A(H1) and 39% A(H3) viruses.

The extraordinary level of detailed reporting we see here continues year in year out, such is the concern to know in advance what the world may be up against. While the great fear – often exaggerated by the media – is that avian flu may kill millions, the truth is that human flu is still a far greater problem in terms of the number of deaths it causes each year.

Set up in 1952, the WHO Global Influenza Surveillance Network works as a global alert system, with the aim of trying to spot emerging influenza virus types with the potential to cause a pandemic. The WHO also has four Collaborating Centres worldwide and 118 National Influenza Centres (NICs) in 89 countries – the scale of this set-up is a clear indication that the threat of influenza is taken very seriously indeed.

NICs work full time monitoring the progress and nature of flu within their national boundaries – they collect specimens, isolate and identify viruses and send a continual stream of specimens to the four big Collaborating Centres, where high-level testing takes place. The Collaborating Centres' work is the basis for decisions about which strains of influenza will be included in the annual influenza vaccine – it changes every year as the circulating viruses mutate – for the northern and southern hemispheres.

The scale of logistical planning necessary to cope with a flu pandemic is huge, and raises all sorts of practical, financial and ethical questions. In poorer countries resources would inevitably be more limited than in wealthy nations. What are the ethical implications of this? Even within western nations what would the practical, on-the-ground tactics be in the face of a virus that could just as easily infect the planners as the population at large? How would drugs be distributed? Who would be given priority access to scarce drug resources?

Across the world governments both local and national are struggling to agree that sometimes vast sums of money should be spent to prevent something that may never occur. As a United States official report put it:

Because State and local officials will likely face considerable difficulties in justifying the development of a sophisticated communication system for a problem which may or may not occur in the near term – i.e. pandemic influenza – justification and marketing of such a system to policy makers and legislators should be based on a more generic approach such as responding to chemical/bioterrorism events …

Planning for a future avian-flu pandemic – or any other pandemic for that matter – involves value judgments as well as scientific ones. When we decide to try to achieve a particular outcome there will always be winners and losers given that resources are finite. When we cannot help everyone the cost will be measured in terms of human suffering and loss of life. These factors are important and will inevitably impinge on scientific factors, although they are beyond the scope of this book.

On the medical front, plans to date have assumed that the central policy in reducing the impact of a new virus should be the use of vaccination. But a vaccine cannot (given our current technical abilities) be produced until the pandemic is underway, so stockpiling is not possible. Even if sufficient vaccine is then produced for whole populations, the question arises, who will get it first? Similarly, with antivirals, which we can at least stockpile, which would be the priority groups? Women and children, or health workers? The elderly or the young? Antiviral drugs would protect those who could not be vaccinated for some reason, but there would still be a great discrepancy between availability and demand.

It would make sense for decisions about priority groups to be taken in consultation with the populations concerned, since these decisions will have profound ethical as well as scientific implications. This idea has yet to be addressed by the World Health Organization or any national government.

The search for vaccines

While the WHO makes plans for coordinating any response to a pandemic, scientists continue their behind-the-scenes work studying individuals who have become infected with, for example, avian flu. They also work on the genetic make-up of all other influenza viruses. Scientists have even managed to reconstruct the Spanish flu virus of 1918.

Studies of individuals who have succumbed to rare types of influenza, particularly avian flu, have yielded a wealth of information from which it may eventually be possible to develop far more effective preventative strategies. In the field of AIDS research, for example, tiny genetic differences in a very small number of individuals who have resisted full-blown AIDS despite being HIV positive have given scientists important clues as to the way forward. The same is true within studies of influenza. One of the most remarkable discoveries emerged from studies of two Vietnamese who caught – and survived – avian flu.

Blood from the two survivors was used to create antibodies that cured mice infected with the H5N1 virus. In a remarkable experiment 20 mice that were infected with H5N1 were given the antibodies three days after being infected. All 20 made a good recovery while a control group of five mice infected at the same time, but not given the antibodies, died. Another healthy group of mice was given the antibodies and then exposed to H5N1 – none became infected.

There is still a great deal of work to be done in this area, but the success of these experiments does give cause for some optimism where avian flu is concerned. Despite the perennial problem that the antibodies would work only until the flu virus mutates, the principle of using the antibodies in the blood of survivors of any flu pandemic is a good one, particularly if any resultant drug can be combined with antiviral drugs such as Tamiflu.

Work on vaccines continues apace despite the fact that an effective avian-flu vaccine remains elusive. Those vaccines so far created have worked, but they have only produced a good immune response when used in high doses. Vaccines incorporate a weakened or killed version of a pathogen and stimulate the immune system without harming the host, so that when the real pathogen attacks the subject, the immune system responds quickly enough to prevent illness because it has already been primed to do so. Highly effective on stable viruses, vaccines are not nearly so effective once the patient is infected. Nor can they automatically keep pace with a rapidly mutating virus such as flu – which is why flu vaccines are updated annually.

One of the most recently trialled vaccines contained H5N1 – the bird-flu virus. It was grown in eggs before being rendered inactive – in other words it was made much as standard flu vaccines are made. But to be effective it had to be administered in two doses of 90 micrograms each –12 times more than is required in standard flu vaccines. At these levels it was effective, but only in roughly 50 per cent of cases. Vaccines that need to be used in these doses would not be particularly effective in the event of a pandemic where the need is to immunize large numbers of people very quickly. The quantities needed would be too great to produce at the speed that would be required.

One fascinating development in the search for a cure for influenza was the recent discovery that the virus that causes the common cold appears to offer some protection against pandemic strains of flu. Mice and chickens were successfully vaccinated with an adenovirus-based DNA vaccine against different strains of H5N1 bird flu. The American teams who carried out the tests used a crippled adenovirus, which cannot replicate, as a carrier for the gene for the main surface protein of H5N1, haemagglutinin (HA). This seems to have stimulated a highly effective immune response. The scientists made vaccines using the HA from the H5N1 flu that killed people in Vietnam in 2005, and with the HA from the H5N1 that jumped to humans in Hong Kong in 1997.

In both cases the vaccines protected both mice and chickens from the virus from which the HA was sourced. The most exciting aspect of this work was the discovery that each vaccine also protected against the other strain – something that just doesn't happen with standard vaccines made of killed flu viruses. The reason appears to be that standard vaccines induce antibodies against the flu virus, but they do not create cell-mediated immunity, in which white blood cells called T lymphocytes are also primed to attack the virus. The adenovirus-HA vaccine produced both.

The results of this research mean there is a real possibility that a vaccine based on induced cell-mediated immunity against a particular year's flu virus would still work against the slightly mutated strain that appeared the following year. This might mean that the need to create new vaccines each year would decrease, and it might be possible to stockpile vaccines.

Meanwhile British scientists have been trying to develop a vaccine that will give lifelong protection against all strains of flu. Existing flu jabs focus on a pair of proteins on the surface of the virus, but as these constantly mutate it is impossible to prepare in advance for each new strain. The new vaccine is based on other proteins, common to all flu viruses.

A universal flu jab is the holy grail of researchers, which explains why it is not just British scientists who are searching intensely to find it. Pharmaceutical companies across the developed world know that the company that first discovers and markets an effective vaccine against all types of flu virus will earn billions of dollars.

Modern treatments – antivirals

In the United Kingdom an estimated 12,000 people die each year as a result of seasonal flu, despite the widespread use – particularly among older people – of vaccines. Some doctors believe that influenza vaccines are just not that good anyway. Even Dr Graeme Laver – an Australian scientist and world authority on flu viruses, who in 1961 developed a new flu vaccine – is not convinced. Indeed, in

December 2007 he stated that vaccines are unlikely to protect the world's population against a likely new version of the flu virus. He has also argued that as vaccines are not especially effective, antiviral drugs such as Tamiflu should be made available over the counter and not just on prescription. Others have argued that this will lead to the overuse of the few effective antivirals we currently have. Overuse could make those drugs far less effective.

Tamiflu is a fascinating drug that works against both human and avian flu. Its unique properties enable it to inhibit the viral neuraminidase protein in the flu virus. Governments are stockpiling Tamiflu, but it is expensive and took years to develop, which partly explains various governments' reluctance to make it generally available, especially if that availability reduced its effectiveness. Tamiflu is enormously complex to make – some 30 synthetic steps are required to create it from the natural compound shikimic acid, which is extracted from Chinese star anise, itself a relatively scarce commodity. In some parts of the world the fear of avian flu in particular is so great that it has generated a market for fake Tamiflu currently being sold on the Internet. As with so many drugs that are available on the Internet this causes problems for the authorities who are virtually powerless to stop the trade.

When they were first developed in the 1960s antivirals were hailed as the new antibiotic, but effective against the last great disease group – the viruses. They haven't quite lived up to this promise, but they are still enormously useful, and their arrival created a new and highly fruitful area of research for medical science. Early antivirals worked in a way that was only partly understood. The next great leap forward came in the 1980s when gene sequencing enabled scientists to see deep into the flu virus and learn far more about how it works. Once the chemical basis of the flu virus was understood it was possible to construct antivirals in a far more targeted way – which is how we got Tamiflu.

Unlike vaccines – which attack viruses when they are outside the organism's cells – antivirals can be made, in theory at least, to attack the virus at any stage in its life cycle. The key idea behind antivirals, however, is that they target viral proteins, or parts of proteins, disabling them in the process. The target proteins are those that are least like any proteins or parts of proteins found in humans – this reduces the chances of side effects. The aim is also to target those proteins that are common across many strains of a virus to ensure that the treatment will cover the widest possible range of infections and endure for some time despite the mutation of viruses. Antivirals are designed using enormously complex computer programmes so that they are precisely targeted at the molecular level.

Bird flu – a small threat, for now …

As we have seen above, the recently trialled bird-flu vaccine required massive doses 12 times larger than ordinary vaccines. Scientists think large doses may be required because H5N1 surface proteins within the vaccine – more particularly, the position of the sugar group of proteins – are somehow preventing the immune system responding in the expected fashion when it encounters these surface proteins.

It looks as if bird flu only rarely infects humans because cells in our noses and throats have the sugar component that matches human flu, not avian flu. The virus has to bind to a sugar molecule on the surface of the host cell – if that sugar molecule isn't the right one the virus can't bind to it.

However, it looks as if the sugar molecules on the cells in our alveoli – the fragile air sacs deep within our lungs – *are* right for the bird-flu virus, so if it can get that far into our bodies we may well become infected. Human-flu types, however, only have to reach the sugar molecules on the cells in our noses and throats to have a good chance of infecting us. That seems to be a key difference.

The risk of a bird-flu pandemic will only become a real and present risk if the virus mutates in such a way that it can bind to the sugar molecules in the noses and throats of the human population. While it is only able to infect us by binding to molecules deep in the lungs, it is likely to be knocked out before it reaches those cells. This explains why it has so far tended to infect only those who live very close to their animals – particularly chickens. In southern China it is easy to imagine farmers continually breathing dust filled with chicken excreta and coming into contact with chicken fluids – at this level of exposure infection with avian flu is far more likely.

… a big threat for the future?

Genetic shift – a dramatic genetic leap forward – is the most likely route that the virus could take in order to be able to overcome the sugar-protein barrier to infection.

Influenza-A virus's eight separate gene segments allow influenza-A viruses from different species to mix and create a new influenza-A virus. This usually happens in a pig – the pig is infected with a human influenza-A virus and an avian influenza-A virus at the same time. The viruses mix their genetic information (this is known as reassortment) and the resulting new virus has genes from the human virus combined with a haemagglutinin and/or neuraminidase from the avian virus. This new virus – a virus created by genetic shift – might then be able to infect humans (who would have little or no immunity to it) via nose and throat cells. As in 1918, it could then cause deaths on an unprecedented scale unless we could create a really effective vaccine.

The difficulties in finding an effective vaccine are compounded by the fact that it is possible for the reassortment of the flu virus genes to occur within humans. It would only take an individual to be infected with a human type-A influenza virus to then become infected with avian flu via the deep-lung route described above, and the reassortment could occur that would allow the new virus to transmit rapidly from human to human.

This possibility explains the high level of scientific interest in all those people (so far few in number) who do become infected with avian flu. If any of these people are found to have a new type of flu that shares bird and human flu characteristics scientists will at least have identified the problem early enough to do something about it.

At the time of writing some 275 people have been infected worldwide by avian flu and 167 of those have died. If that mortality figure were extrapolated across worldwide populations the potential death toll would be vast – just as it was in 1918.

The menace of biological warfare

While the world makes ever greater efforts to protect us from all types of flu, there is an increasing fear that influenza – particularly avian influenza – could actually be used as a weapon.

Much as medieval armies conducting a siege sometimes catapulted dead but still infectious victims of smallpox over the battlements of castles, or as Spanish conquistadors used the clothing of smallpox victims deliberately to infect and kill the indigenous peoples of the Americas, so modern terrorists are, it is believed, looking at ways to obtain and develop lethal versions of influenza and other viruses.

The great fear with the few remaining live cultures of smallpox – held in laboratories in the United States, Great Britain and Russia – is that they should fall into the hands of terrorists and be released against populations that have entirely lost their historic partial immunity to the disease.

It is known that al-Qaida and a number of other guerrilla groups have tried – so far unsuccessfully according to the best information currently available – to obtain biological weapons and many chaotic and corrupt states in Africa and Asia are also trying to obtain the means to conduct germ warfare. There is little doubt that a group or 'rogue' state would use a deadly flu virus if they could obtain or develop it and if they felt sufficiently threatened.

The normal safeguard when it comes to biological weapons is that the user cannot be sure that he or she will not die if the weapon is used. It is difficult to see how terrorists would be able to contain any release of the virus. They might, it is true, be able to steal the virus and release it in target countries, but they could not then stop it spreading rapidly to every single country in the world. However, with fanatical religious terrorists such safeguards will not necessarily apply. The major problem with a number of these states and groups is that ultimately they believe that this life is a preparation for a life after death and they are prepared to die, even welcome death, in the cause of what they see as a holy war against those who do not share their views.

If a deadly flu virus were to be released deliberately then those who released it would be at as much risk as their target: viruses do not respect man-made boundaries, nor do they exercise political or religious preferences. If a deadly flu virus, avian or otherwise, does ever strike the world again, we will quickly discover that we have just two choices: to work together or die together.

Glossary

Acute Respiratory Disease Syndrome (ARDS) – A severe life-threatening lung condition characterised by inflammation of the alveoli that destroys the ability of the lungs to transfer oxygen to the blood.

Alveoli – Spherical outcrops of the respiratory bronchioles, the alveoli are found deep within the lungs and are the main sites of gas exchange with the blood. The word comes from the Latin *alveus* meaning 'small cavity'.

Antigenic drift – The process by which mutations accumulate in a virus.

Bacterium (pl. bacteria) – A member of a large group of unicellular micro-organisms, some of which cause disease.

Capsid – The protein coat or shell of a virus.

Clade – A group of organisms evolved from a common ancestor.

Cyanosis – A condition that occurs when the oxygen content of the blood falls below 85 per cent. At this point the skin becomes bluish, revealing the presence of deoxygenated haemoglobin in blood vessels close to the surface of the skin. This was a key condition noted in the 1918 pandemic.

Cytokine storm – A massive overreaction of the immune system.

Darwinism – The theory promulgated by Charles Darwin (1809–82) of the evolution of species by the action of natural selection. Popularly encapsulated as 'the survival of the fittest', this phrase is often incorrectly taken to mean fittest in the sense of healthiest – in fact it refers to the survival of the best adapted for a particular environment.

DNA – Deoxyribonucleic acid, a substance present in nearly all living organisms, especially as a constituent of chromosomes. DNA molecules carry the genetic information necessary for the organization and functioning of most living cells and control the inheritance of characteristics.

Droplet infection – An infection transmitted from human to human by droplets of moisture expelled from the respiratory tract through sneezing and coughing. Droplets thus expelled from the body remain infectious for some time if they do not directly reach another victim.

Ebola – A deadly haemorrhagic virus, unrecorded before the late 20th century.

Electron microscope – A type of microscope employing a beam of electrons rather than light. Because the wavelength of a high-speed electron is very much shorter than that of light, a correspondingly greater resolving power is possible, so that magnifications of up to one million times can be achieved. Electron microscopes enabled viruses to be seen for the first time.

Epidemic – A disease is defined as of epidemic proportions if it infects a particular human population much faster than doctors would normally expect based on past experience. The word comes from Greek *epi* (upon) and *demos* (people). An epidemic is contained within one country. When it spreads across a continent or the world it is known as a pandemic.

Genetic reassortment – A process by which DNA within a chromosome is exchanged with DNA in a different chromosome.

Genetic shift – The process by which two flu strains combine to form a new subtype that has a mixture of the surface antigens (molecules that stimulate the immune response) of the two original strains.

Haemagglutinin – An antigenic glycoprotein found on the surface of flu and other viruses that binds the virus to the infected cell.

Haemorrhagic – Of or pertaining to bleeding or haemorrhage from the circulatory system. Bleeding occurs externally through a break in the skin or internally where blood leaks from blood vessels. A number of viruses, most spectacularly Ebola, cause massive internal bleeding.

Hanta virus – Highly dangerous, rodent-borne virus that causes haemorrhagic fever.

Lymphocytes – Cells found in the blood, lymph and lymph tissues that make up roughly 25 per cent of white blood cells and include immune function B and T cells.

Macrophage – Cells within tissue that have their origin in special white blood cells called monocytes. Both macrophages and monocytes find and destroy pathogens and cellular debris. From the Greek *makros* (large) and *phagein* (eat).

Morbidity – The incidence of disease within a population.

Myxomatosis – An infectious, usually fatal viral disease in rabbits, causing swelling of the mucous membranes. Rabbits in the UK are now to a greater or lesser extent immune to the virus.

Neuraminidase – An enzyme found on the surface of the flu virus.

Pandemic – Any infectious disease that spreads rapidly and easily between humans and is widespread, i.e. it spreads beyond one country, to a continent or the whole world. The word comes from the Greek *pan* (all) and *demos* (people).

Passage – Process by which a virus gains in virulence and lethality as it progresses through a population.

Pathogen – An agent causing disease.

Rhinovirus – The virus that causes the common cold.

RNA – Ribonucleic acid, a nucleic acid present in all cells. Its principal function is to act as a messenger carrying instructions from DNA for controlling the synthesis of proteins.

Surface proteins – organic macromolecules found on the surface of cells and containing carbon, oxygen, hydrogen, nitrogen, and (usually) sulphur; proteins comprise chains of alpha-amino acids and are fundamental components of all living cells. Glycoproteins are a type of surface of a virus; consisting of a carbohydrate and a protein, they perform essential roles in the body and in the immune system.

Virus – A submicroscopic infective agent that usually consists of a nucleic acid molecule inside a protein coat (capsid), only able to multiply within the living cells of a host.

Bibliography

ARBUTHNOTT, JOHN, *An Essay Concerning the Effects of Air on Human Bodies* (London, 1751)

BAKER, SARAH, J., *Fighting for Life* (Robert Hale, London, 1940)

BALFOUR, ANDREW and SCOTT, HENRY H., *Health Problems and the Empire* (Collins, London, 1925)

BARON, A. L., *Man against Germs* (Dutton, New York, 1957)

BARRY, JOHN M., *The Great Influenza* (Penguin, New York, 2004)

BERGER, MAURICE, *Germany after the Armistice* (Putnam, New York, 1920)

BISHOP, R. W. S., *My Moorland Patients* (John Murray, London, 1922)

BRAINERD, ELIZABETH, *The Economic Effects of the 1918 Influenza Epidemic* (Centre for Economic Policy Research, London, 2003)

BULLOCK, W., *History of Bacteriology* (Oxford University Press, 1938)

BURGESS, RENATE, *A Satyre on the Influenza of 1803* (London, 1803)

BURNET, SIR FRANCIS and CLARK, ELLEN, *Influenza* (Macmillan, London, 1942)

BYAM, WILLIAM, *The Road to Harley Street* (Geoffrey Bles, London, 1963)

CASES, BARTOLOME DE LAS, *A Short Account of the Destruction of the Indies* (Madrid, 1545)

CASSON, STANLEY, *Steady Drummer* (Bell and Sons, 1935)

CLARKSON, GROSVENOR, B., *Industrial America in the World War* (Houghton Mifflin, New York, 1923)

COLLIER, L and OXFORD, J., *Human Virology* (Oxford University Press, 1993)

COFFMAN, EDWARD T., *The War to End all Wars* (Oxford University Press, 1968)

COLLIER, RICHARD, *The Plague of the Spanish Lady* (Macmillan, London, 1974)

COLLIS, ROBERT, *The Silver Fleece* (Nelson, London, 1936)

COOK, J. GORDON, *Virus in the Cell* (Dial Press, London, 1957)

CRAWFORD, D., *The Invisible Enemy: A Natural History of Viruses* (Oxford University Press, 2000)

CROOKSHANK, F.G. (ED), *Influenza: Essays by Several Authors* (Heinemann, New York, 1922)

CROSBY, ALFRED W., *America's Forgotten Pandemic: The Influenza of 1918* (Cambridge University Press, 1989)

CUMMINS, S. L., *Studies of Influenza in Hospitals of the British Armies in France, 1918* (Medical Research Committee, London, 1919)

CUSHING, HARVEY, *From a Surgeon's Journal* (Constable, London, 1936)

DALY, J. M., *Antigenic and Genetic Variation Among Equine H3N8 Influenza A Viruses* (Open University, London, 1996)

DAVIS, MICHAEL M. JR, *Immigrant Health and the Community* (Harper, New York, 1921)

DEL MAR, FRANCES, *A Year Among the Maoris* (Ernest Benn, London, 1924)

DOCK, LAVINIA, *History of American Red Cross Nursing* (Macmillan, New York, 1922)

DOS PASSOS, JOHN, *Mr Wilson's War* (Doubleday, New York, 1963)

EISENMENGER, ANNA, *Blockade, 1914-24* (Constable, New York, 1932)

ETHERTON, LT.-COL. PERCY, *In the Heart of Asia* (Constable, London, 1925)

FAIRBROTHER, R. W., *Handbook of Filterable Viruses* (Heinemann, New York, 1934)

FROTHINGHAM, THOMAS G., *The American Reinforcement in the World War* (Doubleday, New York, 1927)

GARRETT, L., *The Coming Plague: Newly Emerging Diseases in a World Out of Balance* (Penguin, London, 1995)

GODSELL, PHILIP, *Arctic Trader* (Putnam, 1934)

GOGARTY, REV. H. A., *In the Land of the Kikuyus* (Gill and Son Ltd, New York, 1920)

GOSSE, PHILIP, *Memoirs of a Camp Follower* (Longman, London, 1934)

GOVE, JOHN, *Epidemics Examined* (London, 1850)

GRANVILLE, JOSEPH MORTIMER, *A Note on the Nature and Treatment of Influenza* (Balliere and Co., London, 1893)

GRAVES, CHARLES, *Invasion by Virus* (Icon Books, New York, 1969)

GRAVES, ROBERT and HODGE, ALAN, *The Long Week-End* (Faber and Faber, London, 1940)

GRAY, DR EDWARD, *An Account of the Epidemic Catarrh of 1782* (London, 1784)

GREGER, MICHAEL, *Bird Flu: A Virus of Our Own Hatching* (Lantern Books, London, 2006)

GUNN, CLEMENT B., *Leaves from the Life of a Country Doctor* (The Moray Press, Edinburgh, 1935)

HALDANE, ELIZABETH S., *The British Nurse in Peace and War* (John Murray, London, 1923)

HAMILTON, ROBERT D., *A Description of the Influenza, with its Distinction and Method of Cure* (London, 1782)

HARLEY STREET DOCTOR, *A Doctor's Diary* (Hutchinson, London, 1925)

HAYS, J. N., *Epidemics and Pandemics* (London, 1993)

HEADLAM, LT.-COL. CUTHBERT, *History of the Guards' Division in the Great War* (John Murray, London, 1924)

HEISER, VICTOR, *A Doctor's Odyssey* (Jonathan Cape, London, 1936)

HENRIKSON, VIKTOR, *A Doctor's Story* (Michael Joseph, London, 1959)

HERDMAN, JOHN, *A Plain Discourse on the Causes, Symptoms, Nature and Cure of the Prevailing Epidemical Disease Termed Influenza* (Manners and Miller, Edinburgh, 1803)

HIRSCH, DR AUGUST, *Geographical and Historical Pathology Vol. 1* (London: The New Sydenham Society, 1883)

HOEHLING, A. A., *The Great Epidemic* (Little, Brown, New York, 1961)

HOOPER, E., *The River: A Journey Back to the Source of HIV and AIDS* (Penguin, London, 1999)

HOOVER, HERBERT, *Memoirs* (Macmillan, New York, 1951)

HUMPHRIES, WILFRED, *Patrolling in Papua* (Unwin, London, 1923)

HUSEREAU, DONALD ROBERT, *An Assessment of Oseltamivir for the Treatment of Suspected Influenza* (Canadian Coordinating Office for Health Technology, 2002)

HUXHAM, JOHN, *Observations on the Air and Epidemical Diseases* (London, 1758)

JAMES, A. T. S., *Twenty-Five Years of the L.M.S.* (London: London Missionary Society, 1923)

KEABLE, ROBERT, *Tahiti: Isle of Dreams* (Hutchinson, London, 1925)

KEESING, FELIX, *Modern Samoa* (Allen and Unwin, London, 1934)

KIPLE, K. (ED), *The Cambridge World History of Human Disease* (Cambridge University Press, 1993)

KOLATA, GINA, *The Story of the Great Influenza Pandemic* (Touchstone, New York, 2001)

LANGDON, ROBERT, *Island of Love* (Cassell, London, 1959)

LUDENDORFF, GEN. ERICH, *My War Memories* (Hutchinson, London, 1919)

LUND, THOMAS WILLIAM MAY, *Behind the Veil: A Reminiscence of Influenza* (Howell, Liverpool, 1982)

MACARTNEY, WILLIAM, *Fifty Years a Country Doctor* (Geoffrey Bles, London, 1938)

MACDONALD, DAVID, *Twenty Years in Tibet* (Seeley Service and Co., London, 1932)

MANN, A. J., *The Salonica Front* (A. and C. Black, London, 1920)

MCCARTHY, MARY, *Memories of a Catholic Girlhood* (Heinemann, New York, 1953)

MCNEILL, W. H., *Plagues and Peoples* (Penguin, London, 1994)

MILLARD, SHIRLEY, *I Saw Them Die* (George Harrap, New York, 1936)
  – *Mr Punch's History of the Great War* (Cassell, London, 1920)

MOORE, HARRY H., *Public Health in the United States* (Harper, New York, 1923)

MURPHY, WENDY, *Coping with the Common Cold* (Time Life Books, 1981)

NATHAN, MANFRED, *South Africa from Within* (John Murray, London, 1926)

OLDSTONE, M. B., *Viruses, Plagues and History* (Oxford University Press, 1998)

PAUL, DR HUGH, *The Control of Communicable Diseases* (Harvey and Blythe, New York, 1952)

PEARSON, RICHARD, *Observations on the Epidemic Catarrhal Fever or Influenza of 1803* (London, 1803)

POTTLE, FREDERICK, *Stretchers!* (Yale, 1929)

POWER, HAROLD, *Bush Doctor* (Robert Hale, London, 1970)

RIDDELL, LORD, *War Diary* (Ivor Nicholson and Watson, New York, 1933)

ROYSTON, ANGELA, *Colds, Flu and Other Infections* (Franklin Watts, London, 2006)

RYAN, F., *Virus X: Understanding the Real Threat of the New Pandemic Plagues* (Harper, New York, 1998)

SAUERBRUCH, FERNAND, *A Surgeon's Life* (Andre Deutsch, London, 1953)

SCOTT, ERNEST, *Australia During the War* (Angus and Robertson, Sydney, 1936)

SHORT, DR THOMAS, *A General Chronological History of the Air, Weather, Seasons, Meteors, Etc.* (London, 1749)

SMITH, KENNETH, *Viruses* (Cambridge University Press, 1962)

SMITH, LESLEY, *Four Years Out of Life* (Philip Allan, London, 1931)

SNELL, SIDNEY H., *A Doctor at Work and Play* (John Bale, Sons and Curnow, New York, 1937)

STAMP, WINIFRED, *Doctor Himself* (Hamish Hamilton, London, 1949)

STUCK, HUDSON A., *A Winter Circuit of our Arctic Coast* (T. Werner Laurie, New York, 1919)

THOMPSON, THEPHILIUS, *Annals of Influenza* (London, 1852)

UGLOW, JENNY, *The Lunar Men* (Faber and Faber, London, 2003)

WATERSON A. P. and WILKINSON L. *An Introduction to the History of Virology* (Cambridge University Press, 1978)

WAUCHOPE, GLADYS, *The Story of a Woman Physician* (John Wright and Sons, New York, 1963)

WESTMAN, STEFAN, *A Surgeon's Story* (William Kimber, New York, 1962)

WILLIAMS, GREER, *Virus Hunters* (Hutchinson, London, 1960)

WILLIAMS, T. G., *The Main Currents of Social and Industrial Change in England, 1870-1924* (Pitman, London, 1925)

WILLIS, *Practice of Physic, Being the Whole Works of That Renowned and Famous Physician* (London, 1658)

WILSON, R. MCNAIR, *Doctor's Progress* (Eyre and Spottiswoode, London, 1938)

WINSLOW, CHARLES, *The Conquest of Epidemic Disease* (Princeton University Press, 1943)

Index

PICTURE CREDITS